THREE MODERNISTS

THREE MODERNISTS

ALFRED LOISY
GEORGE TYRRELL
WILLIAM L. SULLIVAN

by John Ratté

SHEED AND WARD : NEW YORK

TO MY MOTHER

Acknowledgments

I WAS FORTUNATE to begin the study of the interstices of modern church history and modern intellectual history under the complimentary direction of Christopher Dawson, formerly Chauncey Stillman Professor of Roman Catholic Studies at the Harvard Divinity School, and Professor H. Stuart Hughes, and to have had their continuing encouragement in revising a doctoral dissertation. The names of my teachers Dudley Fitts, Myron P. Gilmore, Stuart Hughes, and of my friends and sometime colleagues John Conway, Robert Richardson, and Leon Bramson, must stand for all the others who helped to shape the author, if not the book. The Trustees of Amherst College and the Society for Religion in Higher Education awarded me fellowships for the year 1965-66, and for this support I am grateful. I thank Mr. Holley Shepherd, Archivist of the Harvard Divinity School Library, Mr. Porter Dickinson and the staff of the Reference Desk of the Robert Frost Library, Amherst College, and the Rector and the Librarian of Heythrop College, Oxfordshire, for their courtesy and assistance. And I thank Reverend Robert Richardson, Reverend Dan Fenn, Mr. Brendan Farrington, Mr. Shepherd, and others for their recollections of William L. Sullivan.

Grateful acknowledgment for permission to use copyrighted material is also made to the following publishers: Casterman S. A. Editeurs (Emile Poulat, *Histoire, Dogme et Critique dans la Crise Moderniste*); Cambridge University Press (Alec Vidler, *The Modernist Movement in the Roman Catholic Church*); The Seabury Press, Inc. (Alec Vidler, *20th Century Defenders of the Faith*); E. P. Dutton & Co., Inc. (Alfred Loisy, *My Duel with the Vatican: The Autobiography of a Catholic Modernist*, tr. R. W. Boynton; Friedrich von Hügel, *Selected Letters, 1896-1924,* ed. Bernard Holland); Ernest Benn Limited (George Tyrrell, *Letters,* selected and edited by M. D. Petre); Beacon Press, Boston (William L. Sullivan, *Under Orders, The Autobiography of William Laurence Sullivan,* copyright 1944 by Richard R. Smith); *The Atlantic Monthly* (William L. Sullivan, *The Anti-Religious Front,* Vol. 145 [January 1930], pp. 96-104).

Wives always come last in these lists, presumably because they endure even the writing of acknowledgments. Lou Ratté has seen me and this book over an excessively protracted course with great charity, as much by correcting my judgment as by criticizing the manuscript. For this help and for comparative quiet in the lee of the Abbot of Winchcombe's tithe barn, I am very grateful indeed.

J. R.

Church Enstone, 1965—Amherst, 1967

Contents

Jean: 'In fact, we might as well turn Protestants!'

Shertz: 'Certainly not! An individualist, not to say anarchist, religion like Protestantism leaves us unsatisfied; whereas an organized, social and —how shall I put it—communalized religion like ours—that's just what human nature needs.'

—ROGER MARTIN DU GARD, *Jean Barois*

THREE MODERNISTS

Introduction -
MODERNISM AND HISTORY

THIS STUDY is offered as part of the history of religious opinion at the turn of the century. It illustrates one aspect of the crisis of confidence which seized the clergy of the Catholic Church at that time, as well as the impact of liberal Protestant, secular, social, and scientific ideas on Catholic teaching which was in part its cause.

As the name implies, the so-called "Modernists" were men who wished to make Catholic Christianity relevant to the contemporary world. They were not alone in this hope. Leo XIII had begun his pontificate with the intention of setting the Church so well onto the road of modernization that his successor, even if he were a man of the views of Pius IX, would not be able to turn it back. Under his direction the Church sought accommodation with post-Revolutionary political and social realities, and began to awake "from an intellectual sleep which had lasted over a hundred years." Reconciliation in Germany, support for the Third Republic in France, and Leo's encyclicals on the social question were the fruits of the first effort. The revival of Catholic philoso-

phy, the encouragement of the Catholic institutes, and the
development of a scientific biblical criticism were among the
manifestations of the concomitant surge of intellectual activity.[1]

There was a good deal of ground to be covered. Since
Lamennais had proposed that the Church become the cham-
pion of the people in the urban industrial world, both capi-
talism and socialism had grown into complex forms which
were hardly susceptible to even the most disinterested and
inspiring Christian rhetoric. The symbol of the Church to
the majority of its members and to its radical critics was the
kingdom of God or the kingdom of heaven. It was understood
as a perfect or near-perfect society set in, but against, the
world, its people clearly marked by unqualified adherence to
a complex and rationally ordered system of dogmas, doctrines, and devotions. The whole was maintained in its purity
by a centralized and authoritarian administration properly
possessed of temporal as well as spiritual power. It was a
concept modeled after the jurists and political theorists of
the sixteenth and seventeenth centuries, owing little to the
eschatology of the New Testament because that dimension
of the gospel was not then accessible to Catholic scholarship.
The decrees of Vatican I and the absolutism of curial organization seemed to confirm the notion that the Church was
anything but "a pilgrim pressing on amid the persecutions
of the world and the consolations of God announcing the
Lord's cross and death until he comes" (Vatican II, *Lumen
Gentium*).[2] New directions in ecclesiology clearly depended
on a fresh and liberal attitude toward learning, which would
disprove Lord Acton's suspicion that the Church,

in her zeal for the prevention of error, represses that intellectual
freedom which is essential to the progress of truth; that she allows

an administrative interference with convictions to which she cannot attach the stigma of falsehood; and that she claims a right to restrain the growth of knowledge, to justify an acquiescence in ignorance, to promote error, and even to alter at her arbitrary will the dogmas that are proposed to faith.[3]

But the Church had delayed so long in encouraging free Catholic scholarship that immense efforts were demanded if Catholic thought were constructively to absorb the developments of nineteenth-century science, especially in the fields of history, philosophy, and para-biological social theory.

The problem on which intellectual renewal in the Church was finally focused was the historical character of the Church and of the gospel. No particular scientific advance but, rather, the considerable attention given to the "biblical question" by Protestant and rationalist scholarship all through the nineteenth century made it likely that, once the techniques of modern philology and comparative religious studies were recognized as having some utility to Catholic scholarship, attention would be focused on the study of the New Testament as the ultimate source of all Christian teaching and institutions. The biblical question was a paradigm for the general issue of the proper relationship of religion and science which was being debated in other areas as well. It was especially acute because it echoed and renewed the major theme of the Catholic-Protestant polemic, the relationship between scripture and tradition. Precisely because Protestant scholarship had come to terms with the historical problem in a radical way, the development of biblical criticism in Catholic scholarship also involved its champions in a confrontation with those larger questions on which liberal Protestantism seemed to depart, not merely from the Catholic tradition, but also from the Reformed. Thus it was that men who

were profoundly in touch with the Catholic idea and eager
to do nothing which would in any way challenge authority
were often accused of heretical tendencies because they
adopted liberal Protestant means to counter liberal Protestant ends, insisting to little effect that the principles of a
sound scientific scholarship did not have to lead toward
relativism, indifference, and the variety of other errors which
seemed to the Holy See to mark the all-too-predictable collapse of reformed Christianity into secular liberalism.

Of course, the historical question did not confront Catholic scholarship in a purely philological form. To many the
historical method modeled on physical science and treating
of human facts with an objectivity presumed to equal that
of the laboratory was inseparable from an historicist philosophy. The issues raised, first by the scientific study of early
church history (especially in France) and then by "higher
criticism" of the bible, were also seen in the context of the
debate on evolution and the wider confrontation on the
principles of political and social liberalism which had begun
in 1789. The response of the magisterium had been negative
to these earlier developments; all through the century the
work of Catholic scholars was frustrated by the hostility of
the authorities as well as by the skepticism with which Protestant and secular intellectuals met their bold claim to be
good Catholics as well as good scientists.[4] The condemnation
of *L'Avenir* in 1831 by Gregory XVI had seemed to confirm
the Church's rejection of a Christian interpretation of the
Revolution. The *Syllabus of Errors* (1864) of Pius IX had
apparently ruled out the idea that "the Roman Pontiff can
and should reconcile himself with, and accommodate himself
to progress, liberalism, and modern civilization." And the
decrees of Vatican I, especially the proclamation of papal

infallibility, had seemed to prove to men like Döllinger and Acton that the Church would never come to terms with its history. National events—the problem of the papal states in Italy, the debate between Montalembert's *Correspondant* and Veuillot's *Univers* in France, the rejection of Newman's proposal for an active laity in England—all tended to confirm the view that Western culture and Catholic Christianity were irreconcilable enemies. And the 1880's, crowded with "rear guard actions and abandoned positions"—the work of Renan and Berthelot, anticlericalism in France and the Kulturkampf in Germany—also made it appear that the Church was doomed to lose the battle.

Catholic historians have frequently rehearsed the legitimate reasons for the hostility of the magisterium to the culture of the eighteenth and nineteenth centuries and have emphasized that the papal condemnations, when examined in the context of specific condemnations, were far less sweeping than they appeared to be to contemporary Catholic and non-Catholic opinion.[5] What is perhaps less noted is the fact that there was little in the way of a foundation on which Catholic scholars and scientists could build a structure of disinterested intellectual activity. Until the teaching Church had experienced a profound ecclesiological revival and reform, Catholic learning could not move on from the dull plateau of defensive, negative, and often far from scholarly apologetic on which it had been stuck ever since the struggle with Jansenism. But the prospect for an opening to the world of modern science depended on *proving* the oft-repeated conviction that there could be no real contradiction between faith and science if each kept to its own precinct. That proof, in turn, was impossible without the kind of intellectual freedom which recognizes in advance that science has to produce a good deal of error before it begins to find truth. This vicious circle was sealed by the ideological principles of nineteenth-century Catholic social theory, which saw the middle ages as the model for a re-Christianized Europe and pointed, not to errors *in* the modern world, but to the modern world (that is, the world of the Enlightenment and the French Revolution) as error itself. There was, according to this view, little need to play the devil's game. And it must be admitted that the experience of Catholic scholars who exerted themselves to accommodate official teaching to the latest word on evolution, only to hear that the "fact" which had been secreted into the Catholic world view was now, by virtue of some new research, only a disproved hypothesis, tended to develop a certain skepticism toward the whole scientific effort. Newman commented on the tendency of Catholics "to think that, in other cases, error will eat up error, if they are but patient, without their trouble."[6] Centers of scholarship which had flourished in the seventeenth and eighteenth centuries disappeared with the Revolution and were seldom reestablished. Jean Leflon has commented on the problem in France after the workshops of Mabillon's successors, the Maurists, and of the Bollandists and the Benedictines of St. Vannes were closed: "After 1800 we had the poetry of Chateaubriand, the striking proclamations of Lamennais—but we lacked a center of scientific Catholic research."[7]

The dim picture of inactivity in France was reflected in Italy, Spain, England, and the United States. There were exceptions, most notably in Germany. Beginning with the work of Möhler and Drey at Tübingen, where Catholic and Protestant theological faculties lived in fruitful competition, German scholars exerted themselves to deal with the historical question. In mid-century the work of Giovanni Battista

De Rossi, who brought the principles of a scientific archae-
ology to the exploration of early Christian Rome, provided
the first example of modern scholarship carried on with the
approval, as well as within the confines, of the Roman
Church. From De Rossi came a line of succession leading
through the French historian Abbé Louis Duchesne (whose
researches scandalized Catholic France by disproving the
legends of the apostolic foundation of many French churches)
to his student, Alfred Loisy. In England, Acton and his as-
sociates on the *Rambler* and its successor journals attempted
to educate Catholic opinion, while Newman—in the flawed
attempt to found an Irish University and, especially in his
last years, when the *Essay on Development* was reissued as a
Catholic rather than a transitional publication—provided the
outlines for a historical philosophy as potentially magisterial
as had been Bossuet's in the seventeenth century. But these
efforts, in spite of specific lines of influence, were not coherent
or specifically scholarly. The first general meeting of Catholic
liberals, the famous congress at Malines in 1863, was primarily
concerned with apologetical, political, and social rather than
scientific issues. And, of course, there was little or no encouragement from Rome.

Crucial was the fact that nineteenth-century Catholic
historiography generally did not deal with Christian origins.
Acton concerned himself with the modern period, with brief
forays into the middle ages to challenge the historical basis for
infallibility; Döllinger wrote of the middle ages, Pastor of
the popes, Newman of the fourth century. There was no
school of Catholic historians dealing with the history of the
New and Old Testaments because, strictly speaking, there was
no historical problem in the bible. The study of scripture was
the purview of the theologian, not the historian; and if the

historian did make use of scripture, he did so with the conviction that his source was qualitatively different from any
other kind of evidence. Schweitzer put the situation succinctly:

> In the Catholic Church the study of the life of Jesus [and one
> must add, of the Old Testament] has remained down to the
> present day [1906] entirely free from skepticism. The reason is
> that in principle it has remained at a pre-Straussian standpoint,
> and does not venture upon an unreserved application of historical
> considerations either to the miracle question or to the Johannine
> question, and naturally therefore resigns the attempt to take
> account of and explain the great historical problem.[8]

In fact, by the time Schweitzer reviewed—and ended—the
"first" quest for the historical Jesus,[9] Marie-Joseph Lagrange
of the Ecole Biblique at Jerusalem and other Catholic scholars
had begun to construct a considerable body of critical studies.
But their *approach* to the "great historical problem" was
far different from that of Loisy, whom Schweitzer did note,
for they operated on a principle foreign to the history of the
quest—one most clearly set forth in Leo's encylical letter on
bible studies, *Providentissimus Deus*—namely, that critical
studies need not inevitably lead to theological reductionism.[10]

Nevertheless, Schweitzer's estimate was, in general, correct.
Catholic scriptural historiography was bogged down in a
positivism which produced historical "facts" as subtly destructive of faith as any which emerged from the positivism of
Strauss or Renan. Emile Poulat cites a striking example of
the kind of teaching the New Testament yielded up to
orthodox historiography in these biographical notes on Christ
and Mary from a work of the late eighties:

Jesus Christ, second person of the Most Blessed Trinity, Messiah conceived by the Holy Spirit at Nazareth 25th of March, 7/5 B.C., born of the Virgin Mary at Bethlehem, December 25th, circumcized January 1st 6/4 B.C., baptized January 6, 29 A.D., crucified at Jerusalem April, 3rd 33, resurrected the 5th, ascended into heaven the 7th of May. . . . Mary, conceived without sin around December 8, 23 B.C., and born around September 8, 22, at Jerusalem (or Nazareth), Virgin-Mother of Jesus Christ, December 25th, 7 B.C., died at Jerusalem (or Ephesus) around August 13, 55 A.D., assumption the 15th.[11]

Whether one regards the reign of Leo XIII as an era of fulfillment or of initiation in Catholic intellectual history, there is little question that events like the opening of the Vatican Archives in 1880, the international congresses at Paris (1888, 1891), Brussels (1894), Fribourg (1897), and Munich (1900), the establishment of the Biblical Commission and the encyclical *Providentissimus Deus,* appeared to contemporaries to mark a new stage in the relationship between Catholic scholarship and the Holy See. But these developments also produced an intensification of the polarization of opinion which had existed since the thirties. Liberal Catholic and conservative, at loggerheads when the pope stood on the conservative side, as did Pius IX, were not reconciled when the pope appeared to favor liberal positions. By the very nature of the situation, differences of opinion were fundamentally theological: both sides operated on the assumption, implicit or explicit, that social, political, and cultural problems should be treated on the basis of Catholic principles, with the general end that European society might recover, or rediscover, its Christian character. Therefore, any substantive advances in Christian knowledge were quickly turned to polemical purposes; and conversely, polemic continued to influence scientific topics and treatments.

These divisions within the Church were intensified by developments outside it. Substantial gains were made in the area of church-state relations under Leo XIII: German Catholics, after the suspension of the Kulturkampf, strove to integrate themselves into national life (with unfortunate consequences for a later generation); the struggle between the pope and the kingdom of Italy was relaxed. But in France— the center of Catholic intellectual life in this period—the Dreyfus affair, the papal policy of rallying Catholics to the Republic, the growing temper of anticlericalism focused on the issue of complete separation of church and state, suggested to liberal and conservative alike that Catholicism and modern secular culture were approaching a crisis of major dimensions. In 1903 Maurice Blondel wrote:

With every day that passes, the conflict between tendencies which set Catholic against Catholic in every order—social, political, philosophical—is revealed as sharper and more general. One could almost say that there are now two quite incompatible "catholic mentalities"—particularly in France.[12]

It is to France, then, where social, political, philosophical, and theological questions were so interrelated, that one must turn for the immediate origins of the Modernist crisis. The general movement of events is clear. During the 1880's and 1890's German critical scholarship (in part interpreted through the work of French critics like Renan and theologians like Auguste Sabatier, but in large measure confronted directly by French exegetes) emphasized the limitations of the fundamentalism of Catholic biblical study. This, in turn, suggested that any revision of Catholic positions on specific questions of interpretation, or even the adoption of a more scientific methodology than had been customary, would also call forth a general reassessment of the relationship of theology to dogma.

This second eventuality had already been considered by a handful of philosophically inclined Catholics, most notably Blondel and Edouard Le Roy, both laymen. They had realized that neo-Thomism could not provide an answer to all the problems raised by the development of European philosophy since the sixteenth century and that the Augustinian tradition in Catholic theology was better suited to deal with the anti-rational tendency in the thought of Schopenhauer, Nietzsche, and Bergson and with the more general critical approach to rationalism which issued from Kant. The critical work which Catholics were beginning to produce strengthened their conviction that a new apologetic was called for, one which viewed dogma and doctrine in terms, not of intellect and assent, but of will and action. These exegetes and philosophers —who unfortunately often knew little of each other's work[13] —and assorted historians, social theorists, and publicists were known as "progressives." Their work centered on Catholic institutes like those at Paris and Toulouse. They had their journals and their correspondence and, of course, their opposition, which ranged from the higher clergy to the seminary faculties of conservative bastions like St. Sulpice in Paris. But there were bishops who shared their opinions and had great hopes for a gradual introduction of scientific criticism into Catholic scholarship and a gradual movement away from the "manual theology"[14] by which priests were educated and by which they led their people. The prospect for the future appeared bright.

But a potentially fruitful tension between progressives and conservatives—celebrated in such figures as Mgr. D'Hulst,

rector of the Catholic Institute at Paris; Wilfrid Ward of the
Dublin Review, the spokesman for the progressive position in
England; and Baron Friedrich von Hügel, a philosopher of
religion—was ruled out by a series of developments in the late
1890's and early 1900's. The party of the left, to continue the
political analogy, gradually split into two groups—later
described by George Tyrrell as the "Erasmians" and the
"would-be Luthers."

In most general terms, the Erasmians, who have kept the
name "progressive" in church history, sought only "to make
the traditional faith profit from recent acquisitions in
religious science."[15] They adhered to the classical formulation
of Catholic teaching, respected and deferred to ecclesiastical
authority, and were sensitive to the difficulties of revising
teaching in a religious society which, in theory, embraced a
wide variety of approaches to faith and worship but, in fact,
was dominated by a highly individualistic devotionalism,
which made "scapulars, medals, and the Rosary . . . more
important than the Mass, private revelations dwelt on more
than the Gospels, La Salette talked about by Catholics more
than the Trinity."[16]

On the other hand, the would-be Luthers "wished to find
in the traditional faith an expression which took into account
all the transformations of the human spirit of which the
development of the sciences was both a symptom and an
agent."[17] This division on the left cut through both the
exegetical and philosophical groups, though the original
breach occurred first on strictly critical questions.

During the late 1890's a very small number of exegetes and
historians on the far left, of whom Alfred Loisy was the most
learned and the most eloquent, published, in their own names
and pseudonymously, books and articles which hinted at
radical theological positions through reports of substantive

developments in criticism and early church history. Considerable attention was drawn to the Catholic Institute at Paris when its rector suggested that there could be a "broad" school of Catholic scholarship, complementary and corrective of the older traditions. Subsequently *Providentissimus Deus* was issued as a corrective to this idea and to tendencies which now became known as *Loisyste*. The Biblical Commission was established—with a significant liberal membership—to serve as a guide to scholars on such vexed questions as the authorship of the Pentateuch and the Johannine comma. With the publication of Loisy's *Evangile et L'Eglise* in 1902, the several positions tended to harden. Progressive critics and historians like Lagrange, Grandmaison, and Pierre Batiffol of the Catholic Institute at Toulouse entered into a complex journalistic effort to clarify the radical position of Loisy, to show that it was not really scientific, and thus vindicate their own efforts. But their attempts were overshadowed by a wave of reaction from the extreme right, which lumped together progressives and *Loisystes,* political liberals, and philosophical innovators like Blondel, Le Roy, and Laberthonnière. The uncritical (and *anti*critical) opposition reduced the issue to an either-or: orthodoxy or disaster. As one conservative critic put it,

If the words of Balaam's ass and the apparition of the angel are an invention . . . even though holy scripture reports them as facts, then why isn't the whole history of Balaam an invention, a lie? And if the history of Balaam is an invention, then why isn't the whole bible a mixture of fact and fancy? Who is to sort out the fable from the history, the allegory from the truth?[18]

Leo XIII had hesitated to affirm the condemnation of Loisy's early works. With the accession of Pius X, a pastoral pope of the sort many liberals had hoped would come forth

from the convocation, the indecision of Leo's last years was
resolved into a strong and active opposition to what Pius, as
Cardinal Sarto of Venice, had called "modern Christianity."[19]
Loisy's books were condemned; a cloud settled over the works
of Lagrange, Batiffol, and Duchesne; and although Blondel
himself was never censured, books by Le Roy and Laberthonnière were placed on the Index. Pius X and conservative
clerics in the Curia had not missed the concatenation of
reforming efforts, nor the influence of French scholarship and
philosophy (and, more recently, of the writings of the English
Jesuit, George Tyrrell) on Italian opinion. Thus, proposals
for ecclesiastical reform and for political action by Italian
Catholics came to be linked to the exegetical work of Loisy,
the critical studies of Catholic learning by Albert Houtin,
the "moral dogmatism" of the French philosophers, and the
antitheological tracts of Tyrrell. The work of Hermann
Schell and his students in Germany seemed to confirm the
international character of the crisis.

The magisterium was faced with two questions: What was
actually happening? What was to be done? The answers to
both were given in two statements of 1907—which named,
described, and condemned the heresy of Modernism.[20] The
decree of the Holy Office *Lamentabili Sane Exitu* (a syllabus
of errors reminiscent of that of 1864) listed sixty-five propositions, drawn entirely from the works of Loisy and Tyrrell
with possible allusions to Le Roy's *Dogme et Critique*, which
were to be rejected by the orthodox.[21] The papal encyclical
Pascendi Dominici Gregis—sketched by Pius, but largely
composed by other hands except for the sections on discipline
—presented in a highly systematic form the ideas of "the
Modernist," corporately described as "a philosopher, a believer, a theologian, an historian, a critic, an apologist, a re-

former." At the time and subsequently, both documents were extensively analyzed. Inevitably they provided the outline for conservative attempts to study the crisis to which they were a response. Their limitations, from both the theological and the historical point of view, were recognized by progressives who, while accepting the need for the condemnation, were eager to prove, like liberals in the nineteenth century, that the pronouncements did not utterly preclude any further innovation in Catholic thought, or condemn the substantial achievement of men like Lagrange and Batiffol.

The documents condemning Modernism were themselves synthetic. But their significance would be great from the historical point of view even if they did not substantially reflect the opinions of the "would-be Luthers" of the turn of the century, and this for several reasons. In the first place, the papal condemnation accelerated the process of polarization between those who wanted to modernize the Church, to reform and revive it in the sense which motivated the progressives of Vatican II, and those whom Blondel called the "veterists," subsequently known as the "integrists," who insisted that there could be no change because there was no flaw. In pursuit of the real errors of the so-called "Modernists" (hereafter referred to as such), a pursuit which was as often as not a pursuit of the reputations of men rather than the weaknesses of their ideas, the work and hope of the progressives was long obscured. "The Catholic who began by accepting at face value the *credo* of the Modernist ended by suspecting any Catholic a little more intellectual than himself, who uttered ancient truths in words he had not learnt in the schoolroom."[22] Reformers were accused of wishing to destroy Catholic faith because they wished more and better theology.

As E. E. Y. Hales has recently pointed out, it is difficult to assess the effect of the style and character of the condemnation. Comparing the "explosion" of *Pascendi Dominici Gregis* to "an atomic mushroom cloud," he wrote:

We shall never know how many valuable shoots, which might have brought forth good fruit, were killed, alongside the dangerous errors, when the bomb dropped, nor how many men were prevented, thereafter, from ever thinking at all because some had fallen into error in their thinking. The price that has to be paid when such high explosive is used can be tremendous; a kind of intellectual sterilization may be included when thinking becomes so dangerous.[23]

Baron von Hügel, who gradually detached himself from his friends Loisy and Tyrrell when he realized the extent of their radicalism, encouraged Cuthbert Butler, the church historian, to engage in critical work in 1922. Butler replied:

Years ago I recognized that these things—Xtian origins, New Testament, History of Dogma, etc.,—have been made impossible for a priest, except on the most narrow apologetic lines. . . . The only freedom in biblical things and the rest is that of a tram, to go ahead as fast as you like on rails, but if you try to arrive at any station not on the line, you are derailed. Textual criticism of the most technical kind is the only form of biblical study open. . . . When the Biblical Commission got under way, and the *Lamentabili* and *Pascendi* were issued, I deliberately turned away from all this work.[24]

And Jean Leflon has quoted the eloquent words addressed to him by a professor at the Catholic Institute, a progressive: "If you ever treat of the Modernist crisis, do not forget to tell how much we suffered."[25]

Once only Protestant critics asked the question, "Was it

really essential, in order to get rid of Loisy and his group, that the Vatican should thus arraign the whole movement of modern thought?"[26] The historical fact is that at the time it appeared very necessary. We may have compassion for the emotional and intellectual anguish of those caught up in the crisis; we may regret those whose energies and achievements were dissipated by the pall which fell over Catholic intellectual life in the wake of the condemnation. But we should not be blind to the force with which the rationalist and anti-rationalist criticisms of Christian life struck at the imaginations of those who were charged with a task conceived almost entirely in defensive terms: the *preservation* of the faith. Psychologically, priests who believed in the near-identity of theology and dogma, who held that "every scriptural dictum was reductively a logical statement,"[27] could understand and administer only in the most rigorous manner both the condemnation and its disciplinary measures—particularly the "loyalty oath" for all priests engaged in any kind of teaching.

The same political and social pressure upon dogmatic questions noted above exacerbated the anti-Modernist crusade. Theological integrism, the intolerant assertion of *"le Catholicisme VRAI,"* meant support for the Action Française and similar movements; it meant the condemnation of the Sillon (1910) and the frustration of any attempt to arrest the process of paganization in France. It was psychologically impossible, given the siege mentality of the times, for the magisterium to entertain the notion that "heresy is a by-product of active teaching"[28] or to realize the considerable pathos in the strivings of men like Loisy, Tyrrell, and Sullivan to keep Catholicism even at the risk of losing Christianity. Nor could they realize that the Modernist effort was a significant indictment of the orthodox tendency to lose sight

of the fundamentals of Christianity in the exaltation of a
tradition extremely attenuated from scriptural sources, at
least in devotional practice, if not in official teaching. Tyrrell,
fond of a particular phrase, explained that when he first came
to the Church, he had done so because of its universal appeal
and its care to hold on to any tool whereby faith might be
preserved or extended; care was always taken "lest the baby
be lost with the bath." But when he became disaffected with
Catholicism, it was precisely because there was too much bath
water, too much reason to fear that the baby was drowning.
Yet he and others were so much a product of the "extrinsic"
Catholicism which they sought to reform that, even after
Roman opposition became fixed, they were unable to detach
themselves from the confusion of sacrament with sacramental,
dogma with theology, authentic mysticism with devotional
habit, and so proposed a symbolic Catholicism instead of a
reformed Christian Church.

The substance of *Pascendi Dominici Gregis* demonstrates
the magisterium's inability to realize how much of the Catholic tradition, for better or for worse, the Modernist "devia-
tion" had preserved, and the implications of that effort for
orthodox apologetic. Yet it is also most effective in conveying
the sense of the movement as a subversive clerical conspiracy,
fundamentally different from anything in previous church
history even at the same time that its teaching summed up
all errors advanced since Arius and Nestorius, so that it was
indeed "the sum of all heresies." The theme is sounded repeatedly:

The partisans of error are to be sought not only among the
Church's open enemies, but what is to be more dreaded and
deplored, in her very bosom, and are the more mischievous the

less they keep in the open. We allude, venerable brethren, to many who belong to the Catholic laity and what is more sad, to the ranks of the priesthood itself. . . . There are Catholics, yea, and priests too, who say these things openly: and they boast that they are going to reform the Church by these ravings. . . . But what is most amazing is that there are Catholics and priests who, we would fain believe, abhor such enormities, and yet act as if they fully approve of them. . . . They are to be found among the laity, and in the ranks of the clergy, and they are not wanting even in the last place where one might expect to meet them, in religious communities.

To contemporaries, Modernism as presented in the encyclical must have seemed an enormous plot, all the more impressive for the fact that it was so invisible, for it was "one of the cleverest devices of the Modernists (as they are commonly and rightly called) to present their doctrines without order and systematic arrangement, in a scattered and disjointed manner, so as to make it appear as if their minds were in doubt or hesitation, whereas in reality they are quite fixed and steady."[29]

Although it was in no case the reality, the image of Modernism as a coherent conspiracy was not altogether of the pope's creation. Those men most clearly associated with the crisis by the magisterium—Tyrrell, Loisy, the Italian liberals like Murri and Buonaiuti, and the several contributors to the Modernist journals which carried on a short and vitriolic existence after 1907—varied in their response to the papal documents but generally accepted the name and the concept of a movement. Loisy alone perceived how hopeless the effort was. While he continued to write about Modernism and against Rome, he abandoned any hope that a neo-Catholicism which would sustain human solidarity and the moral progress of civilization through a religious life based on a "symbolist" reading of Christian revelation could ever be brought into existence within the framework of the Church. But Loisy's efforts to deflate the papal synthesis—he called Modernism as defined "a figment of the theological imagination"—were vitiated by the terms of the condemnation. In denying the existence of the movement as defined, he was proving that it was just as the pope had said. Those who continued to hope that, if reform were out of the question, revolution was still a possibility found it to their advantage to exaggerate the extent and coherence of the "movement." The encylical was countered with a "Program of the Modernists" and other documents. Tyrrell, in his last book, spoke of "Modernist Anglicans and Nonconformists—nay, Modernist Jews and Mussulmans."[30] Publicists of the movement estimated that it had affected 15,000 priests in France alone; Tyrrell said 20,000 was a likely figure, adding that if one estimated the situation according to the zeal of the condemnation, 40,000 would be a better figure. Loisy, replying to these estimates, said that 1,500 was a better figure than 15,000. A sensitive contemporary student of the crisis of the French clergy (of which Modernism was only a phase) argued that 150 was even more accurate. There was, of course, no way of estimating how many curés in Aix or Palermo, Strasbourg, Liverpool or Boston had read Loisy's Evangile et l'Eglise, or Tyrrell's Letter to a Professor. Nor was there any way of proving that "troubled" priests had not been troubled by Harnack rather than by Loisy, or by Matthew Arnold rather than by Tyrrell. As several students of the crisis have pointed out, the illusion of a vast movement was increased by the use of pseudonyms on the part of a handful of French critics, most notably Loisy and Joseph Turmel, by Tyrrell during his most productive years, and subsequently by "modernizers" and progressives who wished to put forth the less radical opinions without running the risk of being identified with heretics.[31]

But the impact of the encyclical—and, to a lesser degree, of the syllabus—was not limited to its own day. By 1910 the movement had collapsed and was over. Loisy had disassociated himself from it and had finally received the excommunication for which he had longed; Tyrrell was dead; and the work of the "distant echo" of Modernism in America, William Sullivan, was without impact either on his fellow Americans or on Europe. Innovation was at an end, at least to the eye of authority. But, as has already been suggested, the condemnation provided a ready weapon against *any* proposals for reform or scholarship of all but "the most technical kind." Periodically, especially in postwar France, the specter of Modernism has been raised; and all through the fifty-year period the integrists used the condemnation as a rod with which to beat down any sort of opposition—including the attempts of Benedict XV to end the post-Modernist reign of terror.[32]

The encyclical, being primarily a theological and not a historical document, and a strong though not *ex cathedra* statement of official teaching, has inevitably shaped Catholic treatments of the crisis. Apart from several diatribes, monuments to that inquisitorial atavism in Catholic life which the Modernists protested,[33] the more or less progressive treatments of the crisis were affected by "tensions between faith or theological postulates (which are identified with faith), on the one hand, and positively or apparently established historical fact, on the other."[34] Catholic apologies have long tended to resolve the tension in favor of theology, accepting the decision of the magisterium about a given subject as

a guarantee, not only that the problem should not be looked
into for reasons of faith, but that it need not be looked into
for reasons of intellect. The following statement conveys the
implication that the Catholic is only interested in those
movements of ideas which "made it":

In English-speaking countries particularly, the period is still regarded . . . as a series of false starts resolved by authoritative condemnations: of Americanism (1892), Modernism (1907), the *Sillon*
(1910), the *Action française* (1926); and seen in that light it holds
little interest except to the historian of the past.[35]

It is hardly necessary to emphasize that the "historian of the
past" (what else?) holds the key to the future in order to make
the point that it is difficult to make sense of the turnings of
church history without knowing somehing about the roads
which were *not* traveled.

The "theological postulate" with which the Catholic
historian-apologist had to work has been in most cases
delicately handled. *The Catholic Encyclopedia* tells us:
"Modernism is a composite system: its assertions lack that
principle which unites the natural faculties in a living being."[36] Jean Rivière, who wrote what was until very recently
the only comprehensive history of the movement, contributed
the article on the subject to the *Dictionnaire de Théologie
Catholique* and exerted himself to lay the rumors of "crypto-
Modernism" and "neo-Modernism" which cropped up in the
1920's. He wrote that Modernism was "a collective term to
designate the religious crisis which marked, in the Church,
the turn of the century and called forth the principal acts of
Pius X." He recognized that "even more than 'liberalism'
Modernism is one of those ill-defined terms which do not

contain any precise notion and can for this reason be taken in
a good as well as a bad sense," and gave the example of the
propaganda of the Action Française as an example of the latter. But he argued that the approach which saw Modernism
as a "simple myth," examples of which could be found on
both the far right and the far left, was also invalid. Rivière
followed Loisy in regarding "the necessity for a reform of
Catholic teaching" as the factor unifying diverse tendencies.
He further realized the sincerity of the Modernist insistence
that "this reform must take place within the Church and to
its profit," and he built his comprehensive history on the
principle that the only real point of departure for a sound
history of the movement was the actual work of the men
involved in it.[37] But Rivière, too, had a bias. He wrote in
large part to salvage the reputations of the progressives, especially of Batiffol and his students at the Institute of Toulouse,
and exerted himself to exonerate them by painting the errors
of the "real" Modernists in bold colors and in their own
words (which is not difficult to do). The Manichean approach
to the history of the crisis has been thoroughly abandoned by
Emile Poulat, who has written in the spirit of Henri Marrou:

The history of these combats cannot be written as it has long been
—as a contest between two opposing schools, two distinct tem-
peraments—on the one side, criticism, on the other, tradition; on
the one side the progressives, on the other the conservatives.[38]

Rivière escaped from the exclusive polarization of left and
right, characteristic of the polemic produced immediately
after the crisis, but only in order to accentuate the differences
between the Modernists and the progressives. Poulat, while
clearly recognizing that the reform and renewal of the mid-

twentieth-century Church stem in large measure from the work of the progressives like Lagrange, Batiffol, Grandmaison and the "Blondelians," also emphasizes the initial sincerity of the radicals, their concern for the Catholic tradition, and the reasonableness of many of their criticisms and proposals.

The final historiographical issue raised by the encyclical is scarcely less complex than the problem of sorting out modernizers from Modernists, progressives from heretics. This is the question of the sources of Modernist teaching. The encyclical was hailed by many Catholics as a commanding work of scholarship. Yet, in fact, the general ascription of Modernist error to pride, liberal Protestantism, Kant, and the more general failings of the Enlightenment and the Reformation, gives little help in the search for origins and influences. Many books published soon after the condemnation—most notably, a very long article by several authors in the *Dictionnaire Apologétique de la Foi Catholique*—attempted to remedy this lack, the latter with some success. But these efforts were again limited by the synthetic character of the theological document they attempted to annotate.[39]

The effort to fix the movement in the general context of the history of ideas has taken several directions. The most sweeping, and the least enlightening, are those which trace Modernist ideas back to Voltaire, to Erasmus, to Luther, and even to Socrates.[40] Only slightly less problematic is the line of influence from Kant, suggested by the encyclical and developed by several Catholic critics.[41] Other philosophical attributions were made, most notably to Hegel. All suffer from the fact that by the late nineteenth century the influences of Kant and Hegel were so diffused throughout non-Catholic culture that, when the Catholic began to read beyond the traditional intellectual heritage of the Counter-Reformation and the seventeenth century, he usually met, not one or two individual writers who shaped his thought consistently and clearly along certain identifiable lines, but another whole tradition, one which had been gradually developing since the Renaissance and whose several parts were likely to appear complementary. The very general notion of the limits of the human intellect for grasping direct knowledge of the super-natural (which could be attributed to Kant) was a hallmark of Modernist thought. But this notion shaded off into the belief that some kind of idea or spirit making for human progress in moral growth and the evolution of civilizations was inherent in the process of history, somehow shaping it, possibly even shaped by it at the same time (and this could be attributed to Hegel). But Christian mystics and theologians, like Thomas Aquinas, had long pointed out the limitations of man's knowledge of divinity. Hegel's Idea might be the Holy Ghost. Similarly, by 1900, Herbert Spencer had ceased to be a historical figure and had become instead a symbol for a variety of notions which would be grouped today under the heading of Social Darwinism.

The effort to locate Modernism in the context of earlier Catholic efforts to come to terms with this "alien" culture, and with its Protestant roots, has been more fruitful, though Modernists and orthodox historians rejected the efforts of Edmond Vermeil to trace Modernist ideas back to the work of John-Adam Möhler and Drey at Tübingen in the 1820's.[42] Loisy and Tyrrell both felt that the effort to see Modernism as either a perversion, or a logical extension, of Newman's ideas was unfair—to the Modernists. The progressives thought it was unfair to Newman.[43] The example of great mid-century liberals, especially Lacordaire, and the writings of Mon-talembert are among the few examples of influence that can be documented and assessed as significant.

Precisely because traditional, liberal Catholic, liberal Protestant, and "rationalist" (or "scientistic" or "positivist") strains were woven together in Modernist thought (just as they were in other contemporary movements of ideas), the task of relating Modernism to the general history of ideas can be approached through the study of specific disciplines. Modernist thought can be visualized on the model of atomic structure: one has to imagine a cluster of ideas grouped around a double nucleus. One focus of attraction was the problem of history. Studied scientifically, could the scriptures be regarded as anything more than particularly powerful documents of the religious sense in evolution and, more specifically, of the religious genius of the Jewish people and their Christian successors? Did not scientific history built on the model of physics and biology exclude the supernatural? Loisy wrote:

God does not show himself at the end of the astronomer's telescope. The geologist does not find him in his samples, nor the chemist at the bottom of his test tube. God may very well exist through all the world, but he is in no way the proper object of science.[44]

Could the gospel, even as the product of faith, be anything more than a human history? Since it was "as man, not as God, that Jesus entered human history," it appeared that the historian could say nothing about the nature of the experience which prompted the first Christians to believe what they did about Jesus other than to describe the various religious currents to which they (and Jesus) were subject in their day: late messianic Judaism, and, subsequently, Hellenistic philosophy, Gnosticism, and the competition of state and mystery religions. In theory, these conclusions did not preclude the theological effort. In fact, by historicist principles, they did. For the positivist, if a thing were not historical, it did not exist.

Talcott Parsons describes two main directions of the nineteenth-century "idealistic interest in human action" as "detailed, concrete history on the one hand, the philosophy of history on the other."[45] For the Modernists, the results of detailed concrete historical research on the bible and early church history implied a philosophy of history as universal and binding as Bossuet's or Augustine's. But the philosophical nucleus is more difficult to characterize briefly than its historical counterpart, because it derives only partly from the positivist approach just described and because it is similar in many respects to the philosophical position assumed by the Blondelians. A long debate, which focused on Blondel's essay *Histoire et Dogme* (1905), sorted out the differences to the satisfaction of the participants, though unfortunately not to the enlightenment of conservative opinion. Blondel made it clear that the progressives held neither with those who believed that theology and dogma ruled history (*extrincisme*) or with those who felt that history must rule over theology and dogma (*historicisme*), but sought instead a third position, based on a philosophy of action and will, which would rescue faith from what was in effect a war between two different kinds of positivism.[46] Philosophically, Modernism dealt with questions of pragmatism and voluntarism in religious experience, of course; but it was primarily concerned with a view of the history of religion which would guarantee significance to a "demythologized" Christianity and preserve the institutions of Catholicism. The Modernists found such a philosophy in the application of evolutionary principles to the history of religion.

If this double nucleus is taken as the point of departure for an investigation of the sources of Modernism, or at least for the task of locating it in a context at once larger and more certain than that provided by the Enlightenment or the "idea of the modern," the results are more promising. Although Loisy never attempted to establish personal contact with Renan, he heard the great man's lectures at the Collège de France and aspired to refute him on his own grounds. Certain sources can be found in the works of Harnack, Holtzmann, Weiss, and others. Thus, a tradition of historical research can be traced back to the school of Ranke and its philological antecedents. The complementary sequence in the Catholic tradition would focus on the idea of development and the concept of tradition, and would make connections and comparisons between Modernist historiography and earlier Catholic work, though with considerable caution. Loisy insisted that although his political and social awareness had been stimulated by reading Montalembert, he had learned nothing about the technique or nature of historical study from the liberals. And if Tyrrell admitted a strong parallel between his own case and that of Döllinger, he also argued that it obtained only in their attitudes toward authority, not toward history.

The greatest difficulties come when one attempts to list contemporary influences. The striking parallels between much of Modernist thought and the ideas of the generation of the nineties seldom rest on any clear contacts. Many contemporaries saw Modernism as nothing more than a "form and an episode of the sickness of pragmatism."[47] Tyrrell cited the works of Darwin, Schopenhauer, Bergson, James, Adhemar, Poincaré, Dilthey, and others in his letters; but his friend Henri Bremond told Loisy that at least a third of

Tyrrell's ideas came from Matthew Arnold.[48] Frazer's generalizations about the stages of religious development seemed to
have made a great impact on Tyrrell, especially in his last
book. Loisy, however, from his earliest articles, had rejected
sociological laws and had boasted that he was without general
philosophical education. He read Voltaire's *Essai sur les
Moeurs* for the first time when he was sixty-three, only read
Bergson to refute him after the crisis, and once, when ill with
grippe, read a few pages of Poincaré's *Science et l'Hypothèse*.
He claimed that he had never read Plato, Aristotle, Descartes,
Pascal, Spinoza, Leibniz, Kant or Comte, the man he was often
compared with.[49] Sullivan was more influenced by Acton and
Martineau than by the European Modernists or by liberal
Protestant biblical scholars, and was quite hostile to most
contemporary developments in science and philosophy.

All these historiographical problems are rooted in the
paradox that the Modernist effort at updating the Church
from within had to present the substance of modern science
without appearing to have simply taken it over lock, stock,
and bullets from the enemies of the Church: rationalist,
liberal Protestant, pragmatist, immanentist, Kantian. Loisy
insisted on the originality of his critical work because once
the statement had been made that "Loisy's teaching is German rational-Protestant theology translated into French,"[50]
it was no longer necessary for the conservative to examine the
conclusions of his work on their own merits. Similarly, Tyrrell
polemicized violently against liberal Protestantism—in part,
perhaps, because he felt that he had been overly drawn to
liberal Protestant positions in his early writing—but, primarily, because he knew, as did Loisy, that once an idea could
be labeled liberal Protestant or Kantian, it could be ignored.
The paradox was intensified by the fact that the Modernists

were in revolt against the rationalism of the post-Tridentine Church *and* the rationalism of the secular age, although they tended to underestimate their dependence on the modern culture they sought to manipulate. Loisy's view of history was distorted by a naïve positivism, and Tyrrell and Sullivan were inclined to think too optimistically of a science of religion. This was because—as the "latecomers" to the Enlightenment, in Gentile's phrase[51]—they were overwhelmed by outpourings from the Pandora's box of ideas and notions, hypotheses and laws, data and insight, which had been closed to Catholic thinkers for so long. (In the Modernist crisis it was not the laymen, but the priests, who insisted on carrying on the fight to the end and were more often censured, perhaps because laymen were less inclined to sacrifice all for secular science, knowing it, as they did, more intimately and with fewer illusions as to its power.) This confusion of themes in Modernist thought puzzled even the pope: the Modernists were condemned both as rationalists and as anti-intellectuals in the encyclical.

As this brief discussion of interpretations and sources suggests, generalizations about the historiography of the Modernist crisis are as unsatisfactory as synthetic answers to the nagging question, What was Modernism? The Catholic has been accustomed to ask this question with the fear and trembling that has long attended investigation in those areas which the magisterium has marked with danger signs. Even after all the methodological problems have been rehearsed and the limitations of previous Catholic approaches outlined, he still longs for the reassuring generalization. For the Modernists were, after all, heretics—weren't they? The Modernist crisis, however, cannot be described in a phrase; it was a manifestation of a crucial clash of two cultures, a stage in the process of acculturation whereby Catholic Christianity has come to know the secular epoch.

Nothing dates a man, a work of intellect or insight, or a movement as surely as the term "modern." Many Modernist ideas and positions appear as irrelevant to contemporary concerns as to the orthodox ones against which they were juxtaposed. The critical infrastructure of Modernist ecclesiology, as it was developed by the men studied here, was flawed by positivism. In turn, their whole idea of the Christian gospel and of dogmatic Christology was prejudiced by their idea of Jesus. The potentially corrective and reforming tension between a philosophically disinterested historiography and a propositional—and often unhistorical—theology quickly deteriorated into the irreconcilable opposition of history and transcendence. The men who were to provide the signposts to the future were not those who accepted, however grudgingly, this opposition, but those like Blondel and von Hügel who realized that it was a false one. The Modernists were tending to naturalize religion, as their critics have long pointed out, whereas the tendency of modern Christianity has been much more toward recognizing the spiritual character of nature. The irrelevance of much of Modernist criticism and its Christology, emphasized by the dramatic eruption of the theology of Karl Barth a few years after the end of the crisis, is not the only illustration of the remoteness of the Modernists' thinking from the concerns of the second half of the twentieth century. Their tendency to maintain the juxtaposition of elite and mass in the sociology of the Church and their penchant for other dichotomies and paradoxes— intellect versus will, reason versus experiences, dogma versus the immanent apprehension of divinity—were concomitants of their position on the fundamental issue. Von Hügel wrote:

Under the term Modernist, there are grouped together, as objects
of admiration or of suspicion . . . men . . . holding either one of
two . . . quite irreconcilable points of view; religion conceived as
a purely intrahuman phenomenon, for which no evidence is to be
found beyond the aspirations of humanity, and a religion conceived as having a basis in evidence and metaphysics; as the effect
on us of something greater than ourselves—of something greater
than any purely human facts and desires.[52]

Von Hügel's distinction is neat, but hard to apply at least
to the subjects of this study. Such an unambiguous sorting
out of positions obscures the point that many men who believe
that religion is about God as well as about man, and who admit both historical and metaphysical evidence for its truth,
still feel that, psychologically at least, religion remains a
purely inter- and intra-human phenomenon. Often it is precisely for this reason that they are Christians.

The Catholic in the second half of the twentieth century
appears to be much more sophisticated about the critical and
dogmatic questions which were such a bouleversement for
Modernist, progressive, and orthodox alike. Unhampered by
the Modernist dichtomization of dogma and feeling, he knows
that "every formula in which faith is expressed can in principle be surpassed while still retaining its truth."[53] He is
taught that the gospels are "religious testimonies addressed
to us by the primitive Church," and is not surprised to hear
that the Catholic apologist should be urged to "take more
seriously a seeming discontinuity between the earthly Jesus
and the resurrected Christ, and focus on the constancy,
stability, and permanence of the witness to Jesus."[54] Chastened
by the inheritance of two world wars and the tensions of the
atomic age, he is a critical, cautious, and realistic adherent to

the idea of progress. He is probably aware of the attraction which medievalism and mass-society theory have until recently exercised over the Christian imagination. He is much more conscious of social problems than were the Modernists and much more aware of the sociological complexities of church organization. If he is particularly enlightened, he may even extend his enthusiasm for tolerance and pluralism to the hierarchy.

Various aspects of the radical response to the crisis in which conservative, progressive, liberal, and Modernist were all involved may still have a peculiar resonance for the Catholic today, especially with respect to ecumenism and the questions of authority and tradition. But it is the more general problem of belief that will probably hold his attention. Because they were sidetracked by much that was passing in modern secular culture and because they were themselves so much the products and prisoners of the ecclesiology they sought to reform, the Modernists were unable to give a satisfactory answer to the question which issued from the clash between their childhood faith, seminary training, and pastoral work: How can Christian faith best be taught? But they did attempt an answer. The tragedy and significance of the Modernists lies in the fact that they suffered—as someone had to suffer, as Christians still do suffer—an immediate and paralyzing awareness of the long and apparently irreversible process whereby Christian belief and hope seemed to have disappeared from the world. And even the most assured Christian can learn with compassion about men who wrote as did George Tyrrell:

The silence of God is so inexplicable, so seemingly irrational and willful; the difficulties He throws in the way of belief so incon

sistent with the stress He lays upon belief, that one need not
always be accused of Judaic obstinacy and blindness if one cries
out passionately in the dark for just one word to show that there is
someone there.[55]

NOTES

[1] Robert Rouquette, "Bilan du Modernisme," *Etudes*, Vol. 289 (June 1956),
p. 323.

[2] Gustave Weigel, *Catholic Theology in Dialogue* (New York, 1960), pp. 34–
36. Cf. Robert Murray, "New Testament Eschatology and the Constitution
de Ecclesia of Vatican II," *Heythrop Journal*, Vol. VII, No. 1, pp. 33–42.

[3] Lord Acton, *Essays on Freedom and Power* ("Conflicts with Rome"), ed.
G. Himmelfarb (New York, 1956), p. 244.

[4] Henri Marrou, "Philologie et Histoire dans la Période du Pontificat de
Léon XIII," in *Aspetti della Cultura Cattolica nell'età di Leone XIII* (Rome,
1961), p. 87. Also, on the contemporary setting, H. Holstein, "Au temps du
Modernisme," *Etudes*, Vol. 291 (November 1956), pp. 212–233.

[5] Cf. Roger Aubert, "Religious Liberty from 'Mirari Vos' to the 'Syllabus,' "
Concilium, Vol. 7, No. 1 (September 1965), pp. 49–57, especially p. 56, col. 1.

[6] Cited by J. Derek Holmes, "Newman and Mivart—Two Attitudes to a
Nineteenth-century Problem," *Clergy Review*, N. S., Vol. 1, No. 11 (November
1965), pp. 861–862.

[7] Jean Leflon, in *Aspetti*, p. 111.

[8] Albert Schweitzer, *The Quest of the Historical Jesus*, tr. W. Montgomery
(New York, 1961), pp. 295 n.2, 296. Scholars in touch with Protestant work
knew how serious the situation was. Cf. Maurice Nédoncelle, *Baron Friedrich
von Hügel: A Study of His Life and Thought*, tr. M. Vernon (London, 1937),
p. 96. Another layman, François Lenormant, was one of "the first to see that
the New Criticism had some truth in it." Cf. Georges Weill, *Histoire du
Catholicisme Liberal en France, 1828–1908* (Paris, 1909), pp. 242–260, for the
history of Catholic attitudes toward Church studies before 1880.

[9] Cf. James M. Robinson, *A New Quest of the Historical Jesus* (London,
1959), pp. 13, 26–47.

[10] Marrou points out how little effect Dilthey's distinction between natural
and human sciences had on men inspired by Renan's view of religion as "an
exact science of spiritual things." Positivist historiography, condemned in
Providentissimus Deus as a false criticism, was based on a double error; its
practitioners believed that history was like physics, and they believed that
physics was as simple as introductory school and university courses made it
appear. Marrou, "Philologie et Histoire . . . ," in *Aspetti*, p. 98. Cf. also
Robinson, *New Quest*, pp. 28–29, 39.

11 Emile Poulat, *Histoire, Dogme et Critique dans la Crise Moderniste* (Paris, 1962), p. 619.

12 Maurice Blondel, *The Letter on Apologetics, and History and Dogma*, tr. Alexander Dru and Illtyd Trethowan (London, 1964), p. 221.

13 "Loisy, who reproached his adversaries for ignoring exegesis, was accused by them of ignoring theology. Blondel, who reproached the *Loisystes* for their 'philosophical blindness,' admitted his own critical blindness." Poulat, *Histoire*, pp. 614–615. Cf. René Marlé, ed., *Au Coeur de la Crise Moderniste: Le Dossier Inédit d'une Controverse* (Paris, 1960).

14 Cf. Charles Davis, "Theology in Seminary Confinement," *Downside Review*, 265 (1963), pp. 307–316.

15 George Tyrrell to Baron von Hügel, December 23, 1907; Poulat, *Histoire*, pp. 614–615. The progressive and Modernist approaches to faith are contrasted in E. Hocédez, *Histoire de la Théologie au XIXᵉ Siècle* (Paris, 1947), Vol. III, pp. 103–190; Roger Aubert, *Le Problème de l'Acte de Foi* (Louvain, 1958), pp. 388–392; Poulat, *Histoire*, p. 269 and passim.

16 Maisie Ward, *Unfinished Business* (New York, 1964), p. 52.

17 Poulat, *Histoire*, p. 615.

18 *Ibid.*, p. 149.

19 Pierre Fernessole, *Pie X, Essai Historique* (Paris, 1953), Vol. 2, pp. 191–192. Pius also spoke of the intellectual dangers in his very first official statement.

20 Fernessole, *Pie X*, Vol. 2, pp. 196–200; Jean Rivière, *Le Modernisme dans l'Eglise, Etude d'Histoire Religieuse Contemporaine* (Paris, 1929), pp. 334, 351–372.

21 Rivière, *Modernisme*, pp. 333–348, 381–388; Alfred Loisy, *Simples Réflexions sur le Décret du Saint-Office "Lamentabili Sane Exitu" et sur l'Encyclique "Pascendi Dominici Gregis"* (Ceffonds, 1908).

22 M. Ward, *Unfinished Business*, p. 51.

23 E. E. Y. Hales, "The Americanist Controversy," *Month*, N. S. Vol. 31 (January 1964), p. 36. Cf. also Leonard Swidler, "Freedom and the Catholic Church," *Theology Today*, Vol. XXI, No. 3 (October 1964), pp. 334–341, especially p. 337: "No one will ever know the number of books that never saw the light of day because of lack of ecclesiastical permission."

24 Alec Vidler, *20th Century Defenders of the Faith* (London, 1965), p. 37.

25 Leflon, in *Aspetti*, p. 111.

26 H. L. Stewart, *Modernism, Past and Present* (London, 1932), p. 321. See the Bibliographical Note in this volume for other Protestant discussions of the crisis.

27 Weigel, *Theology in Dialogue*, p. 35.

28 Marrou, "Philologie et Histoire . . . ," in *Aspetti*, p. 89.

29 For the full text of the encyclical, see the official translation reprinted in Paul Sabatier, *Modernism* (New York, 1908), pp. 232–233, 246, 255, 323.

30 Rivière, *Modernisme*, p. vii; George Tyrrell, *Christianity at the Crossroads* (London, 1910), p. 10.

[31] The argument is summarized by Fernessole in *Pie X*, Vol. 2, pp. 161–166. On the question of pseudonyms, cf. Rivière, *Modernisme*, pp. 561–564, and Poulat, *Histoire*, pp. 621–677.

[32] In addition to the article of Rouquette mentioned above (Note 1) and that of Holstein (Note 4), cf. L. de Grandmaison, "Une Nouvelle Crise Moderniste Este-Elle Possible?" *Etudes*, Vol. 176 (1923), pp. 641–647; Jean Rivière, "Chronique de Théologie Fondementale: La Crise Moderniste devant l'Opinion d'Aujourd'hui," *Revue des Sciences Religieuses*, January–April 1940, pp. 140–182; L. J. Lefevre, "Le Cinquantenaire de 'Pascendi,'" *La Pensee Catholique*, No. 47 (1957) pp. 52–53, "Cri d'Alarme," No. 48, 1–6; Luigi Paggiaro, *Il Modernismo a Cinquanta Anni dalla sua Condanna* (Padua-Rome-Naples, 1957), especially pp. 183–210. On the intentions of Pius in making a synthetic, rather than a personal, assault on the radical position, and the status of the teaching of the papal documents, see Rivière, *Modernisme*, pp. 346, 364–367. For other more recent revivals of the accusation, see Notes to the Conclusion in this volume.

[33] For example, J. Godrycz, *The Doctrine of Modernism and Its Refutation* (Philadelphia, 1908).

[34] Hubert Jedin, "General Introduction to Church History," in Karl Baus, *From the Apostolic Community to Constantine* (London, 1965), p. 3.

[35] Blondel, *Letter on Apologetics*, p. 18; cf. also p. 9: "The Modernist controversy . . . appears as a defunct episode."

[36] "Modernism," in *The Catholic Encyclopedia*, Vol. X (New York, 1911), p. 415 (article by A. Vermeersch).

[37] Jean Rivière, "Modernisme," in *Dictionnaire de Théologie Catholique* (Paris, 1929), Vol. X (Part 2), col. 2010; Rivière, *Modernisme*, p. xiii; cf. Alec Vidler, *The Modernist Movement in the Roman Catholic Church* (Cambridge, England, 1934), p. 9.

Poulat has been criticized for his "sociological" approach to the crisis. Canon Roger Aubert, the dean of French church historians, remarks that "the historian cannot stop at the description of phenomena, but must try to move on to motivations," as he concludes his assessment of a book described by the author as "an imaginary colloquy" with the discordant voices of the past (*Revue d'Histoire Ecclesiastique*, Vol. LXI, No. 1 [1966], p. 229). Presumably the resolution of this methodological problem depends on an exhaustive examination of unpublished sources, especially the Loisy papers. Cf. also the assessments in the *Revue Historique*, Vol. CCXXX (1963), and the *Nouvelle Revue Théologique*, Vol. LXXXV (1963).

[38] Marrou, "Philologie et Histoire . . . ," in *Aspetti*, p. 93; cited in Poulat, *Histoire*, p. 613.

[39] "Modernisme," in *Dictionnaire Apologétique de la Foi Catholique* (Paris, 1916), Vol. III, cols. 591–695. The tradition continues with Lucio da Veiga Coutinho, *Tradition et Histoire dans la Controverse Moderniste, 1898–1910* (Rome, 1954), which approaches Loisy and Tyrrell in large part through the Catholic literature generated by the crisis.

40 Stewart, *Modernism, Past and Present* is the most extreme example; most students have been willing to stop at Rousseau and/or Luther. Cf. F. A. Forbes, *A Short Life of Pius X* (London, 1925), pp. 67–68.

41 For instance, Rivière, *Modernisme*, pp. 37–40; "Modernisme," in *Dictionnaire Apologétique de la Foi Catholique*, cols. 655–665.

42 Edmond Vermeil, *Jean-Adam Möhler et l'Ecole Catholique de Tubingue (1815–1840)* (Paris, 1913), pp. ix–xiv, 451–473. L. de Grandmaison, "L'Ecole Catholique de Tubingue et les Origines du Modernisme," *Recherches de Science Religieuse*, Vol. IX (1919), pp. 388–409. Loisy on Vermeil: Alfred Loisy, "*Mémoiries pour Servir à l'Histoire Religieuse de Notre Temps*, 3 vols. (Paris, 1930–31), Vol. III, pp. 267–270. Generalizations about romanticism are frequent; cf. Coutinho, *Tradition et Histoire*, p. 42. A recent discussion of Modernism in the context of historical method is G. Martini, *Catholicesimo e Storicismo: Momenti di una Crisi del Pensiero Religioso Moderno* (Naples, 1951). The German origins of Blondel's thought are examined in J. J. McNeill, *The Blondelian Synthesis* (Leiden: 1966). The image, if not the ideas, of Lamennais was recognized; cf. W. G. Roe, *Lamennais and England: The Reception of Lamennais's Religious Ideas in the Nineteenth Century* (Oxford, 1966), pp. 143–151.

43 Vidler, *Modernist Movement*, pp. 51–59. The French debate is summarized by L. Gougaud, in *Revue du Clergé Français*, Vol. LVII (1909), pp. 560–565. Tyrrell began the public discussion in England; for its sequence, see the *Tablet*, N. S. Vol. LXXIX (CXI) (January 4–25, 1908), pp. 7–9, 47–48, 86–88, 122–125.

44 Alfred Loisy, *Autour d'un Petit Livre*, 2nd ed. (Paris, 1903), pp. 9–10.

45 Talcott Parsons, *The Structure of Social Action*, quoted in H. Stuart Hughes, *Consciousness and Society: The Re-orientation of European Social Thought 1890–1930* (New York, 1958), p. 186 n. 3.

46 Poulat, *Histoire*, pp. 513–609; François Rodé, *Le Miracle dans la Controverse Moderniste* (Paris, 1965), pp. 91–132.

47 Leclere, *Pragmatisme, Modernisme, Protestantisme*, p. 3; cited in Albert Houtin, *Histoire du Modernisme Catholique* (Paris, 1913), p. 32.

48 Vidler, *Modernist Movement*, p. 159 n. 2. Another third may have come from Bremond.

49 Albert Houtin and Felix Sartiaux, *Alfred Loisy, Sa Vie, Son Oeuvre*, ed. Emile Poulat (Paris, 1960), p. 193 nn. 6, 7.

50 Pesch, *Glaube, Dogme, und Geschichtliche Tatsachen*, pp. 44–45; cited in Aubert, *Acte de Foi*, p. 375.

51 M. C. Casella, *Religious Liberalism in Modern Italy* (London, 1965), Vol. I, p. 83; G. Gentile, *Il Modernismo e i Rapporti fra Religione e Filosofia* (Bari, 1909).

52 Friedrich von Hügel, *Selected Letters, 1896–1924*, ed. Bernard Holland (New York, 1927), pp. 333–334.

53 Karl Rahner, *Theological Investigations, Vol. I* (Baltimore, 1961), p. 44. Cf. Leslie Dewart, *The Future of Belief: Theism in a World Come of Age*

(New York, 1966), p. 78: "The fact of which we have recently become aware is not that Christian doctrine has begun to develop in recent times, but that it has *always* existed in a process of development. It is only the awareness of this fact that is new." Dewart, considered "utterly radical" (Harvey Cox) for suggesting that Catholic Christianity must transcend Hellenic categories, is extremely cautious in phrasing his criticism of the rejection of development in *Lamentabili* (see *Future of Belief*, pp. 89–90), but even so he has been misunderstood as endorsing the position of Pius X (Michael Novak, "Belief and Mr. Dewart," *Commonweal*, February 3, 1967, p. 485).

[54] Review of Avery Dulles' *Apologetics and the Biblical Christ* by Joseph Cahill, in *Theological Studies*, Vol. 25 (1964), pp. 260–263.

[55] George Tyrell, *The Autobiography and Life of George Tyrell*, ed. M. D. Petre, 2 vols. (London, 1912), Vol. I, p. 121.

Part One - ALFRED LOISY

I

ALFRED LOISY remained a Roman Catholic priest for twenty years after he had decided that the only statement in the Apostles' Creed to which he could give historical assent was that Jesus suffered under Pontius Pilate.

The encyclical *Pascendi Dominici Gregis* clearly had as its leitmotiv the clerical character of the Modernist movement. Though there were others who carried on the illusion of orthodoxy longer than Loisy, it was his "faithless priesthood" which symbolized the dangers of Modernism to his generation. One of his radical contemporaries, who feared the implications of criticism for his own faith as well as for Catholicism, expressed sentiments shared by many liberals and progressives as well: "The orthodoxy of this priest, who said his Mass every day, confessed fortnightly, and always expressed his opinions on ecclesiastical subjects with respectful reserve, inspired me with complete confidence." Undoubtedly it was Loisy's combination of scholarship and priestly dignity, as well as the good grace with which he submitted to abuse from real and self-appointed authorities, which made him the focal figure of the hopes of many who felt new life stirring in the Church in France. Before Modernism was named, those who hoped for a reconciliation of biblical criticism and orthodoxy were called *Loisystes*.[1]

After Loisy was sure that there was no hope that this reconciliation could be achieved through the radical evolutionary and symbolist interpretation of Catholicism which he proposed, he turned from mystification to candor. In rapid succession he published a series of letters confirming the worst suspicions of his critics. He made a study of the papal documents of 1907 and assigned, from his own works, sources for the propositions condemned. He also produced new critical studies which unambiguously stated positions on vexed points of New Testament interpretation which he had previously set forth in conditional form. It became quite clear that not only did he think that theology and history were separate studies, as, in 1902, he had admitted in *L'Evangile et l'Eglise (The Gospel and the Church)*, the most famous book of the crisis, but he also believed that historical conclusions must rule over theological speculations. In 1913, when Modernism was dead and the attention of the religious world had been drawn to other matters, he published a memoir of his early years and of his part in the Modernist crisis; in this work, titled *Choses Passées*, he took pains to point out from how early a date and in how many ways his own religious opinions differed from the orthodoxy his scholarship was supposed to defend. Finally, in 1930 and 1931, he published three immense volumes of *Mémoires*, which repeated the revelations of the autobiography of 1913 and added a detailed narrative, unflattering to the liberals and the progressives as well as to the superorthodox. On the basis of this material and because of various introductions to new editions of his Modernist books, a debate arose about Loisy's vocation. Was he "false priest" or "*clerc qui n'a pas trahi?*"[2]

The answer depends on one's ideas about orthodoxy and priesthood. To a sympathetic Anglican student of Modernism, Loisy was "genuinely pious and devout; he was inspired by motives that were at once altruistic and mystical [and] (until the final break in 1908) the discipline and dignity of his priestly life were always unexceptionable."[3] But these motives, even when they have been admitted by Catholic critics, have not, in their eyes, altered the fundamental scandal of his duplicity. Attempts to reassess his position in the history of Catholic thought are doomed from the start by the problem of his vocation, even though it has been made clear that much of what is now commonplace in Catholic criticism was first broached by Loisy. From the historical rather than confessional point of view, the relationship of Loisy's vocation (as he understood it) to the new apologetic for Catholicism which his critical studies generated is nevertheless significant. The question which haunted Pius X was, How can these men be priests? The question which troubled the Modernists was, How can the Church survive?[4]

Less ambiguous than the character of Loisy's vocation was the power of his scholarship. Kant once predicted that if religion ever became a philological matter, entirely dependent for its continuity on "the critical knowledge of ancient languages," then the man who knew them would "drag all the orthodox believers, in spite of their wry faces, wherever he may choose. For in the matter which, according to their own admission, carries with it the probative force of the whole, these believers cannot measure themselves with that scholar."[5] There had been Catholic philologists and critics before Loisy, men who had tried to use their knowledge to reshape the orthodox view of Christian origins and Catholic history. There had been Protestant and rationalist critics as well. Loisy's attempt gained its force from the fact that by the time he essayed to drag orthodoxy on a scientific leash, rationalism had triumphed and Protestant Christendom had apparently succumbed to modern critical scholarship. But when Loisy began his solitary study of Hebrew and then moved on to study the bible in the context of criticism and the comparative history of religions, Catholic Christianity was, officially speaking, fundamentalist in its approach to Christian origins.[6]

II

ALFRED FIRMIN LOISY, by his own opinion and that of his schoolmates, was destined for the priesthood, and "probably fitted for nothing better." Born in 1857 in the small village of Ambrières (Marne), he hoped to be a farmer like his forebears, but was too sick and weak. He prayed to Our Lady of Lourdes for better health, watched the uhlans commandeer his grandfather's bed and board, and grieved when the fall of Napoleon III canceled prize-day at school. In his first confession he revealed that at the tender age of eight he had reflected on the tediousness of his petty existence and said aloud upon a hillside, "God is not good." Precocious in school, he remained silent until he could recite the whole alphabet.

Loisy, like Tyrrell and Sullivan, followed the tradition of foreshadowing maturity through childhood memories. Sympathetic reconstruction of the states of mind in which their autobiographies were written affects the estimate of what significance can be attributed to anecdotes which prefigure later developments. When Loisy wrote his first memoirs, he was more disillusioned than were Tyrrell or Sullivan when

49

they came to reflect on their vocations. He was derisory about
the significance of what were undoubtedly authentic and moving experiences for a peasant boy for whom there seemed to be
no alternative other than the priesthood. When a new curate
came to Ambrières, Loisy was deeply impressed by the emotion with which the young priest said his first Mass; suddenly,
Loisy relates, he knew that he would someday do the same.
Reflecting on the episode in middle age, he insists that he did
not then regard the notion as a sign from heaven, and then
adds: "Yet it was from that day, in all probability, that I was
marked for the sacrifice." The double meaning of "sacrifice"
can be taken as intended, but it seems likely that the young
boy, if not the older man, really did regard the premonition
as a sign from heaven.[7]

Retroactive value judgments do not obscure the picture of
a lonely and intelligent boy, timid, unathletic, envied and
admired for his success in school, left on his own for two years
of private tutoring, physiologically and psychologically un-
disturbed by adolescence, eager to assert his personality and
to compensate his parents for their disappointments, convinced that a sacrifice on his part might "spare them every
mischance." Ignorant of other careers, unaware that the
Church had "no monopoly on devotion," he reacted strongly
to the classic stimulus, the retreat (given in this case by a
Jesuit exile from Bismarck's Kulturkampf) demanding a decision for God. In October 1873 Loisy, aged 16, decided to
bypass the *baccalaureat* and go directly to the seminary at
Châlons.

The decision was made much of by Loisy's former friend,
the Ultra-radical historian of Modernism, Albert Houtin,
who argued that Loisy had no vocation at all and only wanted
to further an academic career. Loisy admitted that at the

time his vocation seemed to be that of the professor, but maintained that he would have entered the seminary in any case, sooner or later. The premature departure from the *collège* had a less ambiguous significance. Two additional years would have directed him toward science and literature, so that when he entered Châlons, he would have been set on a career as a secondary school teacher and taken theology and the rest of the course as a reinforcement rather than as a challenge to adolescent piety and fervor. His entry into the seminary was appropriately marked: Returning alone from the station, where he had said farewell to his unhappy father, he met "an intelligent looking man" who uttered a cry of horror at the sight of the young boy in the soutane and went off muttering against the Church—"that baby snatcher!—that abuser of parental confidence!"[8]

The seminary, in spite of efforts at reform by the bishop, was typical of its day. Adrien Dansette has given a succinct picture of the atrophy of French Catholic intellectual life at the time. The vast majority of the clergy, ignorant of the way in which the Kantian critique, positivism, and historical criticism had "cut swathes" through ecclesiastical history, "lived in a watertight compartment"; and those few who recognized the problems left them to the scientists to solve. But unfortunately, "there were no Catholic scientists worthy of the name." All difficulties were temptations from the devil. Dogma was not distinguished from theology—or blind prejudice.[9]

Châlons was not quite watertight, however. A liberal professor of philosophy assigned papers on Lamennais, as well as on Lacordaire and Montalembert. Loisy thus gained from the liberal Catholics of the mid-century a moral and democratic fervor, a taste for history, but no rigorous training in it.

The great influence of the seminary was negative. Loisy was deeply disturbed by the contrast between the pious faith he had learned at Ambrières and the tensions and automatic rationalism of manual theology as it was taught at Châlons. Salvation by faith, yet salvation by works; Christ as true God, Christ as true man; Trinity and unity; original sin and sacraments—all were logically interrelated propositions. Their theological explication was as authoritative and automatic as their dogmatic statement. "Now that I was required to think of all these things rationally and not merely to feel them, I was thrown into a state of prolonged disturbance." In this first religious crisis there was no question of losing the faith. Unbelief was unthinkable, something which was only found "among people who were affronted by the moral standards of Christianity and who felt a personal interest in the non-existence of God and a place of eternal punishment." His confessor dismissed as a scruple his "obsession" with the meaninglessness of theological definitions. Nor did Loisy consider leaving: his "will to serve God and His Church in the priesthood remained unshaken." The study of moral theology was also disillusioning. It contradicted Loisy's growing conviction that morality was "a general aspiration towards the good, not the meticulous obedience to a set of rules drawn up by experts." He sought relief in prayer, study, and the Third Order of St. Francis.[10]

But relief came from a different quarter. Loisy began to study Hebrew on his own, and found that he had a flair for languages. He was freed from the "torture," anxiety, and the "morbid effect" induced by philosophical and theological studies, and "regained almost instantly the serenity of mind" of which theology and philosophy had deprived him. He began a comparison of the Septuagint and the Vulgate, without commentaries to aid him, happy in a state of artificial scholarly primitiveness. It was peculiar work for a seminarian to do on his own, five hundred years after Erasmus and the Complutensian Polyglot; but it marked the merger of religion and scholarship for Loisy. Even St. Thomas, whose discussion of the Trinity had seemed to him a "huge logomachy," was now useful—for information on the exegetical tradition in the commentaries on Paul, rather than for philosophy or "enlargement of the spirit."[11]

Although Loisy's independence and liberalism caused him some difficulties, he was ordained in June 1879. Like Sullivan, but unlike Tyrrell, Loisy discussed the event at length. He recognized a conflict between desire and belief, and yet he "believed, and willed to believe, that Catholicism was the absolute truth." Lying awake on his cot on the eve of the ceremony, scarcely reassured by the encouragement of his spiritual director, he reviewed "all the arguments . . . for the truth of Christianity," a rational exercise from which he had not been liberated by Hebrew studies. He could find no flaw in the argument, but suspected that there was one and "that it lay somewhere in the premises," i.e., in the origins of Christianity. By morning he was so exhausted that he could no longer think, but his will "remained inflexible." He heard the bishop charge the candidates with their last moment of freedom to reflect and change their course, and then went forward "without a tremor." "We bent low before the altar, and the litanies of the saints were recited over us. The tragic error of my life was consummated."[12]

Loisy made the point repeatedly in his memoirs that the will to believe had triumphed over real inner conviction. "He who wishes can say that I was more sure of my vocation than of my belief. It is possible, though faith is to a large

degree a matter of will. And then, were not my belief and
vocation each as solid as the other?" What was clear to him
then was that he was sure he wanted to serve "in the Church,
the cause of truth and good." "The consciousness of that will"
took him to ordination, and kept him in the priesthood until
he judged that there was no possibility of such a service. The
fact which most troubled Loisy's critics after the crisis—his
notion of serving humanity *in* or *through* the Church, rather
than serving the Church whether he personally felt it was
fulfilling its mission or not—antedated his critical discoveries.[13]

Loisy's suspicions about the "premises" of the rational
arguments for Catholic truth were not entirely the product
of solitary study. He had spent a few months as a special
student at the newly opened Catholic Institute at Paris,
where he had impressed, and been impressed by, the great
historian of the early Church, Abbé Louis Duchesne. Two
happy years of study, parish duty, and long visits with his
family ended for the young cleric when Duchesne got Loisy
released from his diocese and invited him to Paris as a
graduate student and instructor in Hebrew. The contradictory
influences of Châlons were now intensified. On the one hand,
the doyen of orthodox exegesis, the Abbé Vigoroux of St.
Sulpice, was carefully explaining in his lectures that the ark,
contrary to rationalist criticism, was quite large enough to
contain all the species known to Noah. The Flood had
covered only the then-known portions of the earth, and
calculations had been made proving that the ark was capable
of holding 6,666 species, allowing so much space to each
couple. On the other hand, Ernest Renan was shocking
Institute students (who attended—and fled—his lectures at
the Collège de France) by hinting that Jeremiah might have

had something to do with the writing of Deuteronomy. And Loisy himself, busy working over a comparative edition of the gospels which Duchesne had given him for vacation reading, had come to the conclusion that the nativity narratives of Matthew and Luke must have come from different sources and—here was the difficulty—"were not capable of being reconciled so as to make consistent history."[14]

Loisy began to dream of mastering the learning of the apostate Renan—in order to refute him. For Loisy's critical discoveries—from the question of the historical record for the nativity of Jesus, he soon moved on to the accounts of the resurrection—caused him no theological doubts. It was clear to him that the gospel writings had to be as freely interpreted as they were composed; they were not historical texts, and it was foolish to treat them as though they were. Pseudo-historical apologetics for the Old Testament, like those of Vigoroux, shattered, rather than sustained, its religious meaning. To Loisy it was obvious that the sacred books were written as all books were written, by men, "only with less exactness and care than many." The orthodox argument for the inerrancy of scripture needed reinterpretation. The bible might well have been inspired, but if the Holy Spirit had been involved, it had not been to make "historical sources of the first rank." Renan had abandoned the idea of an inspired revelation. Orthodoxy insisted on it in the face of historical fact. Loisy dreamed of finding a *via media* as savant and Christian, and prayed for twenty years of health so that he might pursue Christian learning "to the edification of the Church and the discomfiture of her enemies."[15]

His confidence was soon shaken. The year 1883 was one of discovery and disillusion. In his journal for that year he sketched a dialogue with the "ideal" Church in which he

wished to serve. This ideal Church was willing to admit that
her apologists in the nineteenth century had not understood
that they were allowed to reconsider the old formulas, "that
indeed, they might almost forget them, in order to preserve
to the world the truth of which I am the custodian." But
she was unable to see that much more was needed if she were
to live. Loisy's ideal Church was speaking the "progressive
line" in agreeing, albeit conditionally, to his arguments that
Catholicism had become an abstract system which no longer
had meaning even to believers, that its understanding of its
origins contradicted historical fact. But Loisy knew that
progressivism was no longer enough. When the "Princess of
immutable verity" expressed confidence that a new generation of interpreters of her truth would be raised up to dissipate
accusations of ignorance, Loisy insisted that she had no idea
how difficult their work would be: "It is not your formulas
that you must translate for us into a speech intelligible to the
men of our age; it is rather your ideas themselves, your absolute affirmations, your theory of the universe, the conception you have of your own history, that you must renew,
rectify, and reconstruct."[16]

Loisy's vocation, as distinct from that allowed to the
liberals and progressives, was now taking shape. He felt that
it was essential to engineer more than a mere translation of
the formulas of Catholicism. What was needed was a whole
new way of looking at dogma itself. The insight that a new
translation (even a whole new philosophy of dogma like that
later proposed by the followers of Blondel) was not adequate
to cope with what Loisy regarded as the historical facts
antedated by twenty years his Modernist essays. But, according
to his own testimony, he had not yet discovered how the
transformation of the idea of dogma and revelation was to be

made, nor had he realized what such an undertaking would mean for their "truth." And he was not yet convinced that his critical conclusions were absolutely right. (The discovery of the corroborative work of German scholars, which he soon began to study, would give him that conviction.) He did not yet have any general philosophical notions, such as those he later found in Newman, to help him toward a context in which he might draw out the critical conclusions so reinforced. "Without having read Kant, or the Germans, or the positivists," he had come to doubt the "objective reality" of the conclusions of Catholic metaphysics. Although he was willing to admit the influence of Renan and the negative effect of seminary rationalism, he considered that, by the piecemeal progress of his research, he was only gradually and involuntarily becoming "detached" from traditional belief.[17]

The year 1883 also marked the beginning of a pattern of official rejection of his work. Magisterial criticism was to be balanced in the next decade by unofficial enthusiasm. His doctoral thesis was refused publication because it suggested that the element of revelation in scripture was "proportioned to the time and the environment" in which its several books "emerged." The rector of the Institute, the progressive Mgr. D'Hulst, was nevertheless interested in Loisy's work and allowed him to continue teaching. His reputation began to grow. He made the acquaintance of Baron von Hügel. Their correspondence charted the ebb and flow of hope for a reform in the official attitude toward bible study. Equivocation grew, but in secret. In 1886 he confided to his journal an absence of "the slightest religious feeling." Devotional practices were no longer of any value as an antidote to his growing conviction that Catholic belief was "an obstacle to the intellectual development of humanity." Yet he felt that as long as her spirit, rather than the letter of her tradition, was emphasized, the Catholic Church remained "the essential institution" for man's progress. And, although victimized by the subtleties of theologians, she still was the repository of morality and social order. Ecclesiastical discipline was superannuated; traditional liturgical forms were meaningless; the literal sense of theological formulas was becoming less and less credible. However, "to attempt a reorganization of the moral life apart from Christ and his Church would be utopian." The problem was not whether Catholicism was true Christianity, but whether Christianity or any other religion could substantiate historically its claims to be supernatural. Loisy's comparative studies (he had by now branched out into Assyriology) were leading him to generalize his doubts about scriptural inspiration into a critique of the concept of revelation in all religions.[18]

Loisy's tenure of a position in which he could transform the Church from within was brief. At the Institute his course in biblical history lasted less than two years. He proposed in his syllabus an investigation of the questions of inspiration and interpretation which would be guided by "the general principles contained in the decisions of the Church." He treated the bible "only as a matter of history," not as a question of "legislation covering doctrine." His equivocation was "enormous," but he justified it on the grounds that the Church was moving in his direction. He held that if the ground were well prepared through a confrontation with the historical problem now, the full implications of criticism which must now be veiled would be "within ten or fifteen years . . . accepted quietly." He never for a moment doubted, either at this time or in later years, that the revolutionary implications of relativism and symbolism in all matters of religious "truth" were the only ones any objective student of religion could accept.[19]

The publication of his revised dissertation brought a new wave of criticism. The seminarians of St. Sulpice were forbidden to attend Loisy's 1892 fall lectures. The tyro had rapidly become an authority and now, in the official view, a danger. Ironically, it was his patron who burst the bubble. Mgr. D'Hulst, who had no real idea of the nature of the apologetic which lay behind Loisy's "scientific criticism," published an essay on "The Bible Question." In this study he suggested that work like Loisy's—who was not mentioned by name—might reveal errors of natural knowledge and history in the bible. Such errors, however, would not prejudice the truth of biblical teaching on matters of faith and morals. Loisy's position was actually more to the left than D'Hulst realized. (Loisy was convinced that all historical documents were limited by their time and place of origin: the "inescapable relativity of all works by the hands of man" meant that no document could be wholly in accord, "even in matters of faith and morals, with the truth of any other epoch than the one that fathered it.") But D'Hulst's description of the "broad" school did correspond to the tacit argument of the critical work which Loisy had published, and even that was too much for the authorities. In a complicated maneuver which involved the advancement of Leo's policy of improving church-state relations, Loisy was deprived of his course in exegesis.[20]

There matters might have rested, had Loisy not published his last lecture. Among what now appear to be commonplace critical opinions, there were some hints at Loisy's real views. Statements that Genesis did not contain "an exact and reliable account of the beginning of mankind," that Moses

did not write the Pentateuch, went side by side with suggestions that the books of the bible were more loosely composed than modern historical works. Loisy also argued that
free composition permits free interpretation and that the
Church's work was to adjust the bible to the "intellectual,
moral, and social conditions of ages for which it was never
written." These contentions were enough to produce a demand from the assembly of French bishops that Loisy be dismissed from the Institute.[21]

Deeply embittered, Loisy, who had already broken with
Duchesne, left the Institute. He felt that he had been used as
a pawn in a political maneuver. Mgr. D'Hulst said that Loisy
had thrown himself before a locomotive by publishing his
lecture at the moment the authorities were becoming restive
about the direction taken by Catholic biblical studies. Loisy's
reaction was that the rector had thrown him under the wheels.
In fact, Loisy knew from von Hügel that there was growing
anxiety in Rome: his essay on the Old Testament canon was
to be censured, and a new statement would be issued on
biblical criticism. When *Providentissimus Deus* was pro-
mulgated in 1893, it was generally assumed that the encyclical
letter, although concerned with the effect on biblical studies
of recent archaeological finds and the new literary criticism,
was aimed specifically at the work of D'Hulst and Loisy. As
the subsequent history of Catholic criticism has shown, the
encyclical could be construed either as encouraging or dis-
couraging the application of scientific principles to biblical
study. But to Loisy and less radical critics it seemed, at the
time, to dash all hopes of advance. The reassertion of the
Tridentine and Vatican decisions, that the whole of scripture
was written at the dictation of the Holy Ghost, seemed to
challenge even Loisy's mildest conclusions. He was staggered

by the calm advice that the critic, confronted by "new truth,"
should not assume that it had to conflict with "received
ideas."[22]

But Loisy did not lose heart. After his dismissal from the
Institute, he was appointed chaplain at a girl's school in
suburban Neuilly. There he found himself with plenty of time
for reading and writing. Under von Hügel's direction, he
began to investigate "the whole contemporary movement of
religious thought." If the events of 1889–92 had confirmed
him in his belief that the Church was an obstacle to the intellectual progress of mankind and if he had now lost every
shred of his "childhood faith," he was more than ever convinced that religion was "a tremedous force that had dominated and still did all of human history." In 1913 he wrote
that the bishops would have been wiser to have left him with
his Hebrew grammar and cuneiform texts, since his five
years at Neuilly gave him the leisure needed for further en-
deavoring "to adapt Catholic doctrine to the exigencies of
contemporary thought." He now read "the Germans" so
anathematized at St. Sulpice, became familiar with the comparative study of religion, and read Newman for the first
time. His writing took the form of a large apologetic essay
from which he drew material for pseudonymous publications.[23]

The so-called *"livre inédit"* was centered on an analysis of
three "postulates" of belief which Loisy attributed to the
Church, all three of which he felt modern science—i.e.,
criticism, but also biology and social theory—had made
untenable. The "theological" postulate assumed that the
ideas of God and creation have never changed and never
would. The "messianic" postulate insisted that Christ and the
Church were specifically and consciously predicted in the

Old Testament. The "ecclesiological" postulate stated that
the Church and its hierarchy, dogma, and sacraments were
directly instituted by Christ. Loisy hoped that these postulates
could be adapted in such a way as to conform to the laws of
historical development. These laws were predicated on "a
powerful process of growth, more intelligible and satisfying,
in a sense even for faith, than any tissue of miracles."

The enemy of such an adaptation was the "intellectual
regimen" of the Church itself, whereby theologians countered
a modern theory of personality with the idea of hypostatic
union and answered evolution with the early chapters of
Genesis, "whose authors had assuredly not foreseen Darwin."
"If science had waited for the permission of theology before
going ahead, it would never have taken a step beyond the
fifteenth century." Loisy's proposal was that once the postulates of Christian belief and the lesser dogmas derived from
them could be "discarded as fallacies from a rational (i.e.,
historical) point of view," they could still be "interpreted in
the light of what moral significance they might contain." God,
creator of the whole world some thousands of years ago, the
God-man Christ, and the infallibility of the Church, he admitted in 1913, probably could not have endured an evolu-
tionary-symbolic interpretation. But the "high ideals of justice
and of goodness" which were "the true heart" of the Catholic
tradition would have survived.[24]

Of course, Loisy said rather less than this in print. The
articles drawn from the *livre inédit,* published during the
years 1897–1900 under the pseudonym "A. Firmin," aimed
at fostering a current of "liberal opinion strong enough to
give pause to theological absolutism, while at the same time
safeguarding Catholic unity." These essays were a prelude
to Loisy's Modernist books of 1902 and 1903. He was pre-

occupied in them with the "laws of historical development" that his critical work had implied—and that he found sketched in Newman's *Essay on Development*.[25]

Newman's idea of development served as a screen for Loisy's more radical evolutionary theory of religious history. In recapitulating the essentials of Newman's position, Loisy added distinctive touches. Echoing the famous dictum that "to live was to change," he remarked that not only was change not a sign of error but that many heresies in the history of the Church had resulted from a misdirected zeal for conservation. After reviewing and approving the criteria Newman had established for distinguishing true from false development, Loisy emphasized that the work of evaluation was the responsibility of "the religious life of the community." Like Newman, he linked legitimate development with infallible authority. He then added: "Authority and revelation are correlative terms." Each statement gains resonance in the context of Loisy's real opinion, especially the last. A positive presentation of the link between authority and revelation made it certain that a reinterpretation of one would involve the other.

Loisy's discussion of development was predicated on the fact that Newman, although he had no official standing as a theologian, had adumbrated a "scientific theory of Catholic Christianity" which performed the task set for theology in the first centuries: "to establish a kind of equation, or perpetual correspondence, between the interpretation of revealed dogmas and the intellectual progress of humanity." The theory of development, however, needed to be expanded in the light of advances made in history and criticism. It should be applied not only to the study of Catholic dogma but also to the interrelated problems of Christian origins and general religious history. Christianity had to be seen as a development of postexilic Judaism, which grew out of the religion of the prophets, which in its turn developed from the religion of the Mosaic period, the religion of the patriarchs, and the religion of prehistoric man. The study of this sequence of development, as well as of the growth of Christianity, would show that the great moments of revelation were not revolutions obliterating the past and creating new religions, but "regular transformations in which the religious tradition saw a new dawn, grew in vitality, and increased its sphere of action." When the idea of development was so extended, Loisy implied, there would follow inevitably a reassessment of the relationship between Christian dogmas, the historical context in which they had emerged, and the present religious state of humanity.[26]

Newman was only a point of departure for "A. Firmin." Though, to the uninitiate, it was the application of Loisy's evolutionary relativism to post-apostolic dogmatic formulations which seemed most scandalous, the fundamental issue was its implication for the general concept of divine revelation. This was a philosophical as much as a historical question. Firmin argued that the basic religious ideas were nothing more than "symbols and metaphors, a kind of algebraic notation representing ineffable quantities." Men used such symbols as best they could to capture the ineffable, symbols that changed and developed with man's intellectual and moral progress. In the beginning man had glimpsed the relationship between his own consciousness and God, who was present behind the world of phenomena. Subsequently man perceived new and more complex relationships which were nothing more than precise fixings on particular points of the initial perception. Firmin skirted the problem of God's intention.

To say that revelation was "a kind of divine education proportioned to the intellectual conditions of the men for whom it was destined," or even to argue that it was "divine in its principle, in its object, its spirit," neither affirmed nor denied the traditional notion of an unambiguously trans-cendent statement by God to man. The emphasis was, rather, on the receiving end, on men who "formulated" the revealed perception "in accordance with their intelligence and in the language available to them," that is to say, in accord with the *unrevealed* history and culture in which they happened to find themselves. It was inevitable, of course, that men should assume that the symbols and metaphors of theology were the reality, forgetting that their doctrine reflected the conscious-ness of their particular society as much as it approximated the relationship of man to God. Religious men in general needed to be reminded that truth transcended teaching; and Catholics in particular needed to pay less attention to religious images and more to the realities for which they stood.[27]

To balance this generous treatment of revelation, Firmin sketched the "Catholic" view of authority and tradition. As was more fully the case in *L'Evangile et l'Eglise,* polemic against liberal Protestantism, specifically against Adolf Harnack and Auguste Sabatier, provided the context for the statement of neo-Catholic ideas. The liberals attacked Cathol-icism on two points. They alleged that Catholic tradition was not true to the pure gospel and that Catholic authority was without meaning in the modern world. Historical criticism proved the former contention, they claimed; and Luther, Galileo, and scientific historiography proved the latter. The Catholic Church taught an exaggerated and unhistorical Jesus, and maintained, as divinely given, dogmas which were without scriptural foundation. Firmin answered that, in fact, the pure Christianity of the liberals was pure Protestantism: their supposedly scientific view of the gospel was distorted by a prejudice for individualism which was historically and sociologically indefensible. The rapport between man and God always implied a rapport between man and man. Even the most imperfect religions had sought "the union of men in God, not merely the union of man with God." The social character of religious experience inevitably found institutional expression. An absolute definition of Christianity was impossible. The gospel in its pure form had existed only once, in the remote past, and it was not the whole of Christianity. It was a historical fact that no individual consciousness, even that of Jesus himself, contained the whole Christian experience. Jesus, as the prophets before him, worked to advance "the development of the kingdom of God, and not some psychological experiences from which posterity might gain profit." This remark was ostensibly directed at the liberal Protestant argument that Jesus taught out of his experience the truth that God is our father; but it was as easily applied to the Christological problem, especially the vexed question of Jesus' consciousness of his divinity. Christianity was a living religion and could only be defined descriptively. Its vigor lay, not in some central belief, but in its "action on souls"; and "everything which aids that action, everything which religion draws into its orbit and employs for its ends, shares in the life which it serves."

As for authority, the liberal Protestant error was to attribute to the Catholic Chuch a static conception of dogma which it did not hold. In fact, the Church did not consider its dogmas to be "unalterable and perfect." Rather, "it has been forced in the past, is forced everyday, to complete them, explain them, make them more precise, and to clarify and im-

prove them by additions, explications, and refinements."
However, it had to be admitted that the error was not entirely
the liberals' fault. They had been misled by the regrettable
tendency of the Church to confuse "fidelity to the tradition
with immobility in the tradition, the conservation of the
faith with the manual of formulas," and "the interests of
religion with the temporal advantage of the hierarchy." There
was danger ahead if the Church persisted in this tendency;
but there was also hope, for it was always "repaired and
reformed" in times of crisis.

In any case, authority did not contradict the notion of
revelation; rather, it was its complement. An infallible Church
was the postulate of a revealed religion. Without it there would
be a snapping of the tension between "absolute religious
faith and the inevitable relativity of symbols," between "the
individual character of religious faith and the indispensable
community of belief," with the result that religion would
either become "petrified in lifeless forms" or "dissipated in
complete anarchy of both belief and social structure." For a
religion that ceased to be a Church, or a Church which lost
its authority, existed "in appearance only."[28]

Firmin's articles were well received in learned circles and
by the clergy. Out of his wider reflection on the critical work
of recent years, Loisy had forged a powerful apologetical style.
His writings showed both critical sophistication and philosophical insight and seemed to be examples of the kind of
popularization of theological issues which the Church needed
so desperately if it were to hold the allegiance of priests and
laymen. (The latter were discovering that evolutionary theory
and scientific historiography posed much more complicated
questions to traditional faith than had the vague rationalism
and social and political criticism of the Enlightenment.) The

tone was confident, the language current, the solutions to the problems discussed as straightforwardly as their presentation.[29]

Of course, there was criticism. It came to a head with the last of "A. Firmin's" publications, an essay on pre-Christian Judaism, which was censured, along with the rest of the pieces, in October 1900. The general statements about revelation, dogma, theology, and authority which had already been published were, by implication, more radical than any of the specific historical and critcial opinions with which they were combined; but these were only accessible to the reader who could take the context in stride. In "La Religion d'Israël," however, Loisy limited himself to the more obvious historical issues. And this led directly to the accusation that he was subjecting philosophical statements to critical commonplaces as his way of challenging the semi-Gallican and semi-Scholastic theology of the day. In effect, the pattern of 1883 and 1893 was repeated: the scandal of doubts about the historicity of the Flood and the intellectual achievement of Bossuet obscured more dangerous issues, just as Newman's idea of development screened Loisy's theory of evolution.[30]

Firmin began his swan song with a challenge to false critical knowledge. Even the most conservative critic, he alleged, had left tradition behind, if tradition was still defined by the standards of the seventeenth century, when Bossuet firmly dated the creation at 4004 B.C. and the fall of Troy 308 years before Exodus. The old biblical chronology now appeared to be nothing more than a "slender thread" of speculation thrown across a "bottomless chasm" of ignorance. The outlines of the development of the Jewish religion were clear after the advent of the monarchy; there were some points of light in the period between Samuel and Moses; "but, from Moses back to Abraham, all is darkest night." The first chapters of Genesis did not reveal, nor were they meant to reveal, the way in which man and religion came into the world. They only told us that "man appeared as a created being by the will and power of God," that he was morally disordered from the beginning, and that, in spite of this, God watched over him then and had ever since, ruling the universe with justice and mercy. It was a mistake to think that such a confession of ignorance destroyed revelation. Another "religious set" or sequence could be established on positive historical knowledge (where it existed) which lacked symmetry and simplicity but was "more human than the old apologetic" and preserved the "divine history" just as well.

A survey of the way in which religious beginnings—"a veritable chaos of bizarre opinions . . . puerile superstitions . . . strange practices, often cruel and immoral"—had been gradually reformed in the work of Confucius, Buddha, and Zoroaster culminated in Firmin's discussion of the "single essential reform" which had produced a religion "as perfect, it would appear, as is possible for the human condition." This reform began with Moses, was completed by Jesus, and is carried on by the Catholic Church. It became possible because an obscure Semitic tribe, aided perhaps by the comparative simplicity of nomadic polytheism over that of the settled peoples and by the dominance of animistic over mythic elements, made the decisive step to monotheism.

Firmin made his points for the significance of the religion of Israel through a defense of the meaning of all religious experience. By polemicizing against the positivism of the kind of comparative study of religion associated with Frazer, he was able to reiterate some of the fundamental ideas broached in his earlier articles. This polemic had the same reassuring

effect on his Catholic readers as the criticisms of the liberal
Protestants, especially because it was couched in equally
scientific terms. He first reminded its enthusiasts that the
"so-called law" of evolution which guided religious experience
through the stages of animism, polytheism, and monotheism
was merely a useful hypothesis which could not be proved to
have operated uniformly throughout history. To cast further
doubt on the usefulness of the positivistic approach, he suggested that primitive fetishism might not have been the
same as that observable in contemporary primitive societies;
he pointed to the fact that the progression from polytheism
to monotheism had not occurred in the highly developed
civilization of classical Greece and, therefore, need not have
occurred in the setting of late Roman civilization.

Misapplication of the hypothesis to prehistoric times was
the result of an excessive rationalism which transformed
hypotheses into laws. (This criticism was aimed at traditional
Catholic theology as much as at secular positivism.) Neither
approach was able to understand that an equally powerful
faith in the ineffable lay within the grossest, as well as the
most highly developed, religious symbolism. "It is possible
for the idea of God to have had humble origins (by our own
standards) without religion automatically ceasing to be a great
thing. . . . Even fetishism is a sign of the divine presence";
and, conversely, even the most lofty notion of God which
man has succeeded in grasping "is nonetheless an image, an
idol in the root meaning of the word, in which he tries to
to fix the infinite." Though it might not be able to approximate the simplicity of the original concepts of primitive
religion, modern historical science could at least see, from the
experience of Israel, that "religion, pure and beneficial, was
possible from the beginning, and, moreover, in tribes most
remote from civilization."

The Firmin affair was not an isolated episode. Other men were advancing new ideas anonymously, and Loisy himself published under a variety of pseudonyms.[31] There had been a series of scandals, censures, and suspensions in Cardinal Richard's archdiocese, and rumblings in the provinces as well. The establishment of the Biblical Commission, with a majority of highly qualified and independent scientists in the first appointments, was taken as a sign that in the future the results of research would be judged by a magisterium fully informed on the biblical question. In spite of various disillusioning dealings with the Cardinal Archbishop, Loisy (according to his own witness) continued to hope that, as the liberal-progressive cause advanced and Rome became more and more committed to accepting the results of criticism, a changed climate of opinion would make inevitable the triumph of the more radical ideas which he regarded as at least the unavoidable general conclusion of any theologically unprejudiced research.

Loisy's own position had improved when he received a government appointment to the Ecole des Hautes Etudes, where, in spite of his reputation, he had clerical students for his course of lectures on "The Babylonian Myths and the First Chapters of Genesis."[32] And the seriousness of his hope for the "more open climate" was ambiguously evidenced in his reactions to the Prince of Monaco's attempt to have him made bishop of the Principality and to a possible government appointment to a see in metropolitan France. To win support, Loisy wrote to Cardinal Mathieu, the prelate who represented the French bishops at the Curia. After announcing the forthcoming publication of a reply to Harnack's popular presentation of the liberal Protestant position, Loisy elaborated a politically subtle defense of his candidacy. He regretfully admitted that although he was teaching at a secular institution in a purely scientific capacity, the bulk of his students were in fact clerical, and that his teaching troubled them and the authorities. Though it would mean stunting a "brilliant" academic career, Loisy argued, "from the standpoint of general Catholic interest, it would be more advantageous to place me elsewhere." Yet he did not want to compromise the reputation he had acquired in the last ten years in the academic world "in France and abroad," which, after all, reflected honor also upon the Church. Cardinal Mathieu replied that if Loisy were eager to reassure the authorities, he could do so by censoring his teaching at the Ecole in accordance with Catholic principles. In a second letter appealing for support, Loisy characterized himself as a peasant who disliked change, a valetudinarian unsuited for "the labors of the apostolate," a student happiest alone with his research, but also "a priest who is wounded by unjust oppressions, yet who would be disposed to serve the Church to the best of his ability, according to his conscience."[33]

In fact, Loisy was much more enthusiastic for the appointment than is suggested by these letters, the one vaguely threatening, the other self-satisfied. Even though he insisted that refusal to give him episcopal responsibility was understandable in the "crisis" over bible criticism (which he described as more serious than that impending over the separation of church and state in France), he knew that the elevation would give him personal security from the Cardinal Richards of the Church and would also mean approval for his critical works. Rather than as a gesture of an ambition so gross as to move him to sacrifice his scholarship, his willingness to become a bishop could be understood as part of his long-standing plan of transforming Catholic belief from within. The facts that Loisy, during the weeks when his chances seemed best, exercised careful censorship over his periodical, the *Revue d'Histoire et de Littérature Religieuse,* and disassociated himself completely from Marcel Hébert, a young priest who was openly advocating a symbolist interpretation of Catholicism (based in large part on Loisy's writings), can be interpreted either way.[34]

III

LOISY'S EPISCOPAL CANDIDACY coincided with the composition of a little book which quickly extended his reputation beyond learned circles in France and England. *L'Evangile et l'Eglise,* when it was properly understood, did rather more than confirm Loisy's understated explanation of the reasons for the failure of the Prince's project: "The views of Rome were altogether foreign to my own." Its fame far overshadowed that of the scientific critical studies which Loisy begrudgingly interrupted to produce this work. The book marked the perfection of the apologetic style tested in the Firmin articles, and was premised on the notions of evolution, dogmatic symbolism, and theological relativism set forth in them. It also introduced new materials into the debate over the reconciliation of biblical criticism with Christianity, and became the symbol, to Loisy and many of his contemporaries, of the point of no return for the traditional Catholic faith.

The context of Loisy's essay was a bifurcation within German Protestant scholarship which was only vaguely understood, if it was understood at all, by the educated (but not

"specialist") reading public for whom it was written, a public
which, after 1870, suffered from a religious "Maginot
mentality." From the middle of the nineteenth century on—
from Strauss to Renan and then to Harnack—liberal Protestant theology and rationalist criticism had carried on
parallel and sometimes complementary efforts to reconstruct
from documentary sources the historical existence of Jesus
Christ. The impulse for this work had come from the philological and archaeological achievements of the preceding
century, and it was fostered by a confidence in the ability of
historical research to describe the past "as it actually occurred." The ambitions of religious historiography were
further reinforced by developments in German philosophy.
The Kantian critique of intellectualism and Kant's definition
of religion as "the recognition of all our duties as divine
commands" provided the basis for an interpretation of Christianity as a religion of morality, and thus offered an alternative
to the more complicated dogmatic faith challenged by what
became known as the "higher criticism." For others, like
Strauss and the Protestant theologians at Tübingen, Hegelian
idealism provided an anesthetic for the painful process of
demythologization, or else a principle whereby the contradictions in the various parts of the gospel could be understood
dialectically. Recourse to these philosophical palliatives was
encouraged by the spread of evolutionary theories from
biology into the social sciences. "Whereas formerly men had
always felt that in religion . . . truth in its most perfect form
lay in the past, they were now led to think that the more perfect and even perfectible form, lay in the future. This view
shook the very foundations of old style Protestantism, the
belief in the absolute final and literal truth of the biblical
books."[35]

By the end of the century the liberal Protestant theological consensus had emerged. Historically, it held, Jesus had "attempted to spiritualize the realistic (i.e., material) hopes of contemporary Judaism; that he came forward as a spiritual messiah and founder of an ethical kingdom of God; and that, finally, when the people, failing to understand him, deserted him, he resolved to die for his cause and thus carry it to victory." The critical study of the Synoptics, the analysis of the relationship between the Gospel of John, the Pauline Epistles, Hellenistic philosophical influences, the development of source hypotheses, and, especially, the attempt to arrange the materials of the Synoptics into an orderly pattern of consistent teaching—all this fostered an emphasis on the human personality of Jesus and the moral content of his teaching. On this historical view, a theological position was built which saw the kingdom of God preached by Christ as primarily a this-world ethical construct. "Coming as it did when moral optimism was a keynote of Western society and culture," this assumption of theology into morality, typified by the teachings of Albert Ritschl, "appealed to man's conviction that he could save himself by sanctifying himself." Christianity had become an ethical religion, and Jesus the archetype of the enlightened man.[36]

However, at the very moment when the ethical interpretation of the kingdom and the "social gospel" with which it was uneasily allied had become a kind of orthodoxy, there was revived a different approach to the use of criticism, one sketched at the beginning of the century but since ignored. In 1893 the professor of New Testament exegesis at Göttingen, Johannes Weiss, published his *Die Predigt Jesu vom Reiche Gottes* ("The Preaching of Jesus concerning the Kingdom of God"). Weiss, who later sketched the principles of form criticism and had a considerable influence on twentieth-century German theology, argued for the "consistent eschatological" interpretation of the gospel and insisted that Jesus shared completely the eschatological hope of his contemporaries, saw his mission as the proclamation of an imminent transcendent kingdom of God, and regarded himself as its initiator. This vision of the gospel, reinforced in many aspects by rationalist criticism as well as by its explication in a book by a young Strasbourg pastor, Albert Schweitzer, was highly challenging to the dominant moral optimism and belief in progress.[37]

Weiss's book was published in the year Loisy went to Neuilly. It was perhaps the most significant of the purely critical influences on his work, for the consistent-eschatological approach to the gospel had obvious merits from the point of view of a neo-Catholic apologetic. And Loisy clearly made use of it in his reply to Adolf Harnack's famous lectures, *Das Wesen des Christentums* (1900; English trans., *What Is Christianity?* [1901]).

Harnack, student of Ritschl, professor at Berlin, and author of the seven-volume *Lehrbuch des Dogmengeschichte* ("History of Dogma"), had no sympathy for the consistent-eschatological approach. He did not understand "the eschatological consciousness with which the early Christian communities and Paul were suffused" and "never even caught a glimpse of the utter strangeness of the image of primitive Christianity disclosed by the religious historical school, which even today at first inevitably shocks a reader of the New Testament." Harnack, the quintessential liberal Protestant, wrote in part for the skeptic who asked how modern man could be concerned "with events that happened, or with a person who lived, 1900 years ago." In the spirit of Goethe, he replied that the human mind would never advance beyond the "grandeur and moral elevation of Christianity as it sparkles and shines in the gospels" no matter how great the progress of culture. But Harnack was no mere enthusiast. He insisted that the meaningfulness of Christian faith could be secured historically. He could not distinguish between "the kerygmatic character of the gospel and an 'Enlightenment' doctrine or an ethical appeal"; but he *did* think that he was arguing, insofar as a Christian apologist could, on scientific grounds. Loisy took issue with the ethical appeal, the historical science, and the doctrine of Christ as set forth by Harnack.[38]

It must be emphasized that Harnack's liberalism was much exaggerated in Loisy's treatment. In fact, the German theologian rejected both the view that Christianity was an "ethical or social *arcanum* for the preservation or improvement of things generally" and the comparative evolutionary approach which submerged it in the history of religions, as well as the "purely critical or historicist" view (i.e., the eschatological school) which limited the meaning of Jesus' teaching to its environment. Harnack distinguished two approaches to the New Testament: either it was "in all respects identical with its earliest form, in which case it came with its time and departed with it," or else it contained something which "under differing historical forms is of permanent validity." He stated confidently: "The latter is the true view." There was a "Gospel in the gospel" which could be distinguished from "its contemporary integument" and which was neither subject to, nor the inspiration for, a process of development leading to new beliefs and institutions. "Primitive Christianity had to disappear in order that Christianity remain," and the rest of the history of Christian faith has been a process of the disappearance of the fundamental gospel under cultural overlays and of its reemergence in unaltered purity. To find the essential gospel, one had to proceed between extremes which Harnack defined in a pomological image which was to be the hallmark of the subsequent debate between Modernism and liberal Protestantism. The student of Christian history, Harnack said, had to avoid the enthusiasm of the child who, seeking the kernel of a bulb, "went on picking leaves until there was nothing left." On the other hand, he had to resist those who said that there was no such thing as "kernel or husk, growth or decay, but that everything is of equal value and alike permanent." Harnack described the three kinds of material available to the careful student: Jesus and his gospel, the "first generation of his disciples," and the "leading changes" rung on the combination of the first two throughout history. What was common to all the forms of Christian life would be corrected by reference to the gospel; conversely, the main elements of the gospel would be corrected by reference to history. This dialectical approach would bring the Christian critic "to the kernel of the matter."[39]

Following this method, Harnack surveyed first the gospel and the experience of primitive Christianity, then the rest of the history of the Church. His conclusions were simple and confidently expressed. The Christian religion meant "one thing and one thing only: eternal life in the midst of time by the strength and under the eyes of God." The gospel of Jesus has only to do with the Father, and not with the Son; his teaching, which perfected something that had been perpetually renewed in Jewish religion, owed nothing to the violent extremes of contemporary religious reform and expectation. It consisted of three ideas: the kingdom of God and its coming; the fatherhood of God, as perfectly experienced and revealed by Jesus; and "the higher righteousness and the command of love." Harnack wrote that he feared transforming the first notion into a "pale scheme of ethics" in the sense that it might be misunderstood by moderns as a program of social reform, just as it was misunderstood by some of the followers of Jesus as a mundane kingdom. Rather, he wished the idea of the kingdom to be seen as a personal and immediate teaching. "The kingdom of God comes," according to Harnack "by coming to the individual, by entering into his soul and laying hold of it. The kingdom of God is the rule of God, but not in any external or ecclesiological sense." On the contrary, "it is the rule of the holy God in the hearts of individuals: it is God Himself in His power. . . . The word of God, God Himself, is the Kingdom. It is not a question of angels and devils, thrones and principalities, but of God and the Soul, the Soul and its God."[40]

The kingdom is supernatural, but immanent—"a purely religious blessing, the inner link with the living God . . . the most important experience that a man can have." In spite of his insistence that the whole of the teaching of Jesus was contained in the idea of the kingdom, Harnack was less at ease with that principle, as a subject for historical and theological discussion, than with the other two principles which did not directly involve the problem of eschatology. "God as the Father, and the human soul so ennobled that it can and does unite with Him" was a less troubling "essence" of the gospel. In fact, his enthusiasm for Jesus' discovery of, and response to, divine love led Harnack to an exposition which ignored, if it did not contradict, the precedent reduction of the gospel to the idea of the kingdom. The relationship of man to God revealed by Jesus made Christianity "religion itself" and meant that, in theory at least, it was forever free

from laws, from this-world and other-world tensions, and
from other polarities such as those between reason and ecstasy,
between Judaism and Hellenism.

The third notion, that of "the higher righteousness and
the rule of love" was the projection onto the world of the discovery of Jesus who, in the tradition of the Old Testament,
had brought ethics and religion together into a unity by
adding mercy to justice. Harnack denied this righteousness
any normative expression and any programmatic character.
Christianity as a life was not asceticism, monkery, a program
for social reform, or a utopian dream. It was neither a defense of the social and economic status quo nor a plan for its
overthrow. And, above all else, it was not, as Roman Catholicism wrongly insisted, a form of civilization. It held forth
the prospect of a union among men, but not by any legal
ordinance. It was a high and glorious ideal and the "guiding
star of man's development"; yet, it did not tell man how to
live with men, but with God.[41]

Harnack approached the Christological problem with the
same method, seeking to distinguish the kernel of Jesus' personality from the husk of Logos philosophy and post-apostolic
theological speculation. The kernel was the fact that Jesus
knew God as no man, no prophet, had ever known him before. "Rightly understood, the name of Son means nothing
but the knowledge of God." Of how, and in what way, Jesus
gained this knowledge, little could be said historically. What
mattered was that his message was perfect, and in spite of the
passage of time, "He who delivered it has not yet yielded his
place to any man; and to human life today he still gives a
meaning and an aim—he the Son of God." The messianic
notion in the gospel was a vehicle for the teaching of the
loving fatherhood of God. This was a category of his own

contemporary culture which Jesus used to express the idea that if the union of mankind is ever to come about, it will be through the acknowledgment of one Lord and Master. This meaning which Jesus gave to the messianic notion overwhelmed any it might have had before him (i.e., the eschatological and/or political expectation).[42]

Here, then, was the fundamental gospel: the revelation of God's love for man by one who experienced it completely. Harnack treated less fully the faith of primitive Christianity and the rest of the history of the Church. Belief in the lordship of Jesus was not a Pauline creation; it was, rather, the faith of the primitive community which called him Lord because he had given up his life for it and because its members were convinced that he had been raised from the dead and sat at the right hand of God. The real meaning of his sacrifice was witnessed by the fact that it was the last one: wherever Christian faith had spread, sacrifice had ended. Like Ritschl, Harnack distinguished between the "Easter faith" and the "Easter message and appearances." The appearances of Jesus after his death could not be clearly reconstructed from the biblical materials. As a basis for faith, they were "a foundation unstable and always exposed to fresh doubts," and, along with other miraculous appeals to the senses, best abandoned. Whatever happened at the grave and afterward, "one thing is certain: *this grave was the birthplace of the indestructible belief that death is vanquished, that there is a life eternal.*" "On the conviction that *Jesus lives,* we still base those hopes of citizenship in an Eternal City which makes our earthly life worth living." "Belief in the living Lord and in a life eternal is the act of freedom which is born of God."[43]

The life of the primitive Christian community was one of utter freedom, but even then the struggle to keep the gospel alive began, and with it the integumentation of its essence. The primitive conviction of Christ's imminent return was a "coefficient" of the primitive Christian's life. Like the doctrine of poverty for St. Francis or the consciousness of adoption for the Puritans, it was a reminder to the modern Christian that "the most inward possession, namely, religion," must have an external form and that "it grows, so to speak, in coverings of external rites and cannot grow without them." The tendency of the community to become a Jewish conventicle of expectation was resisted by Paul, who announced that the great event had happened, was not something to come, and that "whoso calleth Christ Lord speaketh by the Holy Ghost." Thus Paul became the carrier of the kernel, though inevitably he too endangered it, first, by making the fact of Christ's appearance in the world the real redemption (thus drawing man's attention away from the essence of the gospel toward the cosmos), and secondly, by fostering unintentionally the rule of "form and circumstance" through his enthusiasm for elements of the Old Testament. The rest of Christian history after Paul was ruled by the regrettable tendency of "the religion of strong feeling and of the heart" to pass into the religion of custom, theology, form, and law. Hellenistic Catholicism was the transformation of the Christian religion into a worship of God "in signs, formulas, and idols." Roman Catholicism compounded Greek orthodoxy's surrender to polytheistic remainders, Greek philosophy, and Eastern dualism by making religion into a legal system and by making salvation a form of contract. The Catholic Church was, in fact, simply the extension of the Roman Empire. Harnack's eloquence peaked in his description of the perversion of the gospel by the bishops (proconsuls), priests and monks (legions), Jesuits (imperial bodyguard), and the pope (Trajan). Peter and Paul were the Romulus and Remus of this perverted secular dispensation.[44]

Harnack ended on a Modernist note. His diatribe against Roman Catholicism, punctuated by a discussion of the flawed dehusking of the Reformation, modulated at the end into a query as to whether or not Rome would save itself from the disappearance of the medieval civilization which it had created and then totally identified with the gospel. The whole outward and visible institution of a church claiming divine dignity was "not a distortion but a total perversion." And yet, there was hope, since the Catholic Church possessed a faculty of adaptability known to no other institution: "it always remains the same old Church, or seems to, and is always becoming a new one."[45]

There lay Loisy's theme. The fashion in which he took it up owed more to his own ambition for a new apologetic for Catholicism than it did to what Harnack had actually said. Loisy was only one of the critics of the lectures who oversimplified and distorted Harnack's presentation of the kernel of the gospel. Reduced to a mere formula—"the fatherhood of God and the brotherhood of man"—the theology of *Das Wesen des Christentums* was shorn of the humility, eloquence, and confident faith which so moved its hearers and readers. Loisy capitalized on the fact that to the contemporary Catholic public, which knew little of the Lutheran orthodoxy of Berlin that Harnack had challenged, and even less about "consistent eschatology," Harnack *was* Protestantism. Loisy believed that the creative impulse (acknowledged by Harnack as existing in the gospel and generating "integuments" intended to preserve but tending to pervert the gospel spirit) either had to be expanded to the whole of church history or else abandoned altogether. Loisy knew, of course, that the

tradition of Catholic apologetic was synthetic, and thought he
could parallel it with his own ideas. He recognized his audience: intellectually sensitive Catholics troubled by the defection of the Protestant liberals from orthodoxy, upset by
the confusion generated by critical questions in Catholic
circles, querulously on the defensive in the world of Herbert
Spencer. By attacking Harnack, Loisy offered them an interpretation of church history which seemed to prove that
Catholicism was true to the gospel of Jesus, not in spite of an
institutional complexity, but precisely because of it. This
was a line of apologetic which would not only satisfy the most
conservative Roman theologian and curial official but would
also conform to the general (hypothetical) laws of religious
growth advanced by the historicist critics, the Hegelian ideal-
ists, the anthropologists, and the enthusiasts for evolution.
Loisy's own radicalism was thus overshadowed by the apologetical and polemical tone and intent of the book. His careful
attention to tradition and dogmatic consistency—elements
which were for him, not concomitants of a unique revelation,
but symbols generated by man's religious imagination under
the pressure of emergent humanity—softened the impact
of critical conclusions as well as philosophical generalizations.[46]

From its first words *L'Evangile et l'Eglise* was pitched on
a low key: a "little red book," ostensibly the response of the
humble critic to the great theologian, of one begging to point
out that historical fact should be the basis for any reasonable
theology. But the attack was swift and direct. Harnack had
proposed to be scientific but had, in fact, built his presentation of the gospel on texts which were secondary in the
evangelical tradition. A truly scientific approach "would have
proceeded on the totality of texts." Loisy thus hinted at what

he referred to in his memoirs as the "ineluctable opposition between the theological and historical points of view." He later maintained that he had been on his best behavior in the book—which, when compared with its successors, was almost courtly in its circumlocutions. But every jibe at Harnack was a blade thrust at the Roman theologians. "Possibly there have been theologians who were historians, who could deal with facts as they appear from evidence intelligently investigated without introducing their own conceptions into the texts they explored." It was clear that Loisy did not think so. The theologian was entitled to interpret the gospel for present needs "provided he does not confuse his commentary with the primitive meaning of the gospel texts," but the historian— and Harnack had presented himself as a historian—had to resist the temptation to modernize the conception of the kingdom. His job was to do nothing but present "the meaning the gospel had for those who first heard it, and, to a lesser degree, for those who set it down in the form we know."[47]

Loisy took up the pomological image with relish. The essence of Christianity might as well be found in the fullness and totality of its life as in its origins:

Why should the essence of a tree be held to be but a particle of the seed from which it has sprung, and why should it not be recognized as truly and fully in the complete tree as in the germ? Herr Harnack does not conceive Christianity as a seed, at first a plant in potentiality, then a real plant, identical from the beginning of its evolution to the final limit . . . but as a fruit, ripe, or rather, over-ripe, that must be peeled, to reach the incorruptible kernel; and Herr Harnack peels his fruit with such perseverance, that the question arises whether anything will remain at the end.[48]

This vigorous attack diverted attention from other introductory statements which hinted that Loisy found the content
of the gospels much more difficult to ascertain than Catholic
tradition allowed. Loisy insisted from the beginning that it
was very difficult, if not impossible, to distinguish between
the personal religion of Jesus and the interpretation of it
by his disciples, "between the thought of the master and the
interpretations of apostolic tradition." All that remained in
the gospels was "an echo, necessarily weakened and confused,
of Jesus' words, a general idea of the impression he made on
listeners who were already well disposed to him and his ideas,
. . . some of the more striking of His sentences as they were
understood and interpreted," and finally, "the movement
which he initiated." The implication that Harnack did not
appreciate the difficulties of using the biblical materials was
misleading: Loisy contrived to create an appearance of disagreement between himself and the historical theologian on
this and many other issues, whereas, in fact, his position was
in all major points identical with that of German criticism.
However, he differed quite radically from Harnack (and from
Christian tradition) when he insisted that the gospel had an
existence independent of those who studied it and that it
could be understood in itself before it was interpreted "in
the light of our preferences and needs." This axiomatic historicism was far in advance of anything posed by the liberals,
and overshadowed the reasonable, if novel, insistence that
"whatever we think theologically of tradition, whether we
trust it or regard it with suspicion, we know Christ only by
the tradition, across the tradition, in the tradition of the
primitive Christians." Loisy insisted that the essence of Christianity was to be found in the work of Jesus rather than in
"scattered fragments" of his teaching, and then argued that,

from the historical point of view, it was very difficult to estimate just what that work was. Finally, by way of introduction to his survey of the history of Christianity, he hinted that there was an essential gospel which was its principle of continuity and change.[49]

The significance of these general statements depended on a discussion of the gospel in its cultural context. This was only added to the book in the second edition (1903) when Loisy had realized that his subtle venture was not going to succeed. Enthusiatic approval of the book, such as that voiced by men like Maurice Blondel, Wilfrid Ward, Baron von Hügel ("just simply superb"), and the more cautious interest of Cardinal Sarto (Pius X), the abbot of Monte Cassino, Cuthbert Butler, and Mgr. Batiffol of Toulouse (who was to be the leader of the more conservative critics in their attacks on Loisy), would have been restrained had this material initiated the discussion in the original edition. Loisy, making a rapid survey of texts from the Synoptic Gospels, argued that the Gospels should be regarded, not primarily as sources for the history of primitive Christianity, but as products of its evolution out of the experience his followers had had of Jesus. Everything in the actual history of Jesus Christ had been transformed in the oral tradition which preceded the Gospels, and in the written Gospels themselves, by the apparent proof of the messianic dignity of Christ given by his resurrection. What the historian found in the Gospels was not so much the life and work of Jesus Christ, but what his followers had made of it after his apparent triumph over death. The parables, for instance, which taught certain quite specific details about the workings of the kingdom Jesus announced, had become mysteries because, in the light of the events of Easter, a divine teaching was, or had to be,

found in them. The baptism of Jesus by John, his experiences
in the desert, the miracles of healing, the transfiguration,
the predictions of the passion and resurrection, were all to
be understood in the form in which they had come down to
us, as messianic interpretations of "actual facts and occurrences" (of a presumably less extraordinary type). There were,
in effect, two gospels in the New Testament: "that of the
immediate witnesses of the teaching and the occurrences" of
Jesus' life, and that of those who understood the meaning
of what they had seen and heard more fully after his death.
Loisy argued that we knew very little of the first gospel (Acts
2:22–30 was probably the safest text); the second was, of
course, the New Testament as we knew it today *and* the rest
of the tradition of Catholic Christianity. This last point (perhaps the most fundamental of Loisy's new apologetic) was
only hinted at, as when he wrote that it was "in the nature
of human affairs" that "the work, genius, and character of the
truly great can only be properly appreciated at a certain
distance when they themselves have disappeared." In the
case of Jesus, his greatness has been "more and more appreciated as the centuries passed by"; and the present was
"ameliorated" by the gospel, just as it in turn was "illuminated
by all the experiences of humanity as it advances in age."[50]

Although the sequence of Christian history was taken up
in several chapters, the distinction between these two gospels
dominated the book. The original gospel was the almost
inaccessible teaching by Jesus of the kingdom of God; the
retroactive enlargement of it was the whole of Christianity,
including the New Testament. Loisy differed most clearly
from Harnack in his treatment of the first. He advanced a
completely eschatological reading of the idea of the kingdom
which he variously characterized as "the proposition of the

gospel of Jesus," the "impulse of will" which gave unity and meaning to everything Jesus said and did, and "the soul of Jesus himself." Through a cursory citation of a wealth of parables and miracles, Loisy argued that the kingdom was quite literally not of this world. The teaching of Jesus anticipated the gospel only in the sense that it was an invitation as well as a description. Harnack's Protestant preoccupation with the individual drama of sin and reconciliation had led him to find a mysticism and moralism in the teaching of the kingdom which was far less historically accurate than the messianic interpretation placed upon it by the primitive Church and the subsequent theological and institutional developments of Catholicism. Contrary to Harnack's view of the kingdom as the inner and a-historical confrontation of God and the soul and of the soul and its God, it was a collective, objective, and future-oriented "great hope." The kingdom *is to come*. It is to be a historical event which will bring the spiritual and physical conditions for true happiness. It is collective, because it is intended to embrace all who love God and who are pardoned by him because of their love ("and God pardons all, provided they pardon themselves"). It is objective, because its coming is the fact that completes and ends history. Finally, it is "in no way to be confused with the conversion of those who are called to it" (though entry into it requires conversion).

The imminence of the kingdom, "the renewal of the world, the restoration of humanity in eternal justice and happiness," so dominated the consciousness of Jesus that he neither preached *for* nor *against* the world as it was. Even his teachings about the nature of man had meaning only in the eschatological context. Hence, for instance, when he said, "You are of more value than many sparrows," it was not intended

as an exaltation of the value of the soul, but as an encouragement to have faith. Or, again, in the parable of the talents,
he was not arguing for an individual relationship with God,
but for preparation for the kingdom. When he compared
the disciples to the birds of the air, it was not only to dismiss
anxiety for bodily needs but to show that "even work . . . is
forbidden or discouraged." The argument was summed up
when Loisy wrote that the second part of the Lord's Prayer
took its meaning from the first: to ask for daily bread is to
express confidence that God will maintain us until the kingdom comes.[51]

Loisy was willing to give some place in the gospel of Jesus
to the ideas of God's love and man's response to it, but his
primary concern was to develop the eschatological understanding of the kingdom. Similarly, he placed great emphasis
on the role of Jesus as messiah ("the vicar of God for the
kingdom of heaven"), whereas Harnack had devalued this
notion as a mere vehicle for the teaching of the fatherhood
of God and its attendant doctrines. More cautiously than
Harnack, Loisy suggested that the nature of the "mental or
moral experience" through which Jesus achieved consciousness of his "divine Sonship" was historically uncertain. What
was certain was that all who heard him announce this sonship
identified it as a consciousness of messianic dignity "or the
pretension to that position." Kingdom and messiah were the
sum of the teaching of Jesus. If this was not the case, then
Socrates dying for reason was wiser than Jesus dying for
faith. Rationally considered, it was clear that if the idea of
the kingdom was "inconsistent with the fact," the gospel as
"a divine revelation" fell to the ground and Jesus became
"no more than a pious man who could not separate his piety
from his dreams, and died the victim of error rather than the

servant of the truth that was in him." Moreover, if Christ was intent on founding an earthly society or even "a particular religion," he was not only less wise than Socrates but less competent than Mohammed.[52]

Loisy forced the eschatological and messianic interpretation of the kingdom and emphasized the complete correspondence between the ideas of Jesus and those of late messianic Judaism, because his own critical studies, along with those of the German critics he had read, convinced him that such was, in historical fact, the gospel of Christ. He was quite aware that a rigorous adherence to a consistent-eschatological reading of the New Testament was a two-edged sword. It cut away the ethical-progressive interpretation of liberalism at ground level, but it also struck below the soil at the roots of traditional Catholicism. In one of the most quoted passages in the book, Loisy put the problem succinctly: "*Jésus annonçait le royaume et c'est l'église qui est venue.*"

This paradox was the point of departure for Loisy's new apologetic; it was the hinge upon which turned the whole revolutionary transformation of Catholicism into a truly modern religion. Jesus had died to bring the kingdom, and it had not come. If this obvious historical fact could not be satisfactorily explained, Christianity was a colossal misunderstanding and was totally irrelevant to the phenomena of modernity. The paradox was intensified by Loisy's allegation that this conclusion was made inevitable, even without biblical criticism, by the excessive rationalism of traditional theology—both Catholic and Protestant—which had obscured the nature of religious symbolism and the relationship between religious insight and the language and images in which religious insight was expressed. The twin ideas of the eschatological kingdom and Jesus as its vicar were, in fact, the

"Israelitish" symbol for "the future of faithful humanity, taking root in the present."[53] There was, then, a more fundamental core within the gospel of Christ for which even his teaching was a historically conditioned integument. The messianic expectations of late Judaism gave Jesus the language for "a shadowy representation of the great mystery, God and the providential destiny of man and of humanity." The true gospel was not endangered by the fact that the kingdom in the form then imagined did not come forth. The messianic idea was itself an inadequate and insufficient representation. To its proponents it was, of course, the reality, but "to the Christian historian, it now appears as the concrete, rudimentary, indistinct symbol of subsequent events. Namely, it symbolizes faith in the resurrection of Christ, in his invisible and constant presence among his own people, and in his eternal glory. The messianic idea also stood for the indefinite progress of the gospel in the world, the regeneration of human kind by Christianity, and the anticipation of the kingdom of heaven in the Church."[54]

The error of theological rationalism was to regard the symbol as the reality. The same criticism was implied in Loisy's presentation of Christology and of the rest of the development of Christianity, from the New Testament to the present day. This "second" gospel bore witness to Christ's teaching as it was transformed by faith; but it was *not* twice removed from "the great mystery," as Harnack had argued. The transformation of the idea of Jesus as the messiah into the Lord of faith, the Logos of God, the second Adam, the Second Person of the Trinity, meant better and richer expressions of what Loisy had earlier called the "impulse of will" or "soul of Jesus" contained in Jesus' teaching of the kingdom. Paul began the process by elaborating the first "theory of Christ" (he was "compelled to explain, since he could not narrate") which was quickly worked into the evangelical tradition. Thus, little by little, beyond what can be called the historical reality of the gospel, beyond even its idealization to suit the messiah, the fundamental dogmas were formed in the atmosphere of faith. The layers soon began to interpenetrate each other; traditions grew upon traditions. The growth of the expressions of the "impulse of will" proceeded both outward, becoming in the vision of John (Loisy refrained from offending by a denial of the orthodox view on the composition of the Fourth Gospel) a "symbolic description of the truth" through the loftiest elements of contemporary religious philosophy, and inward, in the development of a Christian "prehistory" in the several birth narratives, which, if they cannot be regarded as "a definite expression of historical memories," must be recognized by the historian as attestations of faith. Even the more authentic texts for the resurrection are inextricably interwoven with a tradition which cannot be entirely recaptured by historical study; for instance, Paul's declaration that the faith which he brought to the Corinthians he had received "according to the scriptures" suggested to Loisy that "the historical character of the tradition he alludes to must not be exaggerated."[55]

Matters such as the resurrection were, of course, questions of faith, and were, therefore, in the purview of the theologian, not the historian. But the historian was at least able to say that "as far as we can penetrate the economy of things of this world, Jesus lives in humanity to an extent and in a way never experienced by any other human being." If the hope of Jesus for immortality and for the kingdom "has only been actually realized before the eyes of faith . . . the philosophical historian will not hesitate to find even that an astonishingly true fulfillment, when he notes the results that this hope has achieved and its inexhaustible fruitfulness." The "great mystery" was advanced through successive symbolic representations. That was the important thing. To give another example, Paul's "ransom" theory probably influenced Mark and the other narratives of the Last Supper. What matters was that the ideas of sin, punishment, and the expiatory suffering of the just, whatever their source or their influence within the tradition, came together in a "symbolic conception" which had become "vivid in the conscience of mankind" in the particular treatment Paul had given them. Other arrangements of the elements might be possible; but, in any case, the complex was a teaching which should not be "forcibly translated into the expression of an absolute truth." Beyond such statements, and a dismissal of Harnack's distinction between the Easter faith and the Easter events, Loisy kept his own ideas about Christology veiled. As he later remarked, he had said nothing about the divinity of Jesus in *L'Evangile et l'Eglise* because it was not, strictly speaking, a problem of historical exegesis. The historian's craft did not extend beyond the grave.[56]

Loisy had, in fact, argued from critical evidence the novel position that scripture *was* tradition. The formal distinction between theology and history, along with his modest claims to be nothing more than the historian (though a "philosophical" one), gave him a certain amount of leeway in the discussion of primitive Christianity. Even so, his more radical views often erupted; and as several of the phrases quoted above illustrate, he was not averse to giving generous hints. But once he was able to pull away from the classic period of dogmatic formulation, Loisy's explication and defense of the historical development of Catholicism was eloquent and apparently traditional, though suspiciously tautological. "The Church can fairly say that, in order to be at all times what Jesus desired the society of his friends to be, it had to become what it has become; for it has become what it had to be in order to save the gospel by saving itself." He cited, among other examples, the crisis of Gnosticism to prove that the Church was as necessary to the gospel as the gospel was to the Church, and that the true yardstick of its achievement was, in every case, its response to the demands of its environment.[57]

In the early sections of the book Loisy repeatedly called attention to the communal character of the teaching of the kingdom, and he enlarged upon this theme in his presentation of orthodox Catholic positions on the development of the Church. For instance, he accepted the tradition of the apostolic succession at Rome, but insisted that the word as it was handed on in the epistle of Clement originated, not from the personal successor of Peter, but "from the community as the heir of the apostolic tradition." Here again, exegetical accuracy, which demanded that the New Testament and the developments of post-apostolic faith be seen contextually, was complementary to the nonscientific Catholic tradition. Loisy accepted Harnack's argument that Christianity had been overwhelmed by polytheistic remainders and nationalism in the East, but made this evaluation a point of contrast with the Western tendency, which permitted political involvement and the growth of temporal power *only* as means to the preservation of the gospel. If it was true that Rome repeatedly claimed new powers throughout the period of late antiquity and the middle ages, in no case were those powers more novel than the situation which called them forth and to which they were applied. The popes had indeed become

agents of the imperial tradition after the dissolution of the
Carolingian inheritance, acting as "social instructor, tutor
of monarchies, head of the Christian confederation"; but
this political involvement had only occurred as a concomitant
to a process of the enlargement of spiritual power within
the Church. In order to be the spiritual mistress of the new
nations, the Church had to be their tutor in the temporal
order as well; it had to grow in order to endure, because "the
changes which shaped themselves in her were the very conditions of her continued existence." Independence for the various tribal and national churches which struggled to assert
themselves (which Loisy slyly equated with the individualism
of Harnack's essential gospel) would have meant the submer-
sion of Christianity in "superstition and Germanic feudalism." And he posed the rhetorical question: What would
have happened to the religion of Jesus "had the pontiffs suddenly perceived that the essence of Christianity was faith in
God the Father and that their duty consisted in representing
this truth to those who might be willing to make their religion out of this alone?"[58]

Loisy's survey of the modern Church was posited on a
critical paradox. With the new situation in the fourteenth
century, the Church also changed; having acquired temporal
power to preserve and spread the gospel, it now needed to
put that power aside for the same reason. Loisy had argued,
in his circular definition of the Church, that it had always
become what it had to become in order to live. But clearly,
the modern Church had not yet responded to its new environment (as it was to prove in condemning Loisy's work).
His treatment of this problem in *L'Evangile and l'Eglise,*
though ironic, was yet hopeful. There were those who wished
to maintain the Church as "a society regulated in all matters

of thought and activity by a kind of military discipline."
With characteristic fidelity to his ecclesiological principles,
Loisy did not controvert this tendency by contrasting it with
the principles of the primitive gospel, as had Harnack, but
by commenting rather mildly that it was "dangerous and impossible to realize" in the modern setting. He saw in the
future a "general comity of civilized nations [as did Harnack]
wherein the Church, as a spiritual power, in no way political
in the present sense, should lose none of her prestige, none
of her independence, none of her moral influence."[59]

These views clearly challenged the triumphalist interpretation of the Church as a closed and perfect society. They are
not particularly disturbing in the second half of the twentieth
century. Loisy's more perceptive critics were troubled by his
opinions, and by the theory of revelation on which his views
were built, not because they challenged post-Tridentine developments, but because they turned the argument back on
the Christological question. Loisy admitted that there were
certain objections which could be raised to the process of
institutional development he had traced which were "very
grave from the point of view of a certain theology . . . but
of little or no significance to the historian." These objections
focused on the foundations of the Church and the measure
of its correspondence to its founder's intention. Jesus had
created a community, of that there was no question. He had
no idea of his followers as merely an invisible society of those
who have in their hearts faith in God and his goodness. But
neither did he "systematize beforehand the constitution of
the Church as that of a government established on earth and
destined to endure for a long series of centuries." It would
be "absurd" to expect that Jesus had determined beforehand
"the interpretations and adaptations that time would exact"

from the principles for which the Church stood "since they had no reason to exist before the hour which rendered them necessary." And, in any case, it was not only useless but psychologically impossible for Jesus to reveal to his disciples the future of the gospel and the Church.[60]

What was clear was that the Church, in every age, had stood for the idea of the heavenly kingdom; the idea of Jesus as its vicar, messiah, initiator; and the idea of the apostolate, of the teaching of the kingdom. There was no referent in the New Testament whereby fidelity to these three principles could be measured. It was enough that it preserved the thought "that the Savior left" to his hearers "that they must continue to wish, to prepare, to await, and to realize the kingdom of God." The only measure Loisy could allow historically was a consciousness of will—of vocation—which corresponded to his other notion of the gospel as an "impulse of will." And "setting aside all theological subtleties, the Catholic Church, as a society founded on the gospel, is identical with the first circle of the disciples of Jesus if she feels herself to be . . . if the elements of the Church today are the primitive elements, grown and fortified, adapted to the ever increasing functions they have to fulfill."[61]

Much more of the historian's philosophy came to the surface when Loisy moved from the history of Catholicism as an institution—popes, curias, canon laws, political pretensions—to the history of Catholic doctrine. Uncompromising statements on doctrinal matters ("neither the worship of Christ nor the cult of the saints could be a part of the gospel of Jesus, nor does either belong to it"; "the development of dogma is not in the gospel and could not be there") were here, as elsewhere in the book, softened by the force of anti-Protestant polemic and an insistence on the right of the magisterium to develop, in extension of the gospel, what science and Protestantism could not find there. Nevertheless, the blurring of scripture and tradition (which was a common characteristic of both the theology Loisy wanted to destroy and the apologetic he proposed) was inevitably more apparent than it had been in the discussion of the relationship between the gospel, primitive Christianity, the theological "theory" of Paul, the Fourth Gospel, and the Christological controversies of the fourth century.

Loisy argued that, as had been the case for institutional growth, the development of dogma was controlled at every stage of history by the monotheism and messianism of the original gospel, elements in no way altered by being linked to "the science of each age." Without the metaphysics of Plato and Aristotle, the notion of faith in one God would have been incomprehensible to men temperamentally philosophical rather than religious. Similarly, the messianic notion was incomprehensible to the Greeks until it was translated in terms of the incarnation of the preexistent Logos and the divinity of Christ. These developments were not arbitrary or independent. Trinitarian definitions had to wait upon adumbration of the theory of redemption; "but the ideas which supported these definitions existed before them in Christian belief, and their evolution has its starting point in the gospel of Jesus and apostolic tradition." "God does not cease to be one, and Jesus remains Christ; but God is triple without multiplication of Himself, Jesus is God without ceasing to be man, and the Word becomes man without losing its identity."[62]

Dogma was quite simply "divine in origin and substance, human in structure and composition." Until the modern period Catholic theologians had been preoccupied with an absolute and static notion of dogma which placed the emphasis on its unambiguous origins in revelation. What was now needed was careful study of the way in which dogmas had developed which would show "the relative character that [their] history makes manifest." Loisy now made a proposal which was a paradigm of his neo-Catholicism: the Church should proclaim a dogma of development. Though no such dogma could be found explicitly in the New Testament, its very formation would confirm its implicit life in the gospel. Loisy linked this proposed new dogma with the dogmatic tradition in characteristic fashion, enhancing his proposal by associating it with tradition and, at the same time, diminishing the "static" and revelatory element of tradition by associating it with an admittedly modern notion. "The acquisition of this new dogma will have no effect different from that of the old ones. These latter were not contained in primitive tradition, like a conclusion in the premise of a syllogism, but as a germ in a seed, a real and living element, which must become transformed as it grows, and be determined by discussion before crystallizing into a solemn formula."[63]

Loisy closed with a survey of the situation faced by the Church. All churches, orthodoxies, forms of worship, were involved in a religious crisis brought on by "the political, intellectual, and economic evolution of the contemporary world" and by "what one may call the modern spirit." To meet it by rejecting all ecclesiastical forms, all orthodoxies, all traditional forms of worship, would be to "cast Christianity outside of life and of humanity." A better course would be "to make the best of what is, in view of what ought to be, to repudiate none of the heritage which the Christian centuries have transmitted to ours, to recognize the necessity and the utility of the immense development that has taken place in the Church, to reap its fruits and to continue it, because the adaptation of the gospel to the changing condition of humanity is requisite today as always and more than ever." In any case, he added, the book had not been concerned with the difficulties, resources, and possibilities for "an accord of dogma and science, reason and faith, and of the Church and society." "If I have succeeded in showing that Christianity had lived in the Church and by the Church and that it is futile to want to save it by looking for its quintessence, this little volume will have done enough."[64]

IV

THE EFFECT OF *L'Evangile et l'Eglise* on the contemporary
religious scene was that of a bombshell, with an action both
double and delayed. Loisy's friends and other progressives,
who were not necessarily sympathetic to the opinions of
"Firmin" but were enthusiastic for Catholic biblical criticism,
hailed both the strategy and tactics in the book and waited
with pleasure to see the liberal Protestant lines crack. The
arch-conservatives, writing in *Univers* and *La Vérité Française,* knew something was wrong and were busy criticizing
Loisy long before the progressives noticed that they were as
badly wounded as Harnack. Within a few months Loisy was
under attack from two positions within the Church, conservative and progressive; and soon after that the extreme
Modernists and symbolists joined the fray. The conservatives
attacked Loisy for neo-Kantianism, neo-Hegelianism, rationalism, aetheism, and so on, because he insisted that Catholic
Christianity must submit the documents of revelation to the
methods of scientific history. The progressives criticized him
more gently (assuming "good faith" as well as an obscure

orthodoxy) because some of his specific conclusions were incompatible with Catholic teaching and, therefore, cast doubt on the general utility of the critical method. The extreme left disagreed because, although having clearly recognized the total subjection of Christianity to the law of evolution and the circumstantial relativity of all doctrinal development, Loisy persisted in his "fideism" and refused to admit that the object, as well as the subject, of all religious belief and practice was man.

Loisy characterized *L'Evangile et l'Eglise* as "an apology for the Catholicism that should be, and a discreet criticism of actual, official, Catholicism." Some thought the book both discreet and effective. Wilfrid Ward, who was never tempted toward symbolism in dogmatic exegesis and who, as Newman's biographer, might have been expected to distinguish between the Cardinal's theory of development and the exegete's theory of evolution, thought it acceptable apologetic. More sensitive and scholarly critics, such as Père Lagrange, whose own commentaries on the Gospels can be read as a protracted point-by-point refutation of the results of Loisy's critical studies, assumed good faith on Loisy's part and recognized the necessity for a philosophical approach to the methods of criticism, as well as a realistic estimate of their results.[65]

Less in Loisy's defense than in reply to his critics, the liberal papers argued that "just as no one has a monopoly on orthodoxy, no one has a monopoly on love of the Church; and it is possible that those who think themselves its best servants may cause the greatest harm to the Church." On the other hand, the *Revue du Clergé Français,* in which some of Loisy's pseudonymous articles had appeared, wondered if it was sufficient, "to justify the Church, to say that it has become what it had to become to live and preserve the gospel. . . . If in fact the Catholic Church appears to us to be a marvelous institution, does it not also appear to be too exclusively human?" The question was asked (with the answer implied): "Can one claim for biblical criticism a real autonomy comparable to that acquired by philosophy and history?"

Those who thought *L'Evangile* neither discreet *nor* effective were less hesitant. The Abbé Gayraud, a conservative clergyman and deputy, who had not read Harnack at all and had evidently only read Loisy on the run, told his readers that the critics had gone too far:

I fear that the only result of criticism will be to render suspect necessary and legitimate efforts. . . . Let us stand firm on the ground of our tradition. The Christ-God established the Church: that is the sum of Christianity: otherwise, it is nothing but an idol of the Hellenic spirit, and Catholicism an idolatry.

A correspondent of the *Univers*, which had long battled for Ultramontane and conservative causes, thought that *L'Evangile* was nothing but Renanism even vaguer and more insidious than that of Renan himself. Loisy was simply Arian and Nestorian. "Nicaea and Ephesus have replied to Loisy fifteen and sixteen centuries ago, and the faith of Nicaea is eternal." The Creed chanted in Church each Sunday was all the refutation Loisy needed. Loisy was no better than a Protestant reading the bible on his own: the Catholic does good historical criticism when he interprets the text in the understanding of the Church, relying on tradition. The apostles knew the thought of Jesus better than the most subtle critics. Other correspondents for the paper dismissed defenses of Loisy which pointed out that Loisy was often quoting Harnack when it had been presumed he was speaking in his own voice: "If M. Loisy cited M. Harnack there is nothing to indicate that he does not approve and that he rejects the errors summed up in the particular passage. In any case those

errors correspond very strongly with the fundamental assertion of the book."[66]

For conservative critics such as these, what mattered was
that Loisy differed with the common teaching of the Church;
it was unnecessary, therefore, to clarify the differences or
argue whether they were or were not compatible with orthodoxy. In any case, the criticisms of Loisy from the extreme
right missed the more subtle originality of the book. *La
Vérité Française*—"the daily of Catholic faithful to the old
tradition"—wrote: "We have in our midst a self-styled school
of science which is conspiring with the rationalist sects and
the liberal Protestants toward the ruin of the bible. The more
it is left to itself, the more it advances in the work of demoli-
tion." Contributors to this paper linked the *Loisystes* with
Blondel and his philosophical disciples, and with social democracy. They pointed to the criticisms of Abbé Gayraud's
attack as signs of the corrupt state of Catholic opinion (which
was clearly infected with the democratic spirit!), and linked
Loisy with Richard Simon.[67]

The theologians were generally soberer in their estimates
of the book than the pastoral clergy, but critical from the
beginning. Grandmaison, one of the progressives eager for
the development of Catholic exegesis, challenged Loisy's
failure to allow for the role of reason in Christianity and
argued that his theory of development was unfaithful to Newman and smacked of Hegelianism—presumably borrowed
from the Scottish theologian Edward Caird (who was the only
other author cited in *L'Evangile* besides Newman) and, of
course, Harnack. Like Hegel, Loisy argued that the idea of
Christianity could never be fully expressed in any event.
Though Loisy had "exerted himself everywhere in his book
to keep in focus the continuity of the gospel of Jesus," the

result of his exclusively eschatological interpretation was that the first link of the chain was the weakest.[68]

More extreme was the Abbé Oger, who said that "to analyze the mystery of our faith is to annihilate it" and argued confidently that the apostles' testimony to the teaching of Jesus was utterly accurate, "more faithful than a phonograph record," capturing not merely his words but his tone. Loisy had quite wrongly implied that the Church was too strict in its control of intellectual life. The Abbé countered:

The peril is not that the Church over-governs men, but that men do not let themselves be governed by her. The gospel of Jesus Christ is a gospel of liberty but not of independence, and the historians can entertain no reservations in detail, much less in the totality of the action of the Church.

And he closed with the rallying cry, "Let us return to an *integral* and intransigeant Catholicism, in the true supernatural sense of that word."[69]

Lagrange made the most telling criticisms. They were amplified many years later, in a small book occasioned by the publication of Loisy's memoirs. Lagrange admitted that "without question a critical reduction" of ecclesiology must be undertaken:

We cannot pretend to find in the words of Jesus a description of the Church as it exists today, nor the same definitive expression of our dogmas. . . . The question is to know if the dogma of the Church is in seed in the pure gospel and if the development of the seed has been legitimate.

Lagrange found Harnack had given more satisfactory answers to these questions than Loisy, because the former had at least

maintained a moral and social element in the gospel of Jesus.
More serious were the implications of Loisy's radical eschatology. Lagrange wrote:

[Its] unhappy result [was that] whatever the personal faith of the
author, the divinity of Jesus Christ only came upon him retro-
actively, as a development—oh, very legitimate, and without
any substantial change of teaching. [But, Lagrange adds,] people
less accustomed to the subtleties of exegesis will conclude from
this that he was not God at all.[70]

Lagrange saw the tension between Loisy's reduction of the
gospel and his apology for the life of the Church. Only the
Church could guarantee the authority of the gospels because
their historical authority had been destroyed by criticism,
but at the same time Loisy had destroyed the authority of the
Church whereby men might be led to accept its statements
about what the gospels mean. Lagrange concluded: "And why
should we accept the yoke of the Church—for it is a yoke—if
it was not instituted by Jesus Christ and if nothing can prove
that Jesus Christ was God?" In 1932 Lagrange summed up
the results of the debate between the German theologian
and the French exegete. The true notion of the supernatural
had disappeared: there remained nothing but a debate between "the religion of the individual and the religion of
society."[71]

The rush of articles and pamphlets against the book, and
its public condemnation by Cardinal Richard of Paris (sec-
onded by seven other members of the French episcopate)
disabused Loisy of his hopes for *L'Evangile et l'Eglise*. He
decided to defend his scientific freedom by making use of it.
His Roman correspondents had told him that the recent elec-
tion of Pius X would probably lead to the condemnation

which he had hitherto avoided by the use of pseudonyms. Loisy went to the printers with three books which marked the end of his career as a modernizer—and Modernist, for that matter—and fixed a turning point for all those on the left-liberal end of the spectrum of opinion about the relationship of the Church to modern science and society. A commentary on the Fourth Gospel, a revised edition of *L'Evangile,* and a defense of the latter work titled *Autour d'un Petit Livre*—which he had been sketching in letters and which his admirers had been encouraging him to write—appeared together in October 1903. In the last-named, the Loisy who had spoken honestly only to himself in the *livre inédit* of Neuilly, who had spoken "in parables" in his reply to Harnack, now spoke the principles of his neo-Catholicism unambiguously—and polemically.

Ever since his dismissal from the Institute his frame of mind had been "warlike," but his manners in *L'Evangile* had been impeccable. Not so the manners of the second "little red book." In a letter to the distinguished Cardinal Perraud, ultra-orthodox, author of a violent attack on *L'Evangile* in which he had described the effect of the book in terms of the last stages of seasickness, Loisy took note of the fact that the Cardinal was an Oratorian, and then remarked that all the glories of that organization "pale before the noble and serene figure of the great ex-Oratorian, Richard Simon, the father of biblical criticism and the victim of the great Bossuet." In addressing Mgr. Camus, the bishop of La Rochelle, who regarded himself as something of a critic, Loisy agreed that one must not make too great a use of criticism; but "perhaps it would be wiser not to meddle with it at all, than to make so little use of it." These sallies hardly lessened the impact of the book any more than did the anonymity of the corre-

spondents—"a cardinal," "an archbishop"—which stimulated
a guessing game abroad as well as in France. By repercussion,
the refutation of Harnack gained in notoriety. For six months
after the publication of its defense, "the French press busied
itself with the themes of *L'Evangile et l'Eglise* as it once had
with Renan's *Life of Jesus.*"

The letters which comprised *Autour d'un Petit Livre* were
concerned with a variety of topics: intellectual freedom
("ideas are not killed with a stroke of the crozier"), the biblical question, the authorship of the Fourth Gospel, various
problems of ecclesiology and history. But the overarching
concern was Christology, a problem which had been glossed
over in the reply to Harnack but which had emerged as the
major issue in the various critiques of the book. Loisy's treatment of traditional Christology involved the frank explication of the idea of the kingdom as a metaphor for the
evolution and perfection of human consciousness.[72] *Autour
d'un Petit Livre* made explicit the epistemology which had
been implicit in the polemic against Harnack. Its first principle was a sharp distinction between the natural and the
supernatural orders. Loisy argued that all knowledge was of
phenomena, except for religious knowledge, which was acquired immanently. The reality of the world and the reality
of God were distinct. Modern thought had discovered that
the only link between the two realities lay within human
consciousness. In the past, men had tried to bridge the gulf
in external, objective ways, and their ideas had unavoidably
been materialistic. The messianic idea of late Judaism was
one such notion. Originally the messiah was thought of as
bridging the two orders, but their long experience of suffering had led the Jews to materialize the idea, so when Christ
proclaimed his messiahship in poverty and humility, they rejected him.[73]

But what did Christ mean by the kingdom? What understanding did he have of his messianic role? These questions
could be answered by the historian. "The sentiment which
Jesus had of his union with God is beyond all definition."
His thought can only have been of a human type. Loisy advanced this point of view with reference to the patristic belief
in the limitation of Christ's knowledge, but his main argument was that an omniscient Christ was a moral impossibility.
The theologian who found it necessary to believe that Jesus
had infinite knowledge and yet hid it from his disciples
could persist in this notion "if he believes it indispensable."
The historian, however, can only say that Jesus Christ, a man
with a "unique destiny," made a most powerful statement,
in the language of his time, about the essential mystery of
man's relationship to the unknown. In any case, "neither
human language nor human thought were made to hold the
entire revelation of God, to explain at one and the same time
all aspects of eternal truth," to explain the unique statement
of Jesus that truth is not to be held as normative for all time
in its original form. The fact that Jesus occurred in history
did not make him lord of history.[74]

Loisy concluded, on the gospel evidence, that Jesus was
certainly not conscious of himself as a divine being. The idea
of the messiahship did, however, contain the germ of the
idea of his divinity; and this idea grew in order to make his
teaching more comprehensible and accessible, more capable
of opening up "before intelligent faith a larger view of the
world and of humanity." The idea grew through a dialectical
process of obstacle and proof. Christ's death on the cross was
the first obstacle, and the belief of the disciples in the "existence of the Resurrected One" was the proof by which their
faith surmounted it. The Christology of the apostles was a
simple evolution of the messianic idea. Even though but-

tressed by the "apparitions of the Savior and the predictions
of the Old Testament," it was essentially "a great act of
faith" which "saved the messianic idea in its application to
Jesus and allowed Christianity to affirm itself in the face of
Judaism."[75]

The next obstacle came with the movement of the idea of
Christ as the Son of God into the pagan world, a world of
high culture to which the Judaic messianic notion was utterly
foreign. Faith surmounted it in the person of Paul, who devised the scheme of the atonement and taught Christ as a
second Adam: Jesus became the "celestial man" who had pre-
existed with God and who had been predestined by him to
come upon the earth in the fullness of time to repair the
failure of the "terrestrial man." Paul's ideas were themselves
the product of struggle with the Church of Jerusalem, which
resulted in the triumph of the movement of the gospel to the
gentiles. The third confrontation was that between Pauline
and Johannine Christianity and Greek philosophy, traceable
in the last epistles of Paul and the Fourth Gospel. Out of the
idea of the atonement there began to grow wider speculations
as to Christ's role as "intermediary" in the whole of creation.
These notions subsequently came to fruition in the Logos
philosophy of the Hellenistic world. Now the Christian could
"without fear render an accounting of his faith before the
wise ones of the world." For at the same time that it was "the
most vital of religious and the most efficacious of moral doctrines," Christianity had also become "the most beautiful of
philosophies." Further obstacles arose and were overcome:
Nicaea and Chalcedon completed the formulation of traditional Christology by elaborating the trinitarian implications
of the idea of Christ and by giving suitable philosophical
definitions to the relationship of the two natures of the God-
man.[76]

It became clear, as Loisy elaborated these arguments about the messianic idea and the development of Christology, that he saw an analogy between the situation of the modern mind confronting traditional Christology and the dilemma of the Jewish mind confronting Jesus' messianic claims. In each case, ideas, designed to bridge the natural and the supernatural realms, tended to assume the charcteristics of the former. The Jewish mind was unable to assent to the idea of Christ as messiah, and to accept his kingdom as the one promised by God and foretold by the prophets, because of its preconceived and historically conditioned notions of the messiah as a glorious king coming upon the clouds and laying low the enemies of Israel. This was, in part, because of the primitive character of that religious mind, but also because of the inevitable process whereby history materializes—and misunderstands—religious symbols. The primitiveness of the Jewish mind lay in its belief that the two orders of reality could be definitely and permanently bridged at a moment in historical time. Christianity was a kind of new beginning. But the dialectic of adaptation led it to forget that the materialization of the religious idea in dogma, worship, and institutions must not be mistaken for the idea itself. And, more seriously, it persisted in the Jewish illusion that the two orders of reality could be brought into relationship in time and, in fact, came to believe that they had met—even as the Jews believed they were destined to meet in the great banquet they would share with Moses and the prophets.

The crisis of modern faith came from the fact that theologians persisted in confusing the rationalizations of faith with its essential mystery and tried to maintain in an "apparent unity two ideas which cannot be subject to a common measure: the idea of personality in God and the idea of personality in man." Herein lay the whole error of Christology: it claimed to understand the supernatural world with the science of the natural world. Loisy insisted that the concept of the personality of God could only be held as "a symbol of his absolute perfection and of the essential distinction which exists between the reality of God and the reality of the world." From this it followed that it was impossible to conceive historically the idea that this personality could be made manifest in the lower order. However, the persistence of the primitive hope of "seizing God" was not the only flaw in this epistemological approach. Primitivism was compounded by the fact that the psychology used by the theologians was "metaphysical and abstract," and completely at variance with the empirically based psychology of the modern age. The insights of this new psychology were producing a new understanding of God as a force immanent in the human spirit. The religious growth of humanity could now surmount the obstacle which neither Judaism nor traditional Christianity had been able to overcome. It could escape from the paradox of the belief that God is purely transcendent and yet has somehow entered into history.

The Church, unfortunately, persisted in adhering to the psychology of traditional Christology, which was a combination of the human psychology of the Synoptics and the speculative divine psychology of the Fourth Gospel and the Fathers. But this was "a special psychology which is *not* a psychology, because it is not based on observation, but on a process of reasoning which has as its point of departure an unhistorical interpretation of the gospel." The educated laity of the modern world could not accept this nonpsychology, and that was why men of learning were everywhere leaving the Church, soon to be joined, Loisy implied, by men of simple faith as well. The rationalism of theological language, designed to preserve the life of the gospel, now threatened to end it. The Church, in the past, had used intelligence in the service of faith. Loisy asked that men might hope that the Church would use it "to construct the religion of the future," safeguarding "the double revelation of God in the world and in man, the religious idea of the living God and that of *Christ-Dieu.*" This new approach could abandon theological rationalism, without succumbing to secular rationalism, that "paltry heresy" which regards Christ as merely a man (the accusation which had been made against Loisy himself). Christ is God for the faith. But men demand that we explain God and Christ to them. Our definitions are conceived in a language different from theirs; a translation is demanded.[77]

Progressive and Modernist themes were very close in these arguments. Protest against the obscurity and meaninglessness of traditional theological formulations was much needed in Loisy's day. Doubt and unbelief threatened countless men searching "with the Church" for a better understanding of the gospel. Loisy, however, was asking for a good deal more than a revitalization of Catholic theology and a "translation" of the doctrines of the Chuch into a language which modern man could understand. As his letter on doctrinal evolution made clear, his view of revelation was such that the term "translation"—at least in its common meaning—was inadequate. He argued that *L'Evangile et l'Eglise* was indeed an "absurd and impious" book if one revelation and one set of dogmas have absolute value, if "it is not only the object of knowledge which is eternal and immutable in itself, but [also] the form which this knowledge has assumed in human history." Revelation properly understood can only be "the consciousness [*conscience*] acquired by man in his relationship with God." Christian revelation was specifically "the

perception in the spirit of Christ of the relationship which
united him with God, and of the relationship which unites
all men to their heavenly Father." Not only dogma, but
revelation itself, was progressive and subject to the evolutionary fact: "God works in mankind. He reveals himself
according to the capacity of human nature; the evolution of
the faith cannot fail to be coordinated with the moral and
intellectual evolution of man."[78]

At this time Loisy had great faith in God and society; in
later years, great faith in society alone. In *Autour d'un Petit
Livre* he still had the vestiges of a faith in the Church as it
might be, as it had been at its best. And he still insisted that
the gospel as Jesus preached it, though lacking any deliberate
worldly dimension, was effective in history because of its
completely social character. To those critics who had said
that the essence of the gospel as Loisy described it in *L'Evangile* was ecclesiologically meaningless, he replied that, on the
contrary, his whole book intended "to prove that the evangelical principle, in spite of the inevitable limitations of its
initial manifestations, is an inexhaustible source of human
progress, by virtue of its unbounded power of adaptation to
the various conditions of humanity." The social dimension
of the kingdom and the hope of a transformation of human
life were ideas so great—they were such a "revelation," one
might say—that they had a life quite independent of Jesus'
hope for the immediate realization of the kingdom of messianic expectation. Deprived of its original eschatological conception by the fact of history, obscured (it would appear, for
centuries) by dogmatic adumbrations which replaced the insight they were meant to represent, the idea of the kingdom
could still have two interrelated meanings for modern man.
It could stand as a symbol of personal fulfillment and trans-

cendence through self-sacrifice for the greater good of society (or of the nation) and as a symbol for the "reign of justice and happiness" which is the historical goal of human evolution. The value of Catholic Christianity lay in the powerful expression it had given to the aspirations of humanity for more complete consciousness. The Church was the best vehicle for this evolution in the future because it had been its vehicle in the past. It could only be abandoned—and then with the greatest sorrow—if it failed to renew its role, if it failed to see, in response to the promptings of modern science and society, that humanity itself was the progressive revelation of the kingdom of God.[79]

Loisy's personal belief, which had long been at variance with his apologetic hopes, came to be more closely coordinated with his public statements after the publication of *Autour d'un petit livre,* which met with the unified opposition of the theologians and the hierarchy. About a year after its publication, when there was a rumor that perhaps Pius X would not condemn Loisy after all, he wrote to a friend:

Pius X has decided I am not to be a martyr. He is more correct in this decision than he knows. To be a martyr, it is necessary to have at least the *excuse* of a robust faith in the cause which one defends.

The two other "little red books" which he subsequently published, one dealing with the sources in his works for the propositions condemned in the decree of the Holy Office, the other with the general circumstances of his condemnation and the reactions to it, were ostensibly meant to clarify and advance positions soon to be known as "Modernist."

In fact, they only showed how completely Loisy had abandoned the cause. In his journal of that period he wrote:

Christ has even less importance in my religion than he does in
that of the liberal Protestants: for I attach little importance to
the revelation of God the Father for which they honor Jesus. If
I am anything in religion, it is more pantheist-positivist-humani-
tarian than Christian.[80]

His Catholic critics later seized on this remark as proof
of Loisy's unbelief. Guitton commented:

His whole religious system has as its residue a great society, and
he implies that it will be the continuation of the Church of
which the past has been so glorious, and of which he has been a
minister.

Guitton pointed out the paradox of Loisy's Modernist priesthood: "If he abandons the Church, he has no work to do,
his message has no object." The contradiction between his
belief and his priesthood, between his rejection of the
revelation of Jesus Christ and his insistence on the Church,
between his evolutionism and his fideism, were paralleled
by the contradiction in his later thought between a materialistic idea of man "as an accident of creation, like the ants"
and his insistence on collective growth toward an ideal
society.[81]

It was in early 1903 that *L'Evangile et l'Eglise* had been
censured by Cardinal Richard. On December 16, 1903, the
Holy Office published a decree placing five of Loisy's works
(including the two neo-Catholic essays) on the Index. In
early 1904 Loisy accepted the condemnation, and submitted

to it reserving the rights of his conscience and his scientific freedom. A complicated exchange was thus initiated between Loisy and the Holy Office, which continued for the next four years. During these years the debate over the issues which Loisy had raised in his books was taken up by a series of progressive Catholics, beginning with Edouard Le Roy's article "Qu'est-ce qu'un dogme?" in *La Quinzaine,* enlarged in *Dogme et Critique* (1906), and involving Maurice Blondel and Père Laberthonnière of the *Annales de Philosophie Chrétienne.* The ideas of social, intellectual, and especially spiritual reform in the Church were given wide currency in Antonio Fogazzaro's novel *Il Santo.* Later, the work of Le Roy, Laberthonnière, and Fogazzaro was also censured by the Holy Office.

From the limited critical questions discussed by "A. Firmin" in a learned journal, the impulse to examine the relationship of dogma and history had expanded into a consideration of the pragmatic value of Christian teaching, its nature and value as a way of life rather than a system of beliefs. The controversy swelled against the background of the publication of Poincaré's *Science et l'Hypothèse* and the great debate over the Law of Separation passed by the French parliament in December 1905. Outside of France, George Tyrrell in England and Romolo Murri, Ernesto Buonaiuti, and others in Italy expanded the movement. A considerable periodical literature grew up. Then, in 1907, came the naming and the condemnation of Modernism. On March 7 of the following year Loisy was formally excommunicated; a year later he was elected to the chair of the history of religions at the Collège de France, the position once held by the apostate rationalist the young exegete had set out to refute: Ernest Renan.

V

WHEN LOISY was formally excommunicated, a considerable range of his life and work still lay ahead. He polemicized in defense of the Law of Separation, wrote prolifically on critical questions, produced several philosophical works discussing religion in the context of nationalism and social science, argued against Bergson, Catholic critics, and rationalists, and was widely honored throughout the academic world. Yet it is not Loisy the critic and historian of religions who appears as a unique figure in the perspective offered by the second half of the twentieth century, but rather Loisy the innovating priest-critic, the savant of the heady and dangerous days of progressive hope and experimentation. Loisy shared his post-Modernist positions with many of his learned contemporaries. Religions of progress, nationalism, and humanity were characteristic of the years before the 1914–18 war; sober revision of such hopes and dreams, of the postwar period. As a lay intellectual, he was only one of a generation of European scholars who believed in the power of ideas and of men of ideas to change the world, and

only one of that smaller group of intellectuals which included figures as diverse as Durkheim and Troeltsch and
which insisted that the secret to the creation of a healthy
society lay locked up somewhere in the religious phenomenon. Like them, he was disillusioned by what he saw, especially as the decade he had initiated with his memoirs (and
which he did not expect to live out), ground on to disaster.
In 1939 he wrote in his journal: "And now, before the coming events, I feel, above all, my helplessness." And a month
before his death in July 1940: "Never have I realized so
clearly how little a weak man, whose pen is his only weapon,
can do."[82]

In the head-text of his essay *La Religion* (1917), Loisy had
given the kind of translation (here of the Fourth Gospel)
he had demanded in 1902 and 1903: "In the beginning was
the task; and the task was in humanity; and the task was
humanity." Christianity was founded, not upon the notion
of humanity, but upon the transcendental and unverifiable
notion of a plan of salvation devised by the master of the
universe for those he has willed to choose. The religious
sense of human and universal society, however, could be
followed in the historical evolution of religions. And this
religious sense was also the principle of that evolution, just
as the ideal—always more worthy of worship—of a society
both human and universal remains the essential goal of all
religions.[83]

But it was *before,* not after, Loisy had explicitly come to
hold for a religion of humanity which was an exclusively
intrahuman and intrahistorical phenomenon that he made
his most individual contribution to modern history. Although personally convinced that the Christian faith would
be altered out of recognition with any historical form it had

ever previously taken, he had then proposed a reform of Catholicism which in many respects corresponded to real needs in the life of the modern Church. In his memoirs Loisy said of *L'Evangile et l'Eglise*: "I did not confine myself to a criticism of Professor Harnack, but paved the way discreetly but definitely, for an essential reform in biblical exegesis, in the whole of theology, and even in Catholicism generally." Yet, in retrospect, these were merely progressive sentiments. How then are we to explain Loisy's terminus: revolution instead of reform?[84]

First, certain personal characteristics must be noted. From his earliest days Loisy knew books and ideas as reality. He worked by himself. His isolation, even in maturity, was remarkable. He pursued his studies at the Institute alone, and refused an offer to live with Duchesne. He knew very few of his progressive or Modernist contemporaries, and passed his years in the company of books and the chickens he kept on his little farm at Ceffonds. He was ambitious, eager for fame, jealous of his originality. His frequent protestations that he had come to his critical conclusions without the aid of German bible scholarship were not a reflex of the Germanophobia (compounded of *revanchisme* and bitterness over Bismarck's Kulturkampf) which paralyzed Catholic scholarship in France, as much as evidence of his real fear that his revolutionary work would be washed away in the Catholic consensus of the future. This individualism isolated him from a good deal of contemporary work in this field, and encouraged his confidence in the value of his own findings.

Of equal importance was his attitude toward historical science. If there was ever a conversion experience in Loisy's life, it came when he discovered philological studies. Long before the apparently innocent disclaimers of *L'Evangile*, religion had become for Loisy an entirely historical phenomenon, in a personal as well as scientific sense. Here the *crise de conscience* (which occurred when the very simple and simplistic faith of the peasant boy clashed with the rationalism and legalism of the seminary course) was the significant negative factor. Not prayer or pious works, but the tangibles of philology, brought a synthesis, and with it the foundations, of authentic personality. It is significant that Loisy, like other Modernists, knew very little firsthand about the world of natural science from which he drew his metaphors, as well as very little about the general inheritance of post-Enlightenment culture. Like Molière's gentleman, he talked the language of Voltaire, Kant, and Hegel (and the newer tongues of Poincaré and James) without knowing it. Even if one can trace few clear early influences on his work other than the very important impact made in the seminary by his discovery of Lamennais and his school, it is not surprising that he should have spoken in the philosophical accents of late nineteenth-century Europe. Yet the general influence of antirationalist ideas from other parts of the social and human sciences is probably of less moment than the all-pervading influence of biology on one who shared "a fervent, at times somewhat ingenuous, belief in contemporary science." For Loisy, evolution was a good deal more than a hypothesis.[85]

Finally, two other personal characteristics which complemented cultural pressures should be noted. He had a remarkable tenacity of will which was hardly lessened by the persecution directed against him, as a man and as a scholar, by lesser minds in an age of freewheeling and character-shattering religious polemic. And he showed a deep concern for society, a concern accentuated by the social confusion of his time (and inextricably mixed with a militant patriotism). But personal elements blend with the cultural milieu. The latter is not problematic. Loisy's attack on the rationalism of post-Tridentine theology and his confusion of dogma with theological explanation issued from an adolescent religious experience of a type still not entirely abandoned in an age of revived biblical theology and seminary reform.

Perhaps the best that can be done by way of assessing the reasons for the revolutionary results of the apology for Catholicism of which the young seminarian dreamed is to look briefly at the residue of Loisy's religious thought as it appears apart from the *mystification* of its presentation and in the context of liberal Protestantism and the Catholic tradition.

Comparisons with Harnack have often been made. On many matters the agreement between them was great, as Harnack himself pointed out in subsequent commentaries. But Harnack also saw the fundamental difference on which Loisy's more sensitive Catholic critics focused. If Harnack had erred on the side of individualism, Loisy had dissipated religion entirely into secular society. Harnack said in 1903 that Loisy did not understand Protestantism, and noted the following paradox: "This man on his way to heresy has a sort of aversion for the heretical spirit. His conception of religion remains Catholic, inseparable from the idea of community and tradition." Two years later he summarized Loisy's approach as: "Criticize all you want, but leave as the teaching of the Church that which criticism has destroyed: for it is the Church which continues the development." Harnack felt that efforts like Loisy's to force the Church

to accommodate itself to the *section hors rang* of intelligent
Catholics ("secret Protestants who live on from generation
to generation") was doomed.[86]

Their agreement was greatest on critical specifics: the
Virgin Birth as a later tradition, the doubtful character,
from the historical point of view, of the resurrection, the
continuity between the original gospel and the development
of Judaism. Yet, even on critical questions, there was a
fundamental and paradoxical difference between Harnack
and Loisy. Loisy pointed out in his memoirs that, whereas
he had been led by his researches to see the New Testament
growing out of a gospel which was "the work of a Christian
prophet who was intermediate between the Christ of history
and that of John," Harnack was unaware of this "primitive
gospel" and therefore based his treatment of the essence of
the gospel on the Fourth Gospel: a Catholic, rather than
a Protestant, source.

Alec Vidler has noted that it is only necessary to read two
lines of *L'Evangile et l'Eglise* to see the irresistible attraction
theological problems held for Loisy. As theologians (Loisy
preferred the name "philosophical historian"), Loisy and
Harnack differed profoundly. Loisy obscured the "points of
convergence" in the two works by presenting his critical
conclusions within an ecclesiological context. Harnack argued that (unfortunately) the gospel needed the Church, but
had constantly to be distinguished from the Church lest the
gospel itself disappear. Loisy argued that the gospel had
become the Church and that the Church was necessary for
believers because "it alone is equipped to assure, from generation to generation, the slow education of humanity." This
fundamental difference of view on the role of the Church
came, in turn, from two different estimates of the relation-

ship between Jesus and the gospel. As aptly summed up by
Poulat in a phrase: the distance which Harnack placed
between the gospel and the Church, Loisy located between
Jesus and the gospel. For Harnack, the mind or soul of Jesus
was accessible in the gospel. For Loisy, it was not. According
to Loisy, the passage of time had rendered incomprehensible the categories of heavenly kingdom and messianic mission
—and, for that matter, the Christological categories which
succeeded them. But the fact that these categories had come
into existence was historically recoverable, even if the "impulse of will" in Jesus was not. All the categories or symbols
inspired by the spark hidden within the kernel of the twin
gospel of kingdom and messiah (contained in its turn within
the more elaborate growth of the Church) testified to the
extraordinary power of the vision of Jesus: a vision of a
united humanity, progressively released from nature, self-
transcendent through the emergence of the "religious impulse," moving inexorably toward some kind of full
understanding of its relationship with the external forces
creating and shaping it.

Within the context of the Catholic tradition, three aspects
of Loisy's thought stand out: his remarkable insistence on
Catholicism without Christianity, his negative treatment of
the problem of human nature, and his concept of doctrinal
growth. The notion of Catholicism without Christianity was
but one manifestation of what is perhaps the most easily
documented and puzzling theme that can be drawn from
the history of the Modernist crisis: if it is true that Modernism in general was defined "by a pair of oppositions (intra-
confessionally, its neo-Catholicism; interconfessionally, its
anti-Protestantism)," it is also true that the neo-Catholic
element was the more important of the two.[87]

The issue of salvation and progress was, of course, associated with the institutional new-Catholicism. Evil was not
problematic for Loisy. The Church whose institution by
Christ was "not a tangible fact for the historian" was nevertheless "the institution of forgiveness for the heavenly kingdom" in which man worshiped his humanity in Jesus, but
the questions of *individual* salvation and immortality were
not particularly important. On this issue the elitist character
of Loisy's neo-Catholicism becomes clear. The hope of personal salvation—*not* any expectation of the completion of
humanity in history, the culmination of the "slow education
of mankind" which the Church had supervised—had always
motivated the *homme moyen religieux,* for better or for
worse. Even when the "coal heaver" adopted a secular or
materialistic faith, as he did in the nineteenth century, he
did so largely out of hope that the new age would dawn in
his own day. Only the historian and the philosopher could
take the long-range view. Miguel de Unamono saw the tension between Loisy's historicism and the traditional preoccupation of the Church when he asked:

Is it indeed possible for a life, life that seeks assurance of survival
to tolerate that a Loisy, a Catholic priest, should affirm that the
resurrection of the Savior is not a fact of the historical order,
demonstrable and demonstrated by the testimony of history alone?.
. . . Do not the Modernists see that the question at issue is not so
much that of the immortal life of Christ, reduced, perhaps, to a
life in the collective Christian consciousness, as that of a
guarantee of our own personal resurrection of body as well as
soul?

Loisy could not. But he could see generations of believers
responding to "the proposition of the gospel of Jesus" which

increased, yet remained the same, "like an echo which, reverberating from mountain to mountain, becomes more sonorous the farther it travels from its point of origin."[88] Loisy's metaphors were often contradictory. Elsewhere he spoke of the New Testament as containing "but an echo, necessarily weakened and . . . confused" of the words of Jesus. His ambiguity, however, was most serious, not in general metaphors, but in specific biological analogies. For example, he argued that in order to fulfill its commission and be "identical" with the religion of Jesus, the Church had no more need to reproduce the exact forms of the gospel "than a man has need to preserve at fifty the proportions, features, and manner of life of the day of his birth in order to be the same individual. The identity of a man is not ensured by making him return to the cradle." Loisy was describing the growth of dogma and of the institutions of the Church in terms of nineteenth-century biological science, and was thereby rejecting the preepigenetic and dialectical views of development. This meant introducing a purely relativist notion, not only of the formal relationship between ideas and their environment, but between their form and their content as well. Thus, in proposing a "dogma" of development, Loisy was in fact proposing that the Church reject the idea of *any* normative external revelation and admit that there can be no infusion of transcendence either in the past or the future, but only that which is immanent in individual or group consciousness.[89]

What would this "dogma" of development replace? Catholic tradition offered several explanations of itself. The preepigenetic idea explained the elaboration of dogma by analogy with the older theory of biological growth, according to which the embryo contains, in miniature, all the parts of the complete adult organism. The dialectical theory explained the elaboration of one dogma from another by analogy with the syllogistic progression of the minor from the major conclusion. The "explicatory" theory, defended by Bossuet and attacked by Richard Simon, saw dogmas growing by translation and explication from the gospel in which they were fully and definitively stated. The notion of the *disciplina arcani* gave continuity to the growth of doctrine by arguing that Christ had entrusted to the apostles and their successors a secret store of revelation, from which the Church draws what is needed as time demands, according to the divine plan.

The notion of the *disciplina arcani* had no significant defenders. Bossuet was less important than in earlier days. The dialectical theory, which was dominant in orthodox thought after the seventeenth century, admitted progress in doctrinal growth but safeguarded the idea of the deposit by insisting that the apostles "knew *explicitly* all the doctrine which the Church would later draw from the teaching passed from the apostles to the Church *implicitly*." It remained the most widely accepted approach. Newman, of course, was the major spokesman for the preepigenetic evolutionary view, though he did not use the biological analogy. And, in Loisy's day, Newman was far from general acceptance by Roman theologians. Newman had gone beyond the dialecticians by admitting change as well as progress. But he preserved the concept of the deposit of faith, not by using the older notion of the embryo, but by constructing a theory of ideas which saw the Christian revelation as a fundamental idea allowing for a multiplicity of interpretive notions. The idea lived in history; therefore, change in the notions of it was inevitable. "Old principles appear under new forms."

The living idea "changes in order to remain the same." "In a higher world it is otherwise, but here below to live is to change and to be perfect is to have changed often." Newman held that a truly important idea can "only be comprehended in all its aspects through a long period of time and diverse circumstances, which elicit its consequences and its relationships." This is what happens in the development of Christian doctrine. An "idea" has been given to the Church, and developments of doctrine are the God-assisted process whereby the Church comes to comprehend more fully the structure and the relations of the original revelation, to see round the different aspects of the one idea which it has been given.[90]

Loisy's view differed from all of the older theories of doctrinal development—no less acutely from the one which appears closest to his evolutionary approach, the idea-in-history theory of Newman, than from that which is most remote, the notion of the *disciplina arcani*. Loisy had discovered Newman and sketched his views enthusiastically in the Firmin articles. But he had gone beyond Newman long before writing *L'Evangile et l'Eglise*, though his refutation of Harnack might have had as its text Newman's theory as stated above. Newman's development was unsatisfactory to Loisy because it, too, was a product of faith. If it was historically impossible to demonstrate the existence of a secret teaching kept by the popes, it was equally impossible, without Newman's difficult and a-historical theory of "illative assent," to grasp the simultaneous simplicity and complexity of the "idea" of Christianity. According to Newman, God has interjected the one great idea of Christian revelation into time and has decreed how it shall be elaborated. According to Loisy, nothing controlled the evolution of Christianity but the evolution of humanity toward full consciousness;

the idea of the kingdom is the first document of the Christian
version of the progressive revelation of man, and it is preceded by the vision of Jesus, and followed by the development of the Church; neither the idea of Jesus nor the notion
of the kingdom contained their subsequent elaborations in
the way in which Newman's idea of Christianity contained
all the notions of it which men were to hold explicitly. If
Loisy had written only as a critic and historian, much of his
work would present little challenge to the extreme kerygmatic argument that "the historical problem is scarcely
relevant to Christian belief in the resurrection" or to an
enlarged reading of dogmatic development along the lines
Newman set out. But Loisy did not confine himself to criticism, and his theology presented, not an act of faith in Christ
the Lord, or a defense of an infallible Church guided by
the Holy Spirit in its deepening understanding of the gospel
through history, but a notion of humanity itself as the only
depositum fidei.[91]

Loisy's vocation and his religious philosophy cannot be
separated, nor can the currents of secular humanist, Protestant, and Catholic influence on his work be clearly distinguished. Dansette, after remarking that Loisy had "too
roughly and too hastily freed exegesis from a mistaken
obligation to defend indefensible positions" and then gone on
to empty of all dogmatic content "the faith of which he remained officially a defender," concludes that "his attitude
was the outcome of a complicated intellectual approach, defy-
ing logical analysis." If Loisy's neo-Catholicism was a house of
symbols, a museum full of ancient testimonials to a mis-
construed faith, it was so partly as the result of a crisis of
faith, widely experienced by his generation (and acutely
described in Roger Martin du Gard's *Jean Barois*), which

revealed a failure of Catholic teaching to make distinctions between scripture and tradition, between revelation and reason, between dogma and theology, between Christian faith and the intellectual and social categories of a passing world. In one of Loisy's moments of doubt and anxiety, his spiritual director at Châlons had once reassured the young seminarian:

A religion which has satisfied geniuses like St. Augustine, St. Thomas Aquinas, Pascal, Bossuet, and Fenelon is surely not unworthy of our adherence.

Commenting on the advice in 1913, Loisy wrote:

I did not then dream of answering him that these men had not lived in the nineteenth century, and that no one could tell what might have been the turn of mind of a Blaise Pascal who had been born a contemporary of Renan.[92]

Loisy's was such a mind.

NOTES

[1] Albert Houtin and Felix Sartiaux, *Alfred Loisy, Sa Vie, Son Oeuvre* (Paris, 1960), p. 103; Emile Poulat, *Histoire, Dogme et Critique dans la Crise Moderniste* (Paris, 1962), p. 19.

[2] The title of a defense of Loisy by Henri Bremond published under the pseudonym "Sylvain Leblanc," Paris, 1931.

[3] Alec Vidler, *The Modernist Movement in the Roman Catholic Church* (Cambridge, England, 1934), p. 70. Canon Roger Aubert remarks: "In any case, it is the religious thought of Loisy, rather than his character, which interests the historian of Modernism. The major problem at issue is to know if Loisy actually did lose his entire faith—not only his faith in the Church or in the divinity of Christ, but his faith in the supernatural and in God as well—at the moment when he published *L'Evangile et l'Eglise* in 1902" (*Revue d'Histoire Ecclesiastique*, Vol. LXI, No. 1 [1966], p. 222).

[4] Recent discussions of Loisy have been somewhat more dispassionate. Cf.

Robert Rouquette, "Bilan du Modernisme," *Etudes*, Vol. 289 (June 1956), pp. 321–343. Rouquette, after citing the inscription on Loisy's grave (*Qui tuam in cotis tenuit voluntatem*), muses: "Did he remain faithful, in spite of the vicissitudes of his career, to the religious inspiration of his first vocation?" (p. 321).

5 Quoted in Friedrich von Hügel, *Religious and Philosophical Essays*, Second Series (London, 1926), p. 27.

6 Cf. Alfred Loisy, *Mémoires pour Servir à l'Histoire Religieuse de Notre Temps*, 3 vols. (Paris, 1930–31), Vol. I, p. 22.

7 *Mémoires* I, p. 25. Cf. Alfred Loisy, *Choses Passées* (Paris, 1913), English edition, *My Duel with the Vatican: The Autobiography of a Catholic Modernist*, tr. R. W. Boynton (New York, 1924), p. 53. I have at times altered the translation.

8 *Mémoires*, I, pp. 28–33, 134; *Duel*, pp. 57–60; Houtin, *Loisy*, p. 14.

9 Adrien Dansette, *Religious History of Modern France* (New York, 1961), Vol. 2, pp. 293–294.

10 *Mémoires* I, pp. 41–44; *Duel*, p. 66; Houtin, *Loisy*, p. 17.

11 *Mémoires* I, pp. 61, 50–55; *Duel*, pp. 71–78.

12 *Mémoires* I, pp. 53–59; *Duel*, pp. 79–80. The difficulties over Loisy's "liberalism" were not discussed in *Choses Passées*.

13 Houtin assembled a list of quotations from the *Mémoires* and from unpublished material to prove duplicity (*Loisy*, p. 19), assessing the origins of Loisy's priesthood in the light of what the exegete himself called the "enormous equivocation" of the Modernist years.

Assessment of the relative merits of Loisy's *Mémoires* and Houtin's *Vie* is difficult. As Poulat points out, Loisy and Houtin were friends when the biographical sketch was undertaken, and Loisy contributed documentation. After the break, Loisy had no way of estimating the character of the work as other than negative. The *Mémoires* thus take the form of a refutation of an attack the author had not read. "Les *Mémoires* sont ainsi l'oeuvre d'un homme qui refuse d'être vu comme il se devine vu, mais qui se sait vu quand il cherche à se montrer comme il se voit" (Houtin, *Loisy*, pp. vii-viii [Poulat]).

14 *Duel*, p. 85. Duchesne had come to the Institute in 1877, had resigned briefly under fire for his lectures on the history of doctrine in 1885, and continued to attract criticism, especially for his attitude toward the "so-called 'apostolic'" foundations of French churches. He was not, however, directly involved in the condemnation. His *Histoire Ancienne de l'Eglise Chrétienne* was put on the Index in 1912. Loisy paints him as an opportunist who refused to draw the theological implications of his historical work (*Mémoires* I, p. 231, for instance). Poulat calls him the "precursor" of French Modernism (*Histoire*, p. 19). Cf. J. B. Duroselle, *L'Evolution Culturelle, L'Europe du XIXe et du XXe Siècles (1870–1914)*, ed. Max Beloff et al. (Milan, 1962), p. 125: "Duchesne, always occupying the advanced position in dangerous situations from which he extracted himself skillfully, was the founder and master of Modernism." Vidler makes a similar estimate (*Modernist Movement*, p. 76 nn. 1, 2).

15 *Duel,* pp. 90–91. Renan's reputation terrified Roman Catholics long after the scientism for which his name was a synonym had begun to be challenged in the secular world by the work of the new critics of positivism, philosophers like Boutroux and Bergson and journalists like Ferdinand Brunetiere. Dansette, *Religious History,* Vol. II, pp. 138–149.

16 *Mémoires* I, pp. 118–125; *Duel,* pp. 95–96.

17 *Duel,* p. 100.

18 Von Hügel kept Loisy informed on a variety of subjects ("A young English Jesuit, a convert, writes . . . on the Anglican question with an admirable and amusing frankness and shrewdness; and in addition, this good Father Tyrrell admires you" [*Mémoires* I, p. 480]), visited him frequently, and was in turn much influenced in his historical philosophy by Loisy's critical work. Though he originally shared Loisy's view of history "as a kind of physics, whose rules of procedure are analogous to those of the material sciences, and whose object can be given as a datum of immediate observation," Nédoncelle argues that the consequent "setting of Christ on two almost unrelated planes" was "a very un-Hügelian idea" (*Baron Friedrich von Hügel: A Study of His Life and Thought,* tr. M. Vernon [London, 1937], pp. 186–188). Paul Sabatier, advocate of a Protestant modernism and publicist of the Catholic effort, considered von Hügel the "lay pope" of the movement. In fact, von Hügel stood with the progressives, expressed himself with delicacy (even when he wrote for Modernist periodicals like *Rinnovamento* or for journals like the *Hibbert*), and survived to be regarded as "A Forerunner of Vatican II" (*Tablet,* November 20, 1965, pp. 1291–1293). "The Baron, who in Scripture exegesis went all the way with the Modernists, was philosophically poles apart from them. He had an uncanny power of dividing his mind into two compartments, of which the right seemed not to know what the left was about. His friends said he would pass from writing Scripture criticism logically destructive of belief in Our Lord's divinity to an hour of rapt adoration in front of the tabernacle" (Maisie Ward, *Unfinished Business* [New York, 1964], p. 53). In addition to Michael de la Bedoyere's *Life of Baron von Hügel* (London, 1951), a readable personal narrative, and Nédoncelle's essay, two recent works present new material: Jean Steinmann, *Friedrich von Hügel* (Paris, 1963) and Douglas Steere, *Baron von Hügel* (London, 1964). The latter points out the ecumenical character of von Hügel's work. A. Hazard Dakin's *Religious Philosophy of Baron von Hügel* (London, 1934) is a good exegesis of von Hügel's writings on mysticism.

Maurice D'Hulst was one of the founders of the Catholic University of Paris, first rector of the Catholic Insitute, and famous as a spiritual director. Cf. A. Baudrillart, *Vie de Mgr. d'Hulst,* 2 vols. (Paris, 1912–14), a work with which Loisy polemicized (*Mémoires* I, pp. 233–245).

19 *Duel,* pp. 110–112. Loisy was "seized by a consuming pity," with the realization that he was inevitably exposing his students to a crisis similar to the one he had experienced at Châlons. "It was not in my power to spare them this trial, and I realized that dodging the difficulties would not enable them to avoid it." At about this time his friendship with Duchesne began

to cool, when the latter failed to advance him for a chair in Assyriology.

[20] D'Hulst first published an obituary on Renan (*Correspondant*, October 1892) in which he hinted that things might have turned out differently if Renan had been able to go to the Institute instead of to St. Sulpice. (Loisy's comment: Renan in fact knew a good deal about Scholastic philosophy "and he still did not become a precursor of M. Maritain.") More to the point, D'Hulst insisted that it was foolish to expect the modern scientist to believe in Christianity if it could not be scientfically presented. Negotiations over Loisy's position were complicated by D'Hulst's role in the *ralliement*. *Mémoires* I, p. 243.

[21] *Mémoires* I, p. 252; *Duel*, pp. 146–151.

[22] *Acta Apostolicae Sedis* xxvi (1893–94), pp. 269–292. If the encyclical "did not expressly condemn the idea of a critical and historical exegesis," Loisy wrote, it was only because "the very existence of such a science was not so much as suspected" (*Duel*, p. 169).

[23] *Mémoires* I, pp. 359–378. Loisy rejected the idea that he had borrowed his views on the growth of dogma and doctrine from Newman. Von Hügel felt that the "synthesis between Catholicism and modern knowledge," which Loisy attempted to construct in the 1890's, antedated his study of Newman, especially his study of the *Essay* (Friedrich von Hügel, *Selected Letters, 1896–1924*, ed. Bernard Holland [New York, 1927], p. 16). His editor argued that Newman's writings "fell in with and accelerated the line of thought that Loisy was already pursuing." Vidler added: "In any case, he extended the application of the idea of development to lengths of which Newman never dreamed" (*Modernist Movement*, p. 93). Cf. also G. Martini, *Cattolicesimo e Storicismo: Momenti di una Crisi del Pensiero Religioso Moderno* (Naples, 1951), pp. 65–140. Other influences which Loisy did admit were Harnack's *History of Dogma* and the critical works of J. Weiss, H. J. Holtzmann, and A. Reville. He was influenced, perhaps most significantly, by the work of Auguste Sabatier (whose books popularized Schleiermacher and Ritschl in France). Sabatier, "especially by interpretation of Christian dogma as the symbolism of religious feeling, exercised a profound influence not only on French Protestantism but also in Catholic theological circles, thus helping to prepare the Modernist Movement" (*Oxford Dictionary of the Christian Church*, p. 195). Loisy's frequent protestations of his philosophical and theological illiteracy, the more obvious connection between his work and that of Harnack, and the general diffusion of Protestant ideas through the pages of the *Revue Germanique* make it difficult to point to more specific points of influence at this time. Cf. Ernest Rochat, *Le Développement de la Théologie Protestant Française au XIXe Siècle* (Geneva, 1942), pp. 269–272, 427–440; and, on the general impact of German thought, Claude Digeon, *La Crise Allemande de la Pensée Française, 1870–1914* (Paris, 1959).

[24] *Mémoires* I, pp. 359–378; *Duel* pp. 172–187. The *livre inédit* also included Loisy's opinions on the impending separation, for which he later polemicized vigorously.

25 This discussion of the articles follows Poulat, *Histoire*, pp. 79–94.

26 "Le Développement Chrétien d'après le Cardinal Newman," *Revue du Clergé Français*, December 1, 1898, pp. 5–20; this piece was followed, in rapid succession in the same journal, by "La Définition de la Religion," (April 1899, pp. 193–209). "L'Idée da le Révélation," (January 1, 1900, pp. 250–271), and "Les Preuves de la Révélation" (March 15, 1900, pp. 126–153).

27 "La Théorie Individualiste de la Religion," *Revue du Clergé Français*, January 1, 1899, pp. 202–214.

28 A few thought that the articles were by Loisy, though Loisy himself believed that his hitherto exclusive preoccupation with criticism and history guaranteed his anonymity (*Mémoires* I, p. 501). As Poulat has shown, the use of pseudonyms was general; Lagrange himself once published in his own journal (*Revue Biblique*) under an anglicization of his name, "Father Barns" (*Histoire*, pp. 87–88, 637–638).

29 Marie-Joseph Lagrange, *M. Loisy et le Modernisme* (Paris, 1933), pp. 98–99, 124–131.

30 "La Religion d'Israël," *Revue du Clergé Français*, October 15, 1900, pp. 337–363. This essay was subsequently published in book form (1901) and in an enlarged edition (1906); Eng. edition, *The Religion of Israel*, tr. A. Galton (London, 1910).

31 In 1896 Loisy had established the *Revue d'Histoire et de Littérature Religieuse,* in which he published articles and book notices as "Jacques Simon" and "François Jacobé"; meanwhile "Isadore Desprès" was busy in the *Revue du Clergé Français,* pointing out the incompatibility of scientific criticism with *Providentissimus Deus* and attributing to von Hügel critical views which were rather more *Loisyste* than the Baron liked.

32 *Duel,* p. 209.

33 Loisy never found out how his name came to the attention of the Prince. *Duel,* p. 218; *Mémoires* II, pp. 91–166.

34 Houtin, *Loisy,* p. 102; René Marlé, ed., *Au Coeur de la Crise Moderniste: Le Dossier Inédit d'une Controverse* (Paris, 1960), p. 14; on Hébert, cf. Albert Houtin, *Histoire du Modernisme Catholique* (Paris, 1913), p. 67, and *Un Prêtre Symboliste* (Paris, 1925), pp. 122–140.

35 Von Hügel, *Letters,* p. 15.

36 Albert Schweitzer, *Out of My Life and Thought* (New York, 1957), pp. 40–41; J. Pelikan, *Human Culture and the Holy* (London, 1959), pp. 59–60.

37 Albert Schweitzer, *The Quest of the Historical Jesus,* tr. W. Montgomery (New York, 1961), pp. 238–242, 330–397; Bultmann, in Introduction to Harnack's *What Is Christianity?,* tr. Thomas Bailey (New York, 1957), p. x.

38 Harnack, *What Is Chrisianity?,* pp. 3–4.

39 *Ibid.,* pp. 8, 14–15.

40 *Ibid.,* pp. 51, 56.

41 *Ibid.,* p. 62. See also pp. 119–120 for a rousing indictment of the persistence of the medieval myth.

42 Harnack, *What Is Christianity?* pp. 128–129, 130, 142.

43 *Ibid.*, pp. 153, 161, 163.

44 *Ibid.*, pp. 171–172, 178–179, 181, 204, 251–267.

45 The "mischief" which inhibited reform in the Catholic Church was Catholicism's belief in "the sanctification of the political element, and in the inability of this church to get rid of what was once of service in particular historical circumstances, but has now become an obstruction and a clog." *Ibid.*, p. 267.

46 The origins of *L'Evangile et l'Eglise* are discussed in *Mémoires*, II, p. 121. All citations are to the English edition, *The Gospel and the Church*, tr. Christopher Home, new edition with prefatory memoir by George Tyrrell (London, 1908). *Gospel*, p. 4.

47 Poulat, *Histoire*, pp. 113–124; *Gospel*, p. 5 (cf. also p. 50).

48 *Gospel*, p. 19.

49 *Ibid.*, pp. 12–13; Poulat, *Histoire*, pp. 89–102.

50 *Gospel*, pp. 38, 40–41.

51 *Ibid.*, pp. 13, 28–34, 38–39, 50, 55–61, 68–69, 70–76, 82.

52 *Ibid.*, pp. 88–106, 118.

53 *Ibid.*, pp. 124–125.

54 *Ibid.*; cf. also pp. 226–274.

55 *Ibid.*, pp. 45–46, 50, 127.

56 *Ibid.*, p. 125; Poulat, *Histoire*, pp. 485–512.

57 *Gospel*, p. 150. The view is essentially an extension of the point which Loisy had already made about the gospel. Cf. p. 87.

58 *Ibid.*, pp. 156, 162–163.

59 *Ibid.*, p. 174. Cf. p. 83: "The Catholic Church is only bound to the science and political form of the middle ages because it does not choose to detach itself from them."

60 *Ibid.*, pp. 165–167.

61 *Ibid.*, p. 171; cf. p. 176.

62 *Ibid.*, pp. 191–193, 201; cf. pp. 180, 267.

63 *Ibid.*, p. 214.

64 *Ibid.*, pp. 276–277.

65 *Mémoires* II, pp. 225–226; Poulat, *Histoire*, p. 160. Cf. Maisie Ward, *Insurrection versus Resurrection* (London, 1937), p. 198; Jean Rivière, *Le Modernisme dans l'Eglise, Etude d'Histoire Religieuse Contemporaine* (Paris, 1929) pp. 129, 165–171. Loisy evaluated the book himself in the *Mémoires* and in the introduction to later editions. As he became more embattled in his attitudes toward Rome and as his skepticism grew, he tended to describe the work in terms which gave a retroactive justification to his most extreme critics. Cf. Poulat, *Histoire*, p. 122; *Mémoires* II, pp. 159–160, 205–206, 219, 221.

66 Poulat, *Histoire*, pp. 125–129.

67 *Ibid.*, pp. 135–136, 139. It is interesting to note that Simon is today regarded as the hero (and Bossuet as the villain), and Loisy is linked with Le Clerc, Simon's radical critic, and with Bultmann. Jean Steinmann, *Richard*

Simon et les Origines de l'Exégèse Biblique (Paris, 1960), p. 203. Cf. also Paul Hazard, *The European Mind 1680–1715* (Cleveland, 1963), pp. 180–197.

68 Poulat, *Histoire,* pp. 143–146.

69 *Ibid.,* pp. 146–148.

70 *Ibid.,* pp. 150–153. Lagrange gives a dramatic narrative of his first contact and immediate response to the book in *M. Loisy,* pp. 122–123.

71 *Duel,* p. 263; Poulat, *Histoire,* p. 269.

72 *Mémoires* II, p. 158; Alfred Loisy, *Autour d'un Petit Livre,* 2nd ed. (Paris, 1903), pp. 23, 70–71; *Duel,* pp. 238–245; Rivière, *Modernisme,* p. 179; A. L. Lilley, *Modernism: A Record and a Review* (London, 1908), pp. 65–66; *Petit Livre,* p. xxi.

73 *Petit Livre,* p. 151. Loisy later saw *modern* nationalism as a catalyst for progress. Alfred Loisy, *The War and Religion,* tr. A. Galton (Oxford, 1915), pp. 83–87.

74 *Petit Livre,* pp. 137, 139, 142.

75 *Ibid.,* pp. 148, 120–124, especially p. 121. Cf. Poulat, *Histoire,* pp. 485–512.

76 *Petit Livre,* p. 126.

77 *Ibid.,* pp. 151, 155.

78 *Ibid.,* p. 195.

79 *Ibid.,* pp. 192–196.

80 Houtin, *Loisy,* pp. 121–129; *Mémoires* II, p. 397.

81 Cited in Alfred Loisy, *Un Mythe Apologétique* (Paris, 1939), p. 122. Loisy was equally brusque with those who alleged that Jesus was a fiction. Cf. Loisy's *Autres Mythes à propos de la Religion* (Paris, 1938).

82 Maud Petre, *Alfred Loisy, His Religious Significance* (Cambridge, England, 1944), pp. 128–129.

83 Alfred Loisy, *La Religion* (Paris, 1917), pp. 45, 58; *War and Religion,* p. 76.

84 *Duel,* p. 228.

85 Arturo Carlo Jemolo, *Church and State in Modern Italy* (Oxford, 1960), p. 113.

86 Poulat, *Histoire,* p. 94. Cf. also pp. 93, 115. Troeltsch, on the other hand, found Loisy's critique of Harnack quite effective.

87 *Ibid.,* p. 94.

88 *Petit Livre,* pp. 169, 171; Miguel de Unamuno, *Tragic Sense of Life,* tr. J. E. C. Flitch (New York, 1954), p. 71.

89 *Gospel,* pp. 51, 12–13.

90 Owen Chadwick, *From Bossuet to Newman: The Idea of Doctrinal Development* (Cambridge, England, 1957), pp. 20, 43, 149; cf. Vidler, *Modernist Movement,* pp. 58–59.

91 Bultmann, *Kerygma and Myth,* ed. W. H. Bartsch (London, 1953), p. 42.

92 Dansette, *Religious History,* Vol. II, p. 301; *Duel,* p. 74.

Part Two - GEORGE TYRRELL

I

GEORGE TYRRELL was the apostle of Modernism. A concern for the religious life of the common man as well as that of the intellectual was the theme of his work, which he expressed in a multi-faceted critique of the dominance of rational theology over devotion in Catholicism. A Jesuit priest, who had found his way to Roman Catholicism through Anglicanism and the social gospel from Low Church evangelical beginnings, he saw himself as the common man of modern faith, the archetypal victim of the religious crisis of his age, as well as a religious thinker who could do something to set things right. In his autobiography he spoke of himself as a *"corpus vile"* on which he had experimented in a searching effort to find out what true religion was. Though his intellectual debts were great and freely admitted, he had come on his own to what was most distinctive in his thought. Commenting on an allegation that his early articles, written before he had read Blondel's *L'Action,* showed the influence of the French writer, he wrote that Blondel had reached by methodological research what he had stumbled on by luck or

instinct. Still, he found it "a great strength . . . to discover
that I have been talking philosophy."[1]

Talking philosophy was his work even before he was aware
that his own ideas were paralleled by a liberal and progressive
school of Catholic thinkers in England and on the continent.
Tyrrell did no original critical work: what he knew of the
bible question he knew primarily through the works of Loisy,
von Hügel, Weiss, Harnack, Holtzmann, and other leading
contemporary critics. He believed that the central question of
the Modernist crisis was historical, not philosophical. However, directed by training as well as by inclination, he took up
the work of developing the philosophical dimensions of the
neo-Catholicism sketched in Loisy's *Evangile et l'Eglise,*
which he regarded as "the classic exposition of the principles
of Modernism." Like Loisy, he insisted on the opposition between Modernism and liberal Protestantism, and never more
vociferously than after the apparent similarities had been
pointed out in the condemnation of 1907. Unlike Loisy, however, he continued to hope that the Church of the future
might be reconstructed along Modernist lines. The force of
his own theism and of his conviction that men had to have
religion added a tragic dimension to his work, since his
theological and philosophical speculations were based on
critical-historical conclusions which vitiated them from the
beginning—as he himself occasionally apprehended. He dealt
more broadly than had Loisy with the problems raised for
Catholicism by the comparative study of the history of
religions. He tried to set out more clearly the philosophy of
immanentism, which had only been alluded to in Loisy's
books of 1902 and 1903, and he expanded—or, rather, tried
to popularize—the discussion over development and evolution. Also, he sketched the outlines of a sociology of religion

which would help to explain the way in which religions in general, and Catholicism in particular, had moved through cycles of inspired revelation and legal calcification.[2]

Much more obviously than was the case with Loisy, Tyrrell's personality shaped his work and his career. He described himself as a mixture of a German brain and an Irish heart, with the latter element usually dominant. He was mercurial, evasive, not above dissimulating for the cause he held, confusing to his friends as well as to his enemies because of his talent for alternating from one to the other side of an argument as seemed best suited to his ends. He saw himself as a chameleon among men, taking on the opinions of the person he happened to be with, and attributed this peculiarity to a personality flawed in childhood. He constantly suspected his own motives, except for the urge which had brought him to the priesthood. He delighted in paradox and polemic, and was quite unsuited, in his impatience with "economies," to the work of reconciling Catholicism with modernity "without scandalizing either the man in the street or the man in the study."[3]

Tyrrell's personality intrudes into an estimate of his thought for other reasons. Although, ten years before his death, he had come to positions characteristic of his mature work, a process of interaction continued right up until the end between his personal religious convictions and his published writing. Loisy, on the contrary, had moved beyond the position he set forth in the Modernist books more than a decade before their publication. Tyrrell's letters and the life based on them show this process of interaction and make judgment of his published works somewhat more difficult, though in his posthumously published *Christianity at the Crossroads* the lines converged. But the major fact which

blends Tyrrell with his books was his refusal to admit the
Roman position as representative of the Church. He acted
out his Modernism as Loisy did not, saying, "I will never go";
whereas Loisy said, "I will go when I am thrown out." What
he called the "doorstep" policy gave a dramatic flavor to what
became known as *L'Affaire Tyrrell.* Though he had sought
separation from the Society of Jesus, he fought for legalization
of his secular status and his right to the sacraments. He died
insisting that it was Rome, and not he, who had wandered
from the Catholic position.

This is not to say that there was no *mystification* in Tyrrell's
career. Quite the contrary. His personal mysticism was far in
advance of his theological positions as they appeared in articles
and books, and even the less personal reflections on theological questions which he confided to journals and to his close
correspondents were considerably more radical than the ones
for which he was formally censured, first by the Society of
Jesus and then by Rome. Even in *Christianity at the Crossroads* he did not admit, in sketching the possible evolution of
Catholicism into a scientific world-religion, that such a religion had become a personal actuality. But it points out
what is perhaps the major paradox of a life all too easily
described in a long list of paradoxes. Tyrrell summed up the
dilemma of Modernism when he wrote that the difficulty was,
not Catholicism, but Christ and Christianity. He himself remained very much a follower of Christ even when he announced the irrelevance of the mind of "that first-century
Jewish carpenter, for whom more than half the world and
nearly the whole of its history did not exist; to whom the
stellar universe was unknown; who cared nothing for art or
science or history or politics or nine-tenths of the interests
of humanity but solely for the Kingdom of God and His
righteousness."[4]

The power of his personality is so great that it has imposed on the historian the outline by which both Tyrrell's inner religious development and his intellectual work must be organized. Tyrrell saw his whole life as a search for freedom from images of God and images of Christ in whom God was made manifest. He wrote his autobiography with this search as its theme, and announced in his last letters that his imagination was "quite cured of the outside God." When he died in July 1909, of Bright's disease, his desk covered with unfinished polemical and philosophical manuscripts, he had concluded that the real Christ, who redeemed him and who was God, lay within. Tyrrell believed that the inward spirit of God pervaded and transcended the whole universe, revealing to men only "an infinitesimal fraction of its Will and End and Truth and Nature." And, "as regards God and immortality, man was made not to know, but to hope." Adopting wholeheartedly the Weiss-Loisy "consistent eschatology," admitting the myth of the kingdom, the symbolic value of all dogma, the progressive and universal character of religious revelation—all this *confirmed* rather than destroyed his hard-won conviction that man could know God only through the "ideal or eternal man, the Christ." It was only because God presented himself to man "as the Christ, with a human spirit, face, voice, and hands, that we can speak to Him or deal with Him at all."[5]

When Tyrrell wrote a sketch of his life and religious development from childhood to his mother's death in 1884, he was at a point of crisis. Growing doubts about his career in the Society of Jesus, as well as an increasing suspicion that his ideas might not correspond to the general direction of the Church's thinking about modern philosophical and historical problems, fostered what Wilfrid Ward later called a mood of "morbid candour." Tyrrell wondered in 1901 if he had ever done anything other than "play" at religion, taking it apart and putting it together as he had his childhood toys, and whether in the depths of his "self-consciousness" he was not utterly without belief. He felt that he had allowed the "wish to believe" to play upon him, confirming the "melancholy hypothesis" of unbelief. Yet, at the same time, he recognized that his mood affected his judgment of the past, that he tended to project his "present mind and intelligence" into the narrative of stages of his life in which he was obviously incapable of seeing direction and significance.

A sense of troubled destiny prompted Tyrrell to assess the meaning of every circumstance, with the result that the autobiography became an auto-analysis. Birth after his father's death, genteel poverty, an exclusively feminine society, a brilliant and crippled brother whom he loved and envied, "gamelessness" at school, a passion for tinkering and dismantling toys (the family called his play-junk "cricklewockle," after the sound made by an autopsied model train)—all had made some contribution to a life of anxiety and change. Tyrrell saw his childhood and adolescence in terms of an anthropological progression from animism to theism, with a long period of "godlessness" intervening between the immature faith in images and the discovery of religion as a serious, if confusing, matter. But he matched every statement of intentional advance with a disclaimer of some sort. If he suspected a fundamental flaw in his personality and a connection between it and his interest in religion, he was incapable of pushing the auto-analysis to Freudian conclusions. If he knew that his search for God was the pursuit of an absent father, his chameleon relationship with other people the expression of a fundamental lack of identity, and his never-ending battle with the Jesuits, Cardinal Mercier, the Bishop of Southwark, the Holy Office, and Pius X the result of a failure to internalize the authority principle, he did not admit it. If Tyrrell was psychologically ill, he came fairly early in life to working terms with his illness.

The general tone of Tyrrell's autobiography and many of the judgments made in it reflect his sharp disillusion with the theological rationalism adopted enthusiastically in the seminary, and for which a youthful encounter with the arguments of Bishop Butler's *Analogy* had been a preparation. Tyrrell wrote of himself that, unlike Cardinal Newman, he had come to faith *à rebours,* beginning with images and proofs and demonstrations and finding only in middle age the apprehension of God and the self which Newman had at fourteen. His personal rejection of the rationalism which had led him to the Church produced an apologetic of unreason when he came to write for others seeking faith. The emphases on immanent divinity, the inadequacy of religious symbolism, and the pragmatic value of dogmatic formulas (which he was beginning to develop in this apologetic in the late nineties) was reflected in his recollections.[6]

II

TYRRELL WAS NOT a cradle Catholic. His family was Dublin
Protestant, middle class, and with distinguished members (in
other branches) in academic life and government service. His
father was an unsuccessful newspaperman, older than his wife,
a shadow to the son who was born a few months after his
father's death. The religious mood of the impoverished family
—mother, hunchback Willie, sister Louise, young George—
was that of Low Church piety reinforced by a sense of tenuous
class position. When Tyrrell was four, the family went to live
with a Calvinist aunt, where bible reading and hymn singing
(Tyrrell's favorite: "Rocka Vages") further emphasized the
contrast between respectable religion and that of the "helots"
of Roman Catholicism, who worshiped in chapels filled with
"dirt and tinsel and flashy gew-gaws and staring pictures and
images." But the images of God were no less concrete in
Protestantism. At five Tyrrell had a near-crippling fall, which
he reported in characteristic fashion. After the doctor left,
the minister came and prayed over the boy, lecturing him for
disobedience and conjuring up vivid pictures of heaven and
hell. Tyrrell gradually began to feel guilty, but only because

he was told that he should feel that way. He realized that his
being bad was as interesting to others as his being sick. But the
rapt attention he gave the preacher was caused, not by the
latter's eloquence, but by "the abnormal length of his upper
lip." "How can people be so silly as to imagine that a child
of five is capable either of sin or of righteousness, and can
attach the remotest meaning to the jargon of Augustinian
theology?"

School brought success and admiration for erratic bril-
liance, but also a weakening of the boy's faith. Tyrrell discovered that he had responsibility for his character and
glimpsed "lying, not merely the lie" as the issue of behavior,
but found little comfort in the "dubious morality of Samuel
and Kings" in Sunday school. At the age of eight he repeated
the "prescribed formulas," felt neither "the need of God
nor of prayer," and saw religion as a tiresome convention, like
wearing gloves on Sunday. "If I knew that God existed and
that Jack the Giant-Killer did not, it was only because I was
told so." Tyrrell experienced in school that tension between
childhood faith and theology which overwhelmed Loisy in
the seminary. The "human-wise" ways of explaining God and
religion and morality (which had been scarcely adequate to
the nursery) were controverted by metaphysical assertions
meant to be taken immediately as matters of faith. "To say
that [God] was a spirit helped little, since for me (as, also,
indeed, for most adults) a spirit was but an attenuated body,
which, in spite of all assertions to the contrary, labored under
the chief limitations of matter." Whatever belief he had from
the age of ten to sixteen was a matter of refinement and a certain "prudery of taste" which kept him from the more
heinous forms of sin: temptations "inherently disgusting, or
coarse, or at least unredeemed by some sparkle of wit." Dur-

ing these years he lived alone with his mother, who scraped
for the education of the brother and sister away at school, and
went without lunch herself so that George would have money
for "wire or nails or tools or paint" for his tinkering. He took
the pledge at fifteen, and then drank off a glass of port on a
dare. He dabbled in petty theft—the "caddishness" of the
venture wore off after a few tries. By sixteen he was "in moral
skepticism, an unconscious disciple of Nietzsche."[7]

Tyrrell discounted anything that might be considered a
conversion experience in his life. Yet he had several. The first
occurred at sixteen, and within a year of leaving moral chaos
behind, he had progressed to pious High Churchmanship, the
hope of a religious vocation, and the conviction that he would
become a convert to Roman Catholicism. It was a turning
point Tyrrell could not adequately explain. He wrote that at
sixteen he "began to want to believe and to force myself
violently into belief." He had "planned" himself into religion
at sixteen. His wholehearted adoption of Bishop Butler's argument that religion could be soberly defended on a rational
basis was prompted by brother Willie's Trinity College
atheism. He found the birettas and cassocks of High Anglicanism "titillating" and sensed the "sham and unreality" of its
liturgy, but the shock he caused his mother's friends made
Anglicanism as exciting as "a new sin." He said that he had
not been "hooked by any healthy bait," but by a desperate
need to recover "self-mastery." "Underneath all my prayers
and endeavors lay the haunting, but stifled, sense of pretence
and unreality. I was playing at religion, nothing more." His
prayer was "Oh God, if there be a God; save my soul, if I have
a soul." In the same mood, he wrote that he had "drifted into
the Church for a thousand paltry motives and reasons, some
good and some bad . . . much as an ignorant and drunken

navigator gets his vessel into the right port by a mere fluke."[8]

Anglicanism was better than moral depravity, better than schoolboy catechisms, and an advance over the images of Jesus "as an insipid, long-haired female," heaven as a real third story in the house of the universe presided over by "Mrs. Heaven . . . with a huge cap tied under her chin and a red plaid shawl folded across her capacious bosom" and "Gaud" (as distinct from the pagan "gods") as the "Ugly Jane" with her tongue stuck out, threatening retribution. Tyrrell adapted easily to High Church ritual. Still, no effort of will could draw out of Holy Communion "as much sensible improvement in spiritual vigor as from a dose of medicine or a square meal." Tyrrell was startled out of his Anglican playacting by the death of Willie, who had argued against religion but insisted that if there were such a thing, Romanism was the only coherent form, even though Willie himself believed that after death the soul went "where the flame goes when the candle burns out." The loss of his brother made it clear that "there was no logical or defensible resting place between the ark of God and the carrion that floated on the surrounding waters —between divinity and piggery." Reading Montalembert's *Monks of the West* set him thinking of Christianity as a life rather than a truth. Although he was "still clinging to the shadows," he now experienced the first streaks of daylight and "the first drawing towards Christly ideals for their own sake." The same author's life of St. Benedict brought an experience which Tyrrell compared to that of Augustine being told in the garden to pick up the book and read. The words he was directed to corresponded so closely to his need that, in the midst of a "psychological" analysis, he admitted that it was an "illusion" or a "coincidence" which he lived on thereafter.[9]

But if it provided a context for a developing theism,

Anglicanism was logically and sociologically unsatisfying. In the long analysis and defense of his vocation written in 1904–1905 to the General of the Society of Jesus, Tyrrell explained that he had become a Catholic, a priest, and a Jesuit because the Roman Catholic Church was, at least potentially, the solution of the religious problem "in that *milieu* from which I had come and from which I have never been separated in sympathy." Tyrrell's sense of the division in Irish life between Protestant and Roman Catholic Christianity was accentuated by his activities in the High Church. He also sensed, as he ceased to take "thrills and quivers for faith, hope, and charity," the incompleteness of Anglicanism as a theological *via media* between puritanism and the pope. No sooner was he involved in the society and ritual of High Churchmanship than he began to sneak into the helot's chapel. If he did not say to himself, "Well, some day it will end up here," he did recognize that Roman Catholicism was a connected whole and must be "all taken or all left"—including those staring pictures and images. The friendship of Robert Dolling (who had a brief but impressive career as an advocate of a socially relevant Christianity) taught Tyrrell that it didn't matter whether you used two candles or six on your altar, that Christianity stood for sunshine and service rather than for Jansenistic individualism. His friend also encouraged Tyrrell's hopes for a vocation, an idea in the seventeen-year-old which appeared to his thirty-seven-year-old analyst as much a matter of self-preservation as of service. "Then, as now, I felt myself a sort of Balaam, forced, I know not clearly how or why, to slave in the cause of Christ; it was a sort of obsession with me—an *idée fixe.*"[10]

Dolling also told Tyrrell that one intent on finding a *secure* faith would probably be happy only with Rome. With the possibility of his imminent conversion confided to the Roman Catholic landlady (whom Tyrrell had chosen for the family

because of her religion, and with whom he had secretly gone
to Mass), Tyrrell left Ireland for a few months, ostensibly to
observe Dolling's workers' house in London. Miss Lynch did
one final service. On hearing of Tyrrell's hopes for the priesthood, she remarked, "If you become a priest, you must be a
Jesuit. They are very learned and very holy men." Tyrrell
replied, "We shall see about that later." Very little time
elapsed before the conversion, begun little over a year before,
reached its formal conclusion. In 1879 his irritation with
Anglicanism and his own restlessness drove Tyrrell out of a
Palm Sunday service. From the fashionable High Church
setting he wandered into Ely Place in the midst of the Irish
immigrant world. He gives this classic account:

I beheld people descending into the bowels of the earth, whom
I followed, to find myself in the crypt of St. Ethelreda's; where in
the darkness and 'mid the smell of a dirty Irish crowd the same
service was being conducted, in nasal tones, most unmusically,
by three very typical popish priests. Of course it was mere emotion
and sentiment, and I set no store by it then or now, but oh! the
sense of reality! Here was the old business, being carried on by
the old firm, in the old ways; here was continuity, that took one
back to the catacombs; here there was no need of and therefore
no suspicion of, pose or theatrical parade; its aesthetic blemishes
were its very beauties for me in that mood.[11]

After an interval of intense reading—including the *Summa*
of St. Thomas and the *Life of Lacordaire* by Montalembert
(which had also influenced Loisy)—and reflection on the
Catholic liturgy as the utterance of "the great communion of
the faithful, past and present, of all ages and nations" (interrupted by projects like looking up all the Catholic churches in
London), Tyrrell got the final push from Feval's *Les Jésuites,*

which painted a fervid picture of militant heroism and self-sacrifice. After writing a note to Miss Lynch, he presented himself at Farm Street, where, to his disappointment, he received penny-catechism treatment. This made little difference, since he had already converted himself by developing Butler's argument. He added to it an effective, if logically weak, syllogism: given that there must be a church on earth claiming infallibility, and that no church disclaiming infallibility can possess it, that church which alone claims infallibility must possess it.

After a short hesitation waltz with a clumsy confessor, Tyrrell was shriven and "reconciled." Then came the problem of the future. Had he thought of what he would do with himself now, the priest asked. Well, he had once thought of the priesthood, though his past sins would, of course, be an insuperable impediment. Not at all. Was he thinking of the secular or the religious state? Well, rather of the religious. And of any particular order? Well, possibly of the Society of Jesus. When the interview ended, Tyrrell had in his hand a note to the novice master and instructions to see him at once. "Here was posthaste and no mistake: from start to goal, from post to finish, in twenty-four hours. I had come out that afternoon with no intention of being received, and I returned a papist and half a Jesuit."[12]

Since Tyrrell was only eighteen, he was advised against entering the novitiate at once, but was given a year's probation teaching Greek at a Jesuit school on Malta. When the school failed, he continued at the English College there, where the spying on pupils, old-boy hostility toward a convert, and devotional automatism disillusioned him. The rector, an ex-sailor, "satisfied with the penny-catechism, plain-as-a-pike-staff view of the Catholic position," fulfilled the image of

purposeful and self-confident activity Tyrrell had nourished.
He rejected half-formed notions about a retreat to the
Benedictines or a plunge into the secular clergy. His interview
for the novitiate was a forecast of the business ahead. Asked
what was his motive for joining, Tyrrell mumbled about past
sins and reparations, unwilling to plumb his "deepest spiritual
aspirations."

"No," said the examiner, "that's not it"—just as if it were a riddle.
"Well, what is it?" said I. "The glory of God and the salvation of
souls." "Oh, very well: the glory of God and the salvation of souls."
"That's right," he said, and scored it down accordingly.[13]

The novitiate was worse than Malta. Tyrrell was odd, older,
a convert. He was "of the world" in a world of "Church-school
boy vocations where the talk was all of Stonyhurst and The
Mount, of cricket matches and masters and prefects." The new
father figure was the novice master, who saw the Society as a
divine institution to which its priests were bound, if anything,
more strongly than a layman to the Church. The novice
master also introduced Tyrrell to personal devotion to Jesus.
The two teachings quickly clashed. Boudon's *Life of Jesus,* a
book strongly critical of ecclesiastical pomp and circumstance,
revived the "socialistic, or perhaps democratic" sympathies
Tyrrell had received from Dolling. How did one reconcile
the freedom, poverty, and simplicity of Jesus with the
authority of the Society and the complexities of the Church?
The question was, in part, a generalization of Tyrrell's un-
happiness in the regimen of the novitiate. To local irritations
and cosmic questions alike, his adviser gave the answer: "Our
Holy Mother Church knows best" and "more prayer to Jesus."
The only result was a growing sense of "that freedom and

fearlessness of mind which was Christ's strongest characteristic." His counselor, recognizing that the novice was not cut out for the life ahead, said, "If you do not leave now you will only give the Society trouble later on." Tyrrell rejected his advice. Everything seemed to depend on succeeding in the order. "My Jesuit life and my moral and spiritual life were associated together in time, and certainly, at first sight, in some kind of causal relationship."

Whatever advances he was making toward belief were grounded in Catholic structure. Aquinas seemed to advance his release from "figures and idols of imagination," but God remained external. Still, Lacordaire's *Conferences on God* were a great improvement over the devotional equivalent of St. Thomas. The latter instructed him how to elicit an act of love of God "equal to that of the Blessed Virgin and all the angels put together and multiplied by 1,000" by desiring it and renewing it on his beads. Thomas (according to Tyrrell) then suggested that by proceeding by geometrical, as well as by arithmetical, progression, one could, "on the second bead square the act on the first, cube it on the third, and so forth, until the very angels reel[ed] at the contemplation of acts so exceeding their own." Bizarre? No matter; for it was all part of Catholicism—*"the religion as a whole"*—to which he had given his mind.[14]

In the major seminary, to which, like Loisy, he came prematurely, Tyrrell found new freedom and an adviser who cultivated his interest in philosophy. This man remarked that Tyrrell had a good Greek, but not a good Christian, mind, and he himself emphasized the "natural virtues" over against the automatic supernaturalism which Tyrrell had previously encountered. He continued his studies in St. Thomas, in a context much changed from that which Loisy

had known at Châlons. The revival of a purer Thomism encouraged by the encyclical *Aeterni Patris* (1879) had reached
Stonyhurst, although not without opposition. Tyrrell took up
the new teaching, as against "Aquinas filtered through the
brain of Suarez," and caused his masters some discomfort.
Tyrrell never lost his enthusiasm for Thomas, even after he
had ceased to regard Thomism as the philosophy "by which
our religion must stand or fall." He considered it important
that he had studied "the real thing . . . instead of wasting . . .
years on his third-rate commentators and imitators." His
constant advice to students of religion was to read St. Thomas
"not as an authority but critically and historically as a genius."

Tyrrell found Thomas' teaching on the complementary
character of the natural and supernatural realms an antidote
to the complete rejection of this world which was a commonplace of the Catholicism he had experienced. He also saw, in
the progression from reason to revelation, a confirmation of
the course he himself had taken in returning to religion and
then in entering the Church. Tyrrell took two notions from
Thomas which played a major part in his own apologetic
writings even, or especially, when they had become detached
from the rest of Scholastic thought. The first was the idea,
gradually transformed into a conviction, that man could know
the supernatural realm only by analogy. The second, which
was to have more radical applications, was the idea of connaturality. For Tyrrell, this meant that, even though man
knows the divine only metaphorically, by parallel with what
is not divine, the faculty which enables him to recognize reflected truth in inferior images also partakes of the supernatural realm. Tyrrell enlarged the epistemological notion of
analogy into a comprehensive symbolism, and expanded the
Thomistic teaching on connaturality into a theory of divine

immanence. Yet, even when he wrote diatribes against "school theology" and tried to sketch the irrational operation of the divine impulse in man, he always did so with an orderliness which he admitted came from these first studies.[15]

Tyrrell was ordained in 1891. After finishing his training at Malta and North Wales, he served briefly at the Oxford University chaplaincy, did parish work for a few years in Lancashire, and then returned to Stonyhurst to teach philosophy. He was unpopular with his conservative fellow Jesuits for "turning young men into Dominicans," and even a complimentary letter from Cardinal Mazzella, the curial sponsor of the Thomistic revival, could not give him academic security. He worked hard on his lectures and planned to publish them as a book; but by the time he had leisure, he had moved beyond Thomism. In 1897 another sequence of short assignments brought him to his last regular position: confessor, preacher, and retreat master at the Jesuit church, Farm Street, where he had been received almost twenty years before. Although he later derided the "nice, easy Farm-Street-confessor, lady's-lap-dog kind of life," he was successful and popular. He was recommended by Cardinal Vaughan to the prominent biologist St. George Jackson Mivart; and through the guidance he gave to Baron von Hügel's daughter, Tyrrell came to know the Baron as a mentor and friend. (The daughter, unlike her father, had difficulty reconciling modern thought with Catholic faith.)[16]

All during these years Tyrrell had been serving an apologetic apprenticeship, writing reviews and articles for the *Month*, a Jesuit periodical. His first composition was published in 1887. By the time Jesuit censorship of his work began in 1905, forty-eight articles had appeared under his name. With seventeen excepted (rejected by Tyrrell), these writings appeared in 1901 in a two-volume work, *The Faith of the Millions.* (In a letter Tyrrell claimed, in mock seriousness, that he would have preferred as title "The Travails of an Irish Gentleman in Search of a Religion," but the authorities decided otherwise.) The reason for the exclusion of the seventeen essays was a significant change in attitude, from what his friend and biographer, Maud Petre, called the stage of "militant orthodoxy" to the stage of "mediating liberalism." The tone of the rejected articles (and even of some of those he allowed to be reprinted) is startling when they are read in juxtaposition with the autobiography, which would mark Tyrrell as an emergent liberal in 1884. In fact, he had joined the Church to fight for it against *all* its enemies, were they modern rationalists or liberal Protestants. And he did so with gusto for almost a decade. Materialism and agnosticism were dismissed out of court with Chestertonian aplomb: zoophilism and socialism were shown to be equally irrelevant in the face of Catholic truth; even the validity of Protestant marriage was doubted. Tyrrell was already fascinated by comparative religious history and evolution, but the parables of lost and altered religions he wove were aimed at modern godlessness, not at ecclesiastical decay and obfuscation. He made various apologies for these writings in later years. In 1903 he wrote that he had once had "a certain taint of the virus of controversial fever in my blood," argued that it was something everyone had to go through, and insisted that even in the late eighties and nineties he had not cared more for the Church "than for the end to which she is but an instrument, namely, the spiritual welfare of mankind." To a criticism by an exceptionally orthodox writer he replied that he had once had the same "fever" for two or three years.[17]

The fever was progressively lowered during the nineties

until it reached a level well below that of the triumphalism which had attracted Tyrrell and which he wished to defend. To a French student of his work he explained that the essays collected in *The Faith of the Millions* represented the crumbling away of his hope in the philosophy of St. Thomas once it was studied in a critical and liberal spirit. He found the makings of a substitute in John Henry Newman, whom he had discovered only late in the seminary. But Newman (whose works he knew only sketchily) was never the powerful medicine for Tyrrell that he was for many liberals and progressives during these years. This was, perhaps, because scarcely had he begun to make use of Newman's ideas when he was attracted to the critical questions which Newman had hardly known.

Militant orthodoxy also made its mark on a different kind of writing which brought Tyrrell a greater reputation than his occasional essays. This writing was his devotional works, which grew directly out of his work as a retreat and mission master. In a book of conferences for lay brothers published in 1897, he had struck a new note when he wrote that the conception of Catholic truth and the Catholic Church was, like a flower not yet in bloom, capable of yet greater expansion; but the old note was sounded the next year in another book in which he described England as "this de-Christianized country, where Catholics find it so hard, so impossible, to keep mind or heart free from the infectious pestilence of unbelief and moral consumption." It is important to note that, in the crisis which produced the introspective autobiography, Tyrrell's sources were neither St. Thomas nor Cardinal Newman, but the pastoral work with educated laymen troubled by the world of science and democracy.[18]

The major turning point in Tyrrell's intellectual vocation

came at the end of the century, when, in November and December of 1899, he published two short essays. One was entitled "The Relation of Theology and Devotion"; the other, "A Perverted Devotion." In these essays, especially in the former, he sketched the major ideas of an apologetic which, in the next few years, was progressively enriched by the books and men of the contemporary continental religious movement to which Baron von Hügel had introduced Tyrrell. These articles were understood, by both admirer and critic, as a liberal Catholic's defense against Anglicans and rationalists alike. On the key issue of the relationship between modern science and traditional theology, Tyrrell had in fact already begun to move beyond the position of men like Wilfrid Ward.

In personal terms, Tyrrell had discovered that commitment to Roman Catholicism as a means to a secure theism involved accepting a great deal more than he himself found personally necessary or historically defensible; but he also realized that Catholicism was a religious system which had developed historically and universally, which illustrated its claims to ecumenical truth by teaching a wide variety of men, classes, and cultures. His letters of the period preceding the publication of the articles reflect the mood which prompted his new apologetical departure. He repeatedly wrote that he saw his mission as to work for the Church, not merely to be in it. And he was confident that (even if lesser institutions like the Society of Jesus were unable to make the adaptation to the modern world) "when the sloughing season is over, the Church will settle down in her bright new skin." The Church, "rather than any particular clique, has always been my *donna gentile,* my *Beatrice,*—so that my peace does not depend on her handmaidens." His growing doubts about the

Society took the form of references, in correspondence with his new friend Henri Bremond, to Ignatius of Loyola as the "16th century Hecker." Ignatius' dedication to contemporaneity had saved the Church in the crisis of the Reformation, but was not understood by his nineteenth-century followers; the torch had been passed to men like Hecker and the Paulists. For encouragement, he reflected on the fact that the Society had always achieved great things through those of its members who were able to resist its repressive influence. Men of high caliber, whether in the Society or out of it, were entrusted by God with the power and responsibility for truly independent thought. They were the few who labored for the many, "not in *destructionem*, but in *aedificationem*." He frequently felt overwhelmed by the challenge. He wrote to von Hügel:

What a relief if one could conscientiously wash one's hands of the whole concern! But then there is that strange Man upon His cross, who drives one back again and again. My dominant conviction is that what Christ had to say to man is embedded in the Roman system, as gold in the ore, and as I cannot sever them, I take them in the heap.[19]

About the same time he made a confession of faith to Bremond, who was to suffer suspension for officiating at Tyrrell's burial. His faith, he explained, "so far as it must necessarily be rooted in some kind of experience and not merely in propositions and principles accepted on hearsay," was based upon the evidence of "a Power in myself and in all men making for Righteousness in spite of all our downward tendencies." Other reasons and experiences only supplemented this conviction. His "Christianism" was based on

"the concrete and intuitive recognition of the full manifestation of that said power in the man Christ as known to us
historically—so full that I can trust Him and take Him as a
teacher sent by God." The Roman Catholic Church was
"the only authorized representative of Christ on earth. . . .
Whatever truth is revealed is to be found in her general
teaching like gold in the matrix." The neologism ("Christianism") is a sign of Tyrrell's urge toward a formulation of
Christian faith which would be disencumbered of tradition.
There was, however, no suggestion of any breach in his identification of the Catholic Church with the Church of Christ.
The task was to liberate the immanent apprehension of
divinity from the structure of belief which was designed to
enhance, but risked overwhelming, it.[20]

"The Relation of Theology and Devotion" was, in Tyrrell's
opinion, the matrix of his thought. When he reprinted it in
1907, he wrote that he had not really advanced beyond it.
This article was not merely the "germ" of the works that
followed but an "explicit statement . . . a brief compendium
or analytical index" of his apologetic. Tyrrell's wording of the
title was idiosyncratic by conventional Catholic usage. In
the term "theology" he confused, intentionally, both dogma
and the intellectual effort to understand dogma and explain
it. By "devotion" he meant, not the disposition of the will
toward God which was implied in Scholastic terminology,
but the sum of the everyday, active, effective, pragmatic religious life. The confusion of dogma and theology was not
directly apparent: initially, the word "theology" stood for
the Scholastic "essay" at translating the truth of Christianity
into the categories of Aristotle so as to give it a "scientific
unity."

Unity and order, Tyrrell argued, were artificial, in supernatural as in natural matters. The classifications forced upon nature by science were hypothetical and abstract, but this fact was often forgotten. Thus, the economist drew apparently irrefutable conclusions from the abstract and erroneous principle that man's sole interest was in making money. The danger of mistaking the hypothesis for the reality increased in the supernatural realm, where knowledge could only be acquired by analogy, "and with no more exactitude than when we would express music in terms of color, or color in terms of music." "A comparatively concrete idea like Man or King gives us a mine of information about the subject of which it is predicated; whereas Being, Substance, Cause, give us the very minimum of information." By natural reason man knew nothing about angels except what he could deduce *a priori* from the general idea of nonmaterial substance. "To our imagination they are utterly characterless and uninteresting beings; quite different from the Saints, of whom we can sometimes feel the individuality in spite of their biographers." No matter how hard the metaphysician tried, nonanalogous statements describing the supernatural were "mere shreds of truth," "bare ribs" to be fleshed out by "liberal recourse to analogy."

It was also wrong to think that the best combined efforts of the metaphysician and the theologian would succeed. Nonanalogous, or metaphysical statements, and theological, or analogous statements, were unable, even when taken together, to approximate the infinite. Scholasticism itself recognized this fact by teaching that the human mind knows only by connaturality, and must think of everything, even the soul, in terms of the material world with which that mind is itself connatural. All explanations of spiritual or psychological activity were analogous and mechanical. "Thought is a kind of photography or portraiture; free will a sort of weighing process; the soul itself, so far as it is not described negatively, is described in terms of body." The metaphors inevitably became the reality.

The process was extended—disastrously—when man tried to know the world which he inferred from his own spiritual dimension. "The error called 'anthropomorphism' does not lie so much in thinking and speaking of God humanwise— for that we are constrained to do by the structure of our minds—as it does in forgetting that such a mode of conception is analogous." Yet, the "common, human way of viewing" the soul, God, eternity, was less harmful than the abstractions of the metaphysician. The layman said that the soul was a "filmy replica of self interfused with his body." He imagined God "out beyond the shining of the farthest star . . . stretching infinitely far." The layman believed that eternity was simply time without end, century after century, *per omnia saecula saeculorum,* and that "the divine life, like our own, drags on part after part, experience upon experience." The metaphysician, intending to be helpful, said instead that the soul was suffused throughout the body, yet concentrated in every point. God had infinite extension, but also had "punctual" presence as well, so that his existence in eternity was *tota simul,* "all gathered up into an indivisible *now,* into the imaginary crack that divides one second from another." And then the philosopher advised that the common notions be combined with the metaphysical statements. His belief that his definitions, combined with common experience and common notions, could state the truth, and not merely approach "the *locus* of truth," was, if anything, a more grievous error than that of the layman with his clumsy analogies.

Like "Firmin," turning from the general themes of revelation and relativism to the history of Israel, Tyrrell applied to the history of religion his idea of the tension between the concrete and the abstract, the natural and the supernatural, the insights of analogy and the oversights of Aristotelian metaphysics. First, it was clear that the Judaeo-Christian revelation had not been communicated to man in philosophical terms. The God of the Old Testament was no abstraction: he was "frankly anthropomorphic from the first." The history of Judaism was a decline into abstraction. "It would almost seem as if the Incarnation were timed to counteract the weakening of religion incident to the more abstract philosophic theology of later ages" in the history of Israel. It has always been God's will to reveal himself to the *vulgus profanum,* not to the learned man whose philosophizing makes God remote again. "He has spoken their language, leaving it to the others to translate it (at their own risk) into forms more acceptable to their taste."

The corollary of this argument was that the primary obligation of the Church was to the *vulgus profanum,* not the metaphysician. The Church's work was "to preserve, not to develop, the exact ideas which that simple language conveyed to its first hearers," even though it must also be aware "that those human ideas and thought-forms are indefinitely inadequate to the eternal realities which they shadow forth." The Church should be interested primarily only in knowing what the words "This is my body" meant to Peter and Andrew and the rest. A concern with the metaphysics of transubstantiation was legitimate only insofar as "metaphysicians have to be answered in their own language and on their own assumptions." If the Church has said that the soul is the "form" of the body, it has done so only because the question "What is the soul?" has been posed by the morphologist. "It is the

nearest way the truth can be put to him." The work that
theology does in developing abstractions and explanations
can only be justified as a counter or balance to the tendencies
of popular devotion to exaggerate the anthropomorphic
analogy.

Revelation was to be understood, therefore, as a "deposit"
of faith which is both a law of prayer and a law of belief: a
corrective to devotion and theology. Tyrrell made it clear that,
of the two extremes, the ultra-theological was more dangerous
than the ultra-devotional, for the deposit of faith "is perhaps
in some sense more directly a *lex orandi* than a *lex credendi*;
the creed is involved in the prayer, and has to be disentangled
from it; and formularies are ever to be tested and explained
by the concrete religion which they formulate." Theology
must submit to the law of prayer it is intended to preserve,
just as in natural science a hypothesis "must square with the
facts." "Devotion and religion existed before theology, in the
way that art existed before art criticism, reasoning before
logic, and speech before grammar. When it [theology] begins
to contradict the facts of the spiritual life, it loses all its reality and its authority, and needs itself to be corrected by the
lex orandi."

Throughout the article Tyrrell's stance was that of the
confessor protesting that, "by a flash of theological illumina-
tion" which brought more darkness than light, he had more
than once "known all the joy and reality taken out of a life
that fed on devotion to the Sacramental Presence." As an
indictment of what Tyrrell subsequently called "theologism,"
it was extremely effective. Beneath the pastoral protest, however, there were more interesting views on the relationship of
theology to revelation. The emphasis on the meaning which
the words of Christ had for the *vulgus profanum* to whom he

preached implied that the law of prayer and the law of belief alike would have to accept a more accurate contextual understanding of the words if historical science should make it available. Almost parenthetically, Tyrrell challenged the dialectical and explicatory theories of development—and that of Newman as well—by taking what might appear to be an extremely conservative position, namely, that theology was supposed to *preserve* and not to *develop* "the exact ideas" which simple "language conveyed to its first hearers." Though this position could be interpreted as a directive for a biblical theology, Tyrrell did not have that in mind. He was arguing that the content of revelation should be frozen and sealed (outside of its historical context), and not subjected to further exegesis or metaphysical translation. It should be considered, rather, as a guide for moral life and, more significantly, for the life of prayer through which the power making for righteousness within man was liberated from nature.[21]

The second essay, "A Perverted Devotion," carried Tyrrell's contribution to the debate over the nature of punishment in hell which had begun with an article by St. George Jackson Mivart. Tyrrell was directly concerned with two recent responses to Mivart. One, by a Redemptorist priest, had insisted on the harshest traditional interpretation. The second, by a Jesuit, tried, on scholarly grounds, to minimize the conventional teaching through a manipulation of texts, whereas Mivart had tried to reinterpret it through an application of modern scientific notions to Scholastic categories. Tyrrell was more radical than either, insisting on "moderate agnosticism" in the matter. In doing so, he again attacked rationalism in theology, and challenged the "perverted devotion" of the day on moral grounds.

Juliana of Norwich gave Tyrrell the context for his plea

that on the question of hell "we are in the region of faith and
mystery and must await the answer to these riddles in patience
and humility." The mystic had written that "there is a deed
which the Blessed Trinity shall do in the last day . . . the great
deed ordained of our Lord God . . . by which He shall make
all things well; for right as the Blessed Trinity made all things
of naught, right so the Blessed Trinity shall make all well that
is not well." Tyrrell rejected any attempt to "patch up" or
"whittle away" "difficulties against our faith in the absolute
goodness and wisdom of God, arising from the existence of
suffering, the permission of sin, the problem of predestiny."
His text, an appropriately Scholastic one, handled here with
an ironic twist: *magis et minus non mutant speciem.*

Efforts like Mivart's to suggest a temporary surcease of
suffering in hell, or minimizing efforts based on Aquinas'
"subtler time-sense," were useless. They did nothing to al-
leviate a quite proper sense of moral outrage at a "devotion"
which makes God seem less just and kind than his creatures.
Such devotions must be rejected by the Church as expressions
of a crude materialism, if the Church expected to be able to
combat the more sophisticated materialism of the modern age.
Tyrrell linked rationalism and materialism, both in the secular present and the ecclesiastical past. Modern materialism
and modern rationalism—"the last and lowest form"—could
not be dealt with until the Church purged itself of "the leaven
of rationalism that we may have carried with us from earlier
and cruder days, when faith needed the rein more than
the spur." Medieval or ecclesiastical rationalism must be
tempered by a new recognition of the essential mystery of
dogma, or else pious souls within the Church, as well as
"men of good will" outside it, will be scandalized and lost
to religion.

The argument had an ecclesiological dimension. Tyrrell suggested that the boundaries of the Church are not the proper subject for rational and legal definition. Christians who admitted their "mental insufficiency" on this score were, in fact, preparing the way for Christ "by showing [their belief that] something equivalent to a revelation is as much an exigency of our nature as religion is. Thus God's spirit working outside the Church is preparing for Himself an acceptable people." Tyrrell implied that the failure of *modern* rationalism and the movement of men of "good will" away from the materialism which had developed out of "faith in science" would not only prepare these men for religion but would also help (or force) the Church to shake off its *medieval* rationalism. This argument, in turn, involved a cautious approach to immanentism. Revelation as the Church possessed it was essential for true religion; but something else was needed, something which was just as available to the modern rationalist and materialist as it was to the believing Christian, a parallel, or "equivalent," to revelation, a force of irrationalism or "super-rationalism" within man without which external revelation was incomprehensible.[22]

It was the closing appeal that Tyrrell made in "A Perverted Devotion" which attracted and repelled the censor's eye. In the language of the day, the article "offended pious ears" (which prompted Tyrrell to write to Bremond: "I wish Rome would either define pious ears, or give a list of them so that one might know"). Tyrrell was not at all interested in the origins of the teaching on hell. The article was not scientific, as was Loisy's contemporaneous discussion of Old Testament history. Tyrrell was reacting against the modern extension of "Tertullianism" in Catholic teaching, but he was not challenging the doctrine on historical grounds. He was arguing for a "deeper and more spiritual conception of the original dogma." In a sense, his criticisms of this aspect of the teaching of the Church were phrased no less rationally than the criticisms directed against Tyrrell by the Society. But, as was often the case in the Modernist crisis, it was the more peripheral matter which attracted the attention of the authorities, though the Jesuit censors, who provided criticisms which were to be the basis for a revision of the article, saw the deeper challenge when they accused Tyrrell of rejecting the definition of Vatican I that "reason, illumined by faith, when it earnestly, devoutly, and soberly seeks a certain God-given understanding of mysteries," can attain such an understanding. Tyrrell replied: the emphasis must be on the word "soberly." The argument might have been carried on in Latin and allowed to run down, were it not that an article in the popular press highly favorable to Mivart (also under fire for his views on the same issue) referred in passing to Tyrrell as a Jesuit "whose views seem to be as much out of harmony with the spirit of his Society as his abilities are superior to those of his confrères." Pressure on Tyrrell now increased. He published a hedging retraction of the article in June, gave his last retreat in July, and by "mutual agreement" retired from Farm Street to a Jesuit "holiday house" at Richmond, in Lancashire. He wrote to his friends that he was looking forward to a "few months" of much-needed rest. When he left Lancashire, five years had passed and he was no longer a Jesuit.[23]

III

THE RICHMOND PERIOD was for Tyrrell what Neuilly was for Loisy, though there were significant differences. Tyrrell now had the leisure to study more widely. He could now read German, and expanded his horizons from the French philosophers Blondel and Laberthonnière to the works of the German critics and those of the religious thinker Rudolf Eucken. By June 1900 he had read Harnack (in English) and written to von Hügel that it was madness for the Church to go on ignoring "so plain a fact as the growth of Catholicism out of a germ as unlike Catholicism as a walnut is like a walnut tree." The two greatest influences after Harnack were Weiss's book and Loisy's *Evangile et l'Eglise*. He immediately realized the significance of the eschatological interpretation of the gospel, though he did not yet understand Loisy's position. As late as 1905 he was of the opinion that Loisy did not himself understand how radical for theology were the implications of his discoveries, and he thought Loisy held to a Newmanite position on the issue of development. Unlike Loisy, Tyrrell saw his exile from the intellectual milieu much more clearly as a vocational crisis, and worried considerably about his relationship to the Society. He was a priest by personal necessity, since he could not bear to live only for himself. In the autobiography and in letters of this period he emphasized repeatedly his unselfishness in carrying on his intellectual work and his now-stunted priestly duties. He had written, at the time of the publication of "A Perverted Devotion," that his position as a Jesuit was becoming a lie and that schism with the Society might be the result: "I am driven on by a fatality to follow the dominant interest of my life, though it should break the heart of half the world." If he could not continue to be a Jesuit, he would still be a priest and scholar. Yet even on this issue he doubted his motives. Tyrrell wrote:

I must allow for a certain kind of spiritual vanity or ambition in my aspirations after the ideals of sanctity—a desire for self-adornment, analogous to that which makes many thirst after learning and knowledge who care little for truth itself; I wanted to be, for the sake of seeming to myself, and not purely for the sake of being. The top circle in Dante's *Inferno* . . . is what I hope for in my more sanguine moods; but I don't seem to be able to care too much.[24]

Tyrrell was depressed and frustrated by the Society's treatment of his essay. But he quickly recovered. Events in the Church, the influence on his thought from his growing acquaintance with critical work, and the gradual clarification in his mind of the nature of the forces working for and against change in Catholicism—especially the limitations of the liberal position—prompted him to continue work on an apologetic for Christianity which would aid "the moribund Catholics in London in search of a *modus vivendi*." He saw the period in which he lived as a time of crisis in human thought "comparable to those in evolution when life, sense, and reason first come on the scene." Inevitably, there were "seasons of great confusion" after such crises. The confusion of Tyrrell's hope reflected the confusion of the age. After insisting that time was needed for faith to be translated into the modern idiom, he added: "Yet I believe faith will reappear, though I am not so sure that it will be Roman faith —yet even that is the more probable issue—in some sense a certain issue."

The two great problems with which Tyrrell came to terms at Richmond were the questions of authority and doctrinal development. The first was brought to the fore by the actions of the magisterium; the second, by a debate within the liberal Catholic camp itself. Tyrrell dealt with them in print as well as in letters, even though he had been forbidden uncensored publication. The play element had its appeal: "I am writing perhaps more assiduously than when I was free —there is a charm of furtiveness which was lacking then."[25]

A year after the appearance of "A Perverted Devotion," the hopes of Tyrrell and far less radical liberals were stunned by the publication of a Joint Pastoral letter by the English bishops. The Mivart affair had been followed by a good deal of public criticism of the methods of the Holy Office. There had appeared in the *Weekly Register* a month-long debate on "A Plea for Habeas Corpus in the Church." The Catholic Union of Great Britain protested against the tone of *Osservatore Romano's* treatment of English political and religious affairs. The freedom of the Catholic press was made an issue when the *Tablet* declared that it would entertain no criticism of the episcopate in its columns. The mood of suspicion and fear generated by the Americanist controversy in France also made a contribution. The response was the

Joint Pastoral, which made a clear distinction between the
ecclesia docens (the teaching Church, the magisterium), on
the one hand, and the *ecclesia discens* (the learning Church)
on the other. The latter included laity, priests, and bishops
in their private capacity. All were "simply disciples" obliged
to give the "assent of faith" to revealed dogmas, to truths
closely connected with revelation. And they were also obliged
to give "religious obedience" to "that teaching of the Church
which does not fall under the endowment of her infallibility,
but under the exercise of her ordinary authority to feed,
teach, and govern the flock of Christ." Such teaching included
(the emphasis is interesting) "pastoral letters of bishops . . .
many acts of the Sacred Pontificate, and all the decisions of
the Roman Congregation."[26]

The challenge was too great for Tyrrell. To one correspondent he write:

I have just been making myself sick over the Joint Pastoral. . . .
If the bishops themselves had read all that is to be read on modern
difficulties; if they had felt and overcome the temptations to
which the faithful, educated and uneducated alike, are exposed,
one would feel bound to listen to their warnings.

He also lamented the "absolute incompetence of our clergy
as a body to meet the oncoming flood of agnosticism," and
he regretted "the deep somnolence of the bishops."

Tyrrell, who had hitherto felt that liberal Catholics should
work quietly and minimize differences, now changed his
tactics. Henceforth he insisted that creative change could
come only if the extreme positions of both liberals and conservatives were clearly stated. It would no longer be possible
to put new wine in old skins. A break had to be forced.

Tyrrell thereby became involved in a very complex (and anonymous) campaign of letter writing to periodicals in which, as "A Conservative Catholic," he paradoxically insisted that it was the teaching of the Joint Pastoral which was really novel. Its effect was to "cleave the Church into two bodies, the one wholly active, the other all passive." The pope was now pulled out of the Church and put above it. He ceased to be "a part of her" and became instead "her partner, spouse, and Lord in a sense proper to Christ alone." This teaching "sheared" the bishops of their prerogatives and, at the same time, gave them a "tenfold power as the delegates and plenipotentiaries of the infallible and unlimited authority claimed for the pope." Tyrrell called this position, rather misleadingly, the "moral view" of authority, and described its opposite as the "organic" view. The former was built on "various fallacies of metaphor and on puerile exegesis and on a contempt and ignorance of history." In a fashion which he characterized to a correspondent as "intentionally invidious," he attributed the latter view to the "amended Gallicanism" of the liberal Catholics who argued that the pope was truly infallible "only when he profoundly investigated the ecumenical mind."

Functioning as devil's advocate, Tyrrell flashed an Ultramontane "badge of orthodoxy." One conservative writer called it a "badge of folly," but Tyrrell was able to point to the fact that "no maximalist has come forward to repudiate my statement of the case." Tyrrell summed up the position with which he was now personally and intellectually at war. "*L'Eglise, c'est moi* is literally the pope's attitude. He is the steam engine; the episcopate is the carriages; the faithful are the passengers." There was nothing for the layman to do but to "pay his fare and take his seat as so much ballast in the bark of Peter, while the clergy pull him across the ferry."[27]

Tyrrell's position confused many liberals. So did the logic of the argument leading him to defend Cardinal Manning, as did his allusions in books and letters to the propriety of the condemnation of Galileo. Tyrrell maintained, in one article, that both views were compatible with the Vatican decrees; then, in the next, he insisted that the view which he found in the Joint Pastoral appeared to be the official one. He argued that there was no *tertium quid*: the pope either had a mind separate from that of the Church, or else he shared in the "collective mind" and gave it expression. In all of this his position was, of course, the "amended Gallicanism" he derided. His biographer properly points to the episode as proof that Tyrrell had formulated a general and theoretical approach to the problem of authority before he himself was seriously involved with its representatives. Events confirmed him in his view that there were only two possible positions and that the wrong one had triumphed.[28]

Tyrrell's tendency to dichotomize the issue of authority in the Church was less upsetting to the liberals than the correlative bifurcation which he was trying to introduce into the debate over the relationship of science to theology, especially as it focused on the question of the growth of doctrine in the Church. Tyrrell had begun to read Newman's works in 1884, but he had never made a systematic study of the Cardinal's thought. He acknowledged that Newman had "effected a profound revolution" in his way of thinking when he had first felt the limits of Scholasticism, and believed that he understood Newman's thought better for lack of complete study. He was mainly attracted to the *Grammar of Assent*, which he claimed he had read seven times. As late as 1906 he had not read the *Essay on the Development of Christian Doctrine,* but relied for his grasp of Newman's theory on the *University Sermons.* This gap he later corrected, but not until he had broken with those who "exalted his [Newman's] system . . . over his spirit."[29]

The stages of his break with the Newmanites, headed by Wilfrid Ward, Newman's biographer and editor of the liberal *Dublin Review,* were confused by Tyrrell's characteristic tendency to argue both sides of the question and to push to extremes the conservative and liberal positions. However, the chameleon play does not obscure a bouleversement in Tyrrell's position, accentuated by the Modernist controversy and by the attempts of the liberals to rescue Newman's reputation from the condemnations of 1907.

In 1900 Tyrrell wrote to Ward that his own position was "a halfway house": "my aim or programme is, whatever unknown issue may come forth from the working of the opposed but complementary tendencies right and left, to prevent the catastrophe of the exclusive predominance of either, which would result from a schism. Is this more or less your view?" It was. Ward had summed it up, in 1899, in an article in the *Nineteenth Century Magazine.* Catholic scholars requested "provisional intellectual liberty" from authorities who were, of course, responsible for maintaining "principles more vital than anything which concerns the advance of secular learning." The Catholic liberal recognized the tradition of Catholic conservatism "which leads theology to hold by traditional positions until such time has elapsed as makes the assimilation of modifications from extraneous sciences free from all objections." A system of checks and balances was at work. "The critic is the liberal pioneer, whose privilege it is occasionally to be rash, provided he does not dogmatize; the theologian remains the conservative make-weight, and sets his remnant of antiquated positions against the critics' overflow of evanescent novelties." Eventually the dialectic rubbed the jagged edges of critical insight and softened the hard block of theological conviction. "One may well hope to win the attention of Roman theologians . . . to consolidated and moderate expositions of highly probable conclusions in science and criticism, though they may have simply rejected the first exaggerated statements of the pioneers." The liberals and the critics ought to recognize that Science was often as overbearing as Theology: the "intrusions of Ecclesiastical Authority" of the past have been caused "because the man of science despises the clerk and enjoys bullying him." "Aristotle was opposed by the Fathers at one time as dangerous to the faith of the multitudes."[30]

Tyrrell had already written a series of articles agreeing in essence with Ward's position. And his letters admitted that the Church must control discussion, "in the essential interest of truth, lest the . . . minds of millions [be] perplexed in matters of supreme practical consequence," and agreed that the Church could neither "identify herself with 'progress' nor isolate herself from it. Her attitude must always be the difficult and uncomfortable one of partial agreement and partial dissent." Even good art had to sacrifice to save the faith of the philistine. Much of the results of contemporary science was "truth 'in solution' but not attainable apart and in its purity until it has long ceased to be a theme of discussion and excitement. Then it is that the Church will quietly adopt and assimilate what no longer admits of controversy." The secret was to go slow, resist the conservative pressure which sought to drive progressives "to rash deeds and utterances, and if to apostasy, so much the better." For this policy Tyrrell could cite one of the favorite maxims of the Society: "The Kingdom of God cometh not with observation . . . noise should be minimized."[31]

Even before the controversy over "A Perverted Devotion," however, there had been different accents in Tyrrell's moderation. Tyrrell was sensitive—as priest, confessor, and intellectual—to the implications of liberal ideas for devotional life, as was Ward. But even before the discovery of the philosophy of moral dogmatism and the works of the critics, he had a much more radical idea of what dogma—which authority and development were both meant to serve—really was. He also expressed in these writings an elitism which was not characteristic of the liberal school. The liberals bent over backward in their insistence that the Catholic intellectual claimed no special relationship to the magisterium. Tyrrell hinted at a double standard: the responsibilities of the intellectual carried certain rights. Writing on "Our Duty to Fallible Decisions," he agreed that the "motives" for the kind of internal obedience which the layman "rightly yields" to peripheral decisions and pronouncements "remain in force for the expert"; but in his case, they may be "counteracted and weakened by the evidence of the known truth."[32]

In 1902 and 1903 Tyrrell turned against this hopeful approach of the liberals. The wedge was no longer to be driven between the liberal and conservative positions, with the intent of forcing acceptance of the former by grotesque parody of the impossibility of the latter; for the liberal position was fundamentally as hopeless a tool for dealing with modern science and philosophy as was the conservatism it sought to reform. Here again, it is important to note that, like Loisy's, Tyrrell's public utterances—even his pseudonymous ones—were not as radical as the lines of thought which can be glimpsed in his letters. This was not an ill-intentioned duplicity, though it could only appear as that to Tyrrell's critics once it was possible to collate books, articles, and private papers. Tyrrell was sensitive to the charge that his views on authority were *ad hoc,* summoned up from nowhere when he came under fire. He was equally sensitive to the charge of dissembling, and this well before the Modernist condemnation.

In this debate Tyrrell's continuing concern for the preservation of religion was again dominant. To him at least, there did not seem to be anything inconsistent about not *unambiguously* denouncing the liberal-Newmanite position once he had discovered its limitations. As long as there was any hope of introducing even the most moderate adjustment in the official attitude toward modern philosophy and criticism and their implications for the history of religion, then there was also good reason to hope that once these first hesitant steps were taken, later and fuller revelations of the real revolution brought to Christianity by modernity could be made within the context of tradition and without disastrous effect on the masses of the faithful. Mock denunciations would only make the liberal position more attractive. So it was not until *after* his own break with the Church that Tyrrell published, in enlarged form, the criticisms of Newmanism he had sketched in 1903 and 1904.[33]

The Newman controversy focused on a series of articles entitled *"Semper Eadem,"* published in the *Month.* Tyrrell's new dichotomization of the two positions came as a "bombshell" to the liberals. There had been hints beforehand. In 1902, in an article on "The Limitations of Newman," Tyrrell had insisted that it was Newman's "spirit" and not his "system" which should be taken as an example by Catholic scholars. He had made the same point in letters to Ward. Now, however, he pointed out that the liberals and the conservatives were talking about two entirely different things when they said they accepted the idea of development.

The liberals, he argued, were unlimited in their enthusiasm. For them, the idea of development was the "mistress" of theology, because they felt that theology, "like natural science, has for its subject matter a certain ever-present department of human experience which it endeavors progressively to formulate and understand." The conservatives, on the other hand, saw it only as a "hand-maiden" of theology, to be used in the service of something fixed and remote: "our school divinity finds its subject matter in the record or register of certain past experiences, that cannot be repeated and are known to us only through such a record." The second part of the argument was at least generally accurate, since it corresponded to the statement which the bishops had made on development in the Joint Pastoral. But the first part was not. Ward and the other liberals held no such position. Tyrrell was confusing the liberal theory of development of dogma with his own theory.[34]

This was piling paradox upon paradox. At the same time that Tyrrell was arguing that the liberals held such a radical view (which delighted their enemies; the article prompted paeans of praise for Tyrrell from journals which had hitherto criticized him), he was discovering that Newman's own position was disappointingly traditional. In 1906 he wrote to a French critic preparing a book on his break with the Society of Jesus that he had realized that Newman's "acceptance of the Roman Catholic idea of the *depositum fidei* as being a divinely communicated 'credo' or theological summary" made impossible any "synthesis" of Catholic tradition with "evo-

lutionary philosophy." He had said much the same thing to
Ward in 1903:

The Church has "adopted" development just as she adopted
Aristotelianism, i.e., she has enslaved it. The alternative would be
for her to be enslaved by it; to submit her presuppositions to be
criticized by it, i.e., to be accounted for and explained away as by
Harnack and Co. Development is common to the Church and
modern thought as wood is common to a table and a tree. Neither
(the Church nor Modern Thought) can absorb without destroying
the other; neither can yield to the other without suicide.

The solution was coexistence and an "artificial synthesis"
between the two which would reveal how much of Christianity remained "after the miraculous has been excluded."[35]

In the same letter he stated the philosophical reasoning
which led him to hold that the liberal concept of theology
was inadequate. Fundamental was an extension of the
Thomistic idea of analogy into an agnosticism which embraced everything but the religious sense itself. Everything
the Catholic believed was "an analogue or metaphor" sub-
stituting for an original experience of the divine which has
now been "withdrawn from view." Presumably this limitation on knowledge would apply to the basic insights of faith
presented in the gospel as historical events. Tyrrell thus extended to revelation a concept usually applied only to
theology understood as a science, and thereby severely limited
the value of the latter's speculations and explications. Since
revelation and the dogmas defined by tradition were merely
analogues for an experience only accessible in the witness of
those who had faith in its ultimate meaning, traditional
theology ("our school-divinity") was twice removed from the
truth, for "there is no valid inference from analogues."

As for development, Tyrrell argued that there was nothing *de fide divina* but what is "actually (however confusedly) contained in the subapostolic mind." Conventional or traditional theology did not define the *depositum fidei*—"the realities revealed"—but, rather, "the form under which they were deposited." Tradition had treasured everything (including Ptolemaic astronomy) which would help to preserve "the impression produced by Christ's revelation on the subapostolic mind." Conversely, Copernicus and Galileo—and one might add Darwin—were "ecclesiastically" false, even if they were scientifically true. Tyrrell, as his later books made clear, had a great deal of sympathy with this position as well as a great deal of trouble. The Church had inevitably tended to treasure more and more extraneous material and to confuse the faith *definita propter alia* with statements *de fide divina*. If the true idea of development were applied to the more limited definition of the deposit of faith, its content would be severely limited indeed.

Tyrrell saw the difficulties of his approach to traditional theology. He realized that if it were seen as doing nothing more than making analogous statements about analogies, it would have little meaning. And he admitted that "it was the fiction of an unchanged and unchangeable nucleus of sacred tradition that saved the Christianity of the apostles from being quickly transformed out of all recognition." But he counterbalanced this grudging praise for tradition with an insistence that it had done its job. With hope born of Weiss and Loisy, he told Ward that students of Christianity could now get back "across the centuries to the historical Christ," because, "amid all the protective theological accretions, the nucleus of Christianity has been preserved like a fly in amber, or like a mammoth in ice." And, thankfully, outside theology

"the spirit of Christ has lived and developed in the collective
life of the faithful." He predicted that the Church's experience with evolution would reverse that of the thirteenth
century. Then, she had swallowed Aristotle; today, she would
be swallowed in her turn. This seemed only appropriate. In
the middle ages the Church *was* culture. Today, "as in the
apostolic age," she stands outside culture; to transform it, she
must submerge herself in it. "As then, so now, she must stoop
to conquer, and die to live."[36]

The whole Newman episode was reminiscent of Mgr.
D'Hulst's well-intentioned discussion of the various critical
schools of thought. And Tyrrell's letters do not really clarify
the issue, as these extracts, if read alone, suggest. For, in another letter to Ward, he made it clear that he thought Newman "put theology on all fours with natural science in its
relation to its subject matter." He insisted that Newman
came down on the side of a radically new theology: "I have
very carefully studied JHN's sermons on Theological Development, and have no doubts whatever that he held the
pre-Scholastic and patristic idea of the permanence of revelation in the minds of the faithful and never twigged the school-
theory of a mere formula of a long past revelation as the subject matter of theology." Liberal theology—i.e., Newman—
"formulates certain subjective immanent *impressions* of *ideas*
exactly analogous to sense impressions, which are realities of
experience by which notions and experience can be criticized." In Tyrrell's view, Ward's mistake was in not seeing
that this kind of theology could not be combined with the
"impossible school theology which ties us to the categories
and thought forms of the last twenty centuries. If Catholicism
is to live, the school theology must go." This statement seems
to accord with the opinion of J. H. Walgrave: "According to

Tyrrell, Newman conceived Christianity primarily as an idea, that is, not as a *truth once given* but as a *spiritual force* seeking to become incarnate, exteriorized, by adapting itself to its environment." Walgrave quite properly rescues Newman from this interpretation. Tyrrell had already done so. On balance, he held that there was better reason for the conservatives to claim the Cardinal than for the liberals. It was Tyrrell, of course, and not Newman or Ward, who held that development (or evolution) was "the unfolding of a melody, which varies according to the culture of each epoch, and which reiterates, in various forms, the theme of *an ever present intuition of faith.*"[37]

These views were taking more definite shape while Tyrrell worked, in comparative peace, at Richmond. They had already been broached in correspondence and in the "devotional" writings. In *Oil and Wine* (1900) he had written that, "though some kind of doctrinal system is inseparable from religion, yet it is but as the containing bark which ever breaks and mends, and readjusts itself to the growth of the trunk which it encases." Pragmatism and immanence were themes which did not need any complicated analysis of meaning, any logical process of intellection. "We feel a truth before we formulate it; and when formulated it helps us to feel our way to a further truth; but our life is in the feeling, not in the formula, in the foliage, not in the stem." In a 1902 letter written while he was reading Loisy's article on Genesis, Tyrrell described scriptural inspiration in terms of "the progressive spiritualizing and refining of those gross embodiments in which man expresses his own ideas and sentiments about God." Tyrrell was vague as to what determined this process. In *Lex Orandi* it was "the Spirit of Holiness" which controlled the "continual and endless variations of belief and devotion." From them the Spirit "selects and assimilates the good and useful, and throws away the mischievous, by the slow logic of spiritual life and experience."[38]

This all sounded innocent enough. When *Lex Orandi* appeared, it was favorably reviewed in the *Month* as a *devotional,* not as a theological, work.[39] Tyrrell himself sensed more than ambiguity in his position. "Are we honest?" he asked rhetorically in a 1904 letter, referring to those who believed that "the creed ought to have been imposed merely as provisional—as registering the state of theological development of that day; as destined to be transformed into a better symbol." He admitted that there was something "uncandid" in his attempt to credit the Church of the past "with any consciousness of principles which we are only now beginning to realize and formulate. . . ." What he meant, but could not say too plainly, was that the creed might still be used as an expression of certain devotional and "pragmatical" values and of "certain mysterious other-world fact-values, in which they are rooted, even though its historico-philosophical sense became to a large extent untenable." But candor was bound to come:

We cannot go on forever stretching old bottles. When men are sufficiently prepared by an understanding of the principles of religious growth, we shall have to recognize the right of each age to adjust the historico-philosophical expression of Christianity to contemporary certainties, and thus put an end to this utterly needless conflict between faith and science which is a mere theological bogey.

Tyrrell felt, in any case, that he was no less honest than those "who ignore the reality of the 'religious process' by which God progressively reveals Himself to the collective mind that asks and seeks and knocks through its creed and theologies."[40]

Ironically, *Lex Orandi* was a toned-down version of "Dr. Ernest Engels' " much more violent book, *Religion as a Factor of Life*. It showed the impact of French dogmatic pragmatism, though the argument differed little in fundamentals from the articles of 1899. The truths of religion, Tyrrell argued, were like those of history and physical science: directed to life as their end. These truths gained acceptance because "they explain and fit in with the life that we live, and offer means for its expansion; because they enable us to understand and master our physical and social environment and to appropriate its resources." The statements made by science and history, if they did not affect action, would have no meaning except as "curious riddles awaiting solution."

The same test of truth must be applied to theology. The good apologist for religion must not only show the connection between theological statements and the statements made by science and history; he also had to "connect the life of religion with the rest of our life, and . . . show that the latter demands the former." Yet this was not to say that religion was merely an aid to the perfect moral existence. Religion was an end in itself. The perfect moral life was second to the search for an "ever more satisfying effort to utter Him whom we have already found; to express and reproduce in terms of the finite and relative that Absolute and Infinite whose secret presence is given us by the 'religious sense.' " The religious sense—Tyrrell also described it as a "consciousness" —was universal. The soul of every man was *naturaliter christiana* because Christianity was the only "natural" religion. It was not theism plus certain other beliefs. Rather, it was the mature form of theism, which was itself "embryonic

Christianity." The human soul had a lack, an "emptiness":
only Christ could complete it. Therefore, religion must not
be seen as something thrust upon men from the outside "by
force of logic or juridical coercion," but as "the life that is
already within them, nay, of their very selves."

Man's categorical analogies for God would be useless, if
God were "simply in a different category or genus from the
finite"—as the theologians treat him. It was wrong to think
of God as "something" other, without also thinking of him
as the root and source of all being, as "immanent no less than
transcendent—a relation which does not exist between finite
things of wholly disparate categories." Our knowledge of God
should therefore embrace, without limitation of degree or
kind, "whatever perfection of content is predicable of any
possible thing or term of thought." "So understood, the
Scholastic doctrine of analogy steers successfully between the
Scylla of illegitimate dogmatism and the Charybdis of Spencerian agnosticism." Knowledge of God through immanence
was to be seen as intimately bound up with knowledge of
him through transcendence, that is, through revelation. There
was growth and development in the knowledge of God which
man acquires immanently, if not in the knowledge given by
revelation. Tyrrell described this knowledge in terms of the
growth of human personality, constantly in flux, constantly
absorbing its previous states into new states of consciousness.
It continues on, "uttering and evolving its potentialities,
working out the ideal, striving endlessly towards the Absolute" which is in part contained within it.[41]

Traditional sources for much of *Lex Orandi* could be
posited. The discussion of the nature of the soul is Augustinian. The argument for the value of immanent knowledge
of the divine depended on the Scholastic presentation of the

idea of analogy, and a three-page footnote on the traditional teaching of that idea was more than a device to fool the censor. The tone throughout was temperate. The work was a model for a new apologetic.

But if this was Dr. Jekyll, there was also Mr. Hyde. In the same year "Hilaire Bourdon" published—"for private circulation only"—*The Church and the Future (L'Eglise et l'Avenir)*. The pseudonym, the limited printing, the paper cover, the French subtitle (implying that the work was freshly translated), made for mystification; but the argument of the book was far from obscure or ambiguous. Tyrrell mounted a major attack on what he was later to call "Romanism" and the Roman heresy, as well as a defense of the results of criticism. The Scylla which modern religion has to avoid was no longer "illegitimate dogmatism" but the "mediatorial liberalism" of Wilfrid Ward. "M. Bourdon" abandoned all hope that the positions summarized in the appendixes (the rejection of the *spiritu sancto dictante* position taken by the pope in *Providentissimus Deus,* of the argument for the gospel origins of canon law and papal supremacy, and of the "monarchical" interpretation of the Church as the kingdom of God) could ever be reconciled with "official" theology. He also rejected the effort of the liberals "to reconcile the data of science and history with dogmas by giving to these latter a sense which the framers would have repudiated."

What was needed for the Church in the future was a new ecclesiology which would be social, evolutionary, and mystical. It should be free of "theologians and canonists, who lust to tyrannize over the minds of men as intellectual despots" and who present their "purely intellectualist conception of Faith as being belief on testimony." This new ecclesiology would regard the Church, not as an institution in the legal sense, but as "avowedly an art-school of Divine charity," a "way or manner of life that has been committed to her guardianship, rather than a body of doctrine." So understood, the Church would be more like a community of Buddhist monks, and the Catholic's creed would be like theirs: "I put my trust in Buddha; I put my trust in the Doctrine (i.e., of Deliverance), I put my trust in the Community." For the Church was truly the social bond, the community, in which the life of religion, which was the life of charity, was led. As such, it was indispensable, infallible, as firmly established as in any legal definition. "Outside such a society the isolated individual is cut off from the corporate life of Christ; he is deprived of the heritage of the gathered experience and reflections of multitudes of generations from which, as from a starting capital, he may set forth in search of further gains; he is cut off from the stimulus, the infection of enthusiasm, that is yielded by co-operation with others who are animated by the same spirit, who live for the same ideals, as himself." The spirit of Christ dwelt only in the community, because only the community stretched backward and forward through time and embraced it completely. No person—"not even Christ himself"—no nation, no age, exhausted the potential of the Spirit for "a progressively fuller manifestation and embodiment, such as would be impossible were the labor not committed to social co-operation."

The Spirit spoke in the community in action and life, not in words. Doctrines and dogmas, structures of words, the playthings of theologians, were to nature—and the true Church—what a pocket map of London is to the city itself: "a sufficient guide in certain matters for certain practical purposes." The exercise of the understanding was a good thing. However, separation of the understanding from the other spiritual faculties and "deification" of it as an end in itself inevitably led to an "idle, hair-splitting, cobweb-spinning intellectualism." Of course, spiritual realities had to be represented by some nonspiritual symbols, which also provided a guide to speech and conduct in the Church; these would be figurative presentations of realities not knowable in themselves which could offer "guidance by analogy," such as the idea of the kingdom of heaven. " 'The Kingdom of Heaven is like unto . . .' something which it is not; nay, it is not strictly even a kingdom: what it *is* we cannot understand or say, though we can feel and know it."

Traditional ecclesiological elements had to be reunderstood. The creed was "a guide to life as expressed in speech and action," not a rational set of definitions. The Church was not a divine institution, in the sense that its history was foreseen and planned by Christ. Could he have foreseen it all and not forewarned his followers? To believe that Christ, knowing the controversies, the schisms, the doubts, and persecutions of a sundered Christendom, could have deliberately left the truth in obscurity was, "from an apologetic standpoint, antecedently irreconcilable with a belief in His goodness, wisdom, and pity." Moreover, the structures necessary for the preservation of the social and spiritual community were developed out of the *consensus fidelium*. It was from the Church as a whole that the pope and the Curia, the vicegerents of the people, took their power, just as the symbols of the life of the Spirit took their form from the collective historical experience of the society. "The notion of a complete ecclesiastical organism produced abruptly by a divine *fiat* on the day of Pentecost belongs to the same sort of philosophy as the Mosaic cosmogony." It was enough that Christ

believed that the "inspirational impetus" he gave to his followers would last until the consummation of the world.

Biblical criticism had forced Christians to reconstruct their
understanding of revelation, as the product of faith, not its
source. The Church, too, must be reinterpreted. "If this
means a breakdown of theology in both matters, we must remember again, that theory is always inadequate to the fact,
and that divine impulses are often wiser than human after-
reasons." There were various qualifications added to "Hilaire
Bourdon's" radical critique of traditional ecclesiology. He
too, like "A. Firmin," was eager to point out that after the
propositions of theologism had been analyzed, then, "after-
wards, as Catholics, we should take [them] on authority."[42]

The most successful and the most moving of the anonymous
and pseudonymous writings to come out of Richmond was
also the last. Written in 1903 and widely and carelessly dis-
tributed (Tyrrell took few pains to limit the number of
copies of these essays or the "private" knowledge of their
authorship), the *Confidential Letter to a Friend Who Is a
Professor of Anthropology* was a striking example of the
apologetic for the "moribund Catholics" to whom Tyrrell
felt a special vocation.

The letter was ostensibly addressed to a professor who had
consulted Tyrrell about his religious doubts. He had asked
if his inability to reconcile the teachings of the Church with
certain truths of history and science meant that he had sinned
against faith. Should he leave the Church? Tyrrell quickly
reviewed the difficulties that assailed the man of science in
matters of religion, and dismissed the fear of his correspondent that admitting them was an expression of moral failing.
The professor should indeed leave the Church "if theological 'intellectualism' be right; if faith mean mental assent to

a system of conceptions of the understanding: if Catholicism be primarily a theology or at most a system of practical observances regulated by that theology." But the answer was "No" if Catholicism were "primarily a life and the Church a spiritual organism in whose life we participate, and if theology be but an attempt of that life to formulate and understand itself—an attempt which may fail wholly or in part without affecting the value and reality of the said life."

Tyrrell reminded his correspondent that science offered insights into the nature of personality as well as criticism of the bible, and then, through a discussion of modern psychology, he developed the ecclesiology sketched in *The Church and the Future*. He reviewed the distinctions made between the conscious and the subconscious self, defining the conscious self as the "emergent point" of an infinitely complex "resultant" of forgotten and unregistered experiences, both "personal and ancestral." Sudden eruptions from the "collective subconscious" forced the individual to reconstruct his personality, or his understanding of it, from the foundations. This process of change, recognized in individual psychology, was "far more evident, by way of analogy, when we deal with states and societies and communities." The task of good government was twofold. It was supposed to develop the unconscious mind and will of the masses and bring the people into spontaneous sympathy with the laws of growth and development. Thus they were progressively civilized. But this double work was seldom realized. The conscious government of human societies often lagged far behind the "collective subconscious" of the masses, lording uncreatively over the mind and will which it was meant to serve. Then revolution was the only cure.

This was the state of the Catholic Church. It had become
a government out of step with the people. Men having difficulties like the professor's needed to distinguish clearly
between the collective subconscious of "the People of God"
and the "consciously formulated mind and will of the governing section of the Church." Faith in the latter was often
weak, or nil; faith in the People of God was always strong
and invincible. One kept faith in a man whose general behavior was good, even though he had occasional lapses, because one knew that his subconscious life was sound. So with
the Church. On occasion she was untrue to her deepest nature. Then one said to her: *"Nescitis cuius spiritus estis—*
'You do not know your own essential spirit.' " When those
in positions of authority failed to express the true Catholicism, then private conscience resumed the rights and liberties
which it had entrusted to authority. Failure to do this could
be traced to a wrong emphasis on definitions of the shape
and nature of the Church. "We can live and be, without
knowing how to explain and define ourselves." In any case,
it was wrong to identify the Church with priests and theologians. They were a class, and had a class interest in their
definitions. They tended to identify themselves with the
Church much as a politician identified himself with "the
great silent masses of the population too busied about living
to think how or why they live." It was with this class that
the professor and others like him had their quarrel, not with
the Church. "This self-conscious, self-formulating Catholicism of the thinking, talking, and governing minority is
not the whole Church, but only an element (however important) in its constitution."

The future of the Church depended in large part on the
laity, who must come to see their responsibility. Schism was,
of course, out of the question. Voluntary schism should al-

ways be condemned, not on the "philistine ground" that the Church was always right and the schismatics always wrong, but because vital elements of truth were lost to the Church in every schism. Communion with the invisible Church, of which Christ was the bond and the sacraments were the token, was the one thing needful. Of course, communion with the visible Church was also a great *desideratum*, because a society must prepare the way for the coming of the kingdom of heaven, even though the society is itself the kingdom only in a secondary sense. For faith was a life, a search for what Matthew Arnold called "the Power that makes for righteousness." And the Church consisted of all those who took up this search, as Christ took up the cross. "We do not worship Humanity, with the Comtists, but we worship the power that is revealed in human goodness of every sort. . . . In this sense Humanity . . . is a mystical Christ, a collective Logos, a Word or Manifestation of the Father; and every member of that society is in his measure a Christ or revealer in whom God is made flesh and dwells in our midst."

Tyrrell emphasized, after each of several broad definitions of the invisible Church, that the individual man could not begin the search alone, much less complete it. Man needed the help of a visible Church. The Church "of Rome" was at the moment "no more than the charred stump of a tree torn to pieces by gales and rent by thunderbolts." She had been more responsible in the past for schism than the schismatics themselves, having stood then and standing today—as the schismatics never did—for the twin principles of unity and universality. Nevertheless, she was at least an "abortive essay" toward the kind of religious society which would bring all men together into the kingdom of God. The great virtue of the Church as it existed was the breadth of its appeal: "the Trinity, the Creation, the Fall, the Incarnation, the Atonement, the Resurrection, Heaven and Hell, Angels and Devils" were all pieces of a single mosaic, all parts of a multi-colored stained-glass window through which was refracted to men God's light, "pure and colorless." Dogmas, creeds, and sacraments were all aids to fuller participation in the truth of the invisible Church. The mistaken notion of the Church, from which the "Professor" and many others suffered, was the work of the theologians, "mortal, fallible, ignorant men like ourselves," who dressed themselves up in the Church's robes and thundered anathemas in her name. Their "present domination [was] but a passing episode in the Church's history." In his peroration Tyrrell compared theologians to "those most faithful and observant Jews who would give no ear to Christ and his heresy." The Pharisees had maintained that Judaism would conquer the world, and were proved right; for Judaism lived a risen and glorified life in Christianity when Paul expanded it into a new world religion. And, Tyrrell speculated,

May not Catholicism, like Judaism, have to die in order that it may live again in greater and grander form? Has not every organism got its limits of development after which it must decay, and be content to survive in progeny? Wine skins stretch, but only within measure; for there comes at last a bursting point when new ones must be provided. Who can answer these questions? We can only turn the pages of history and wonder and wait.[43]

Criticism of Tyrrell's work was growing in the Society, especially in France. (*Lex Orandi* was to be intensely criticized in the Jesuit journal *Etudes* after Bremond's retirement as editor and Tyrrell's dismissal from the Society.) Throughout 1904–05 Tyrrell negotiated at length with the English Father Provincial for amicable release. Rumors that "a

certain English Jesuit" was about to leave the Society exacerbated the difficulties which Tyrrell and the provincial
discussed. The latter held that Tyrrell was in revolt, not
only against the authority of the Society, but also against
the Church. Tyrrell hedged, contending that he could no
longer in conscience remain under Jesuit obedience. Then
he castigated such obedience as demanding "a readiness to
shift one's convictions at the *mot d'ordre* of superiors," which
really meant an "absence of all convictions." Tyrrell fell back
on his earlier reflections on the limits of ecclesiastical authority. Taking as his model "Our Lord and his apostles who
were excommunicated by lawful ecclesiastical authority for
refusing to be silent," he consoled himself with the reflection
that the excommunication which might follow upon his separation from the Society would be, temporally speaking,
"fairly harmless, since advancing civilization and Christianity
have wrested the weapons of persecution, with the exception
of the *gladius linguae,* from the servants of the gospel of
peace."[44]

The *gladii* soon struck. In December 1905 the *Corriere
della Sera* of Milan published selections from the *Letter to
a Professor.* The Jesuit General wrote to Tyrrell asking if
he were the author. Tyrrell at first refused to answer, and
demanded to know whether he was to be dismissed or secularized. Shortly afterward he admitted authorship, and defended the essay as "medicine for extreme cases . . . the
thousands of educated Catholics" who were not experts in
criticism or history but were reduced "by the mere existence
of such disputes . . . to a state of perfectly inculpable theological confusion, which they easily mistake for loss of faith."
Harm would come only if his authorship of the letter were
made public through a repudiation of it, in which case he
and it might become "a cult and a fashion" like Loisy and

his books. The General demanded a public repudiation if
Tyrrell wished to avoid dismissal from the Society. Tyrrell
then published the letter, expanded with an acerbic explanation of his intentions in writing it. Dismissal and suspension
soon followed. The question of his "regularization" as a
secular priest was then referred to the Sacred Congregation.[45]

From February 1906 until his death in July 1909, Tyrrell
became progressively more and more disillusioned with the
Catholic Church or what he now called "Vaticanism" or
"Romanism" and, at the same time, more convinced that the
principles of Catholicism and its teaching of the Christian
gospel provided the only possible link between the present
religious crisis and the "Church of the Future." His own
experience was interwoven with the gradual shattering of
liberal hopes as the conservative reaction to Loisy's work and
the discussion based on it grew. Tyrrell's bitter reply to the
Etudes critique of *Lex Orandi* confirmed the continental
opinion that he was "the English Loisy." His several attempts
to find a bishop who would sponsor his appeal for a *celebret,*
or permission to say Mass, were unsuccessful, reinforcing his
strong feelings of conspiracy and persecution. The negotiations reached a climax of misunderstanding when, after protracted confusion about the extension of censorship to his
private correspondence (he was willing to accept censorship
of books), a premature notice of his "submission" appeared
in *Osservatore Romano.* Tyrrell speedily revoked his signa-
ture to the letters accepting the terms of restoration, made
the negotiations public, and was in turn reprimanded by the
Vatican press.

Meanwhile, he had seen the Biblical Commission "packed."
The French and Italian liberals and progressives he had at
last met were criticized and then condemned; and, for no
apparent reason, his friends in England were also subjected

to various forms of persecution. He became more impatient at the restraint recommended by von Hügel, who recognized a parting of the ways. Tyrrell's letters of this period reflect growing confusion and despair. After the break with the Society he wrote a memoir of his years as a Jesuit. This was intended as an introduction to a possible collection of papers bearing on his "Relations with the Jesuits" which reemphasized his self-image as a "producer" rather than a "consumer" of religion. He was quite sure that out of the Society—and, in practical terms, out of the priesthood—he still believed what he did when he began his vocation: "to recognize the value of religion, to live for it and work for it, is already to believe." But to others he wrote of his disappointment that Pius X was not turning out to be the pastoral pope for which many had hoped. Tyrrell said that he found it more and more difficult to understand how Rome had "got so many men to believe in her." Perhaps it was because she was, "if not the Mother, at least the Mistress" of humanity, since she spent all her time preserving a faded and meaningless grandeur, exploiting the future in the interests of the present, "preferring the scandal of millions to come to that of hundreds now." As for himself, he believed in a Church "of sorts," but not the pope's sort; "for I believe in every other religion as well." In churches, there was no choice between bad and good, only between "bad and worse."[46]

As his reputation grew through books and contributions to Italian and American, as well as French, periodicals, Tyrrell was approached by admiring Anglicans and religious positivists. He identified strongly with the German liberal historian Ignaz Döllinger and his experience with the Vatican Council, and was in turn identified with Döllinger by Catholic writers. Tyrrell carried on an admiring correspondence with the Old Catholic See of Utrecht, and frequently considered "relapsing" to the Church of England. A good part of his correspondence was devoted to disabusing disaffected Catholics and Anglicans of their notions that schism, a new confessional alliance, or even a new church of excommunicates would help matters. The crisis was universal, and men of good will should stay in their communions, "conscience allowing," and work for their enlargements, even as he was laboring "to stretch and expand Rome." He was now outside the Society, musing on a possible public admission of his having lost hope for Rome; and yet he insisted that the Church could only expand creatively through involuntary schism. He was quite sure that "if the old Churches reform themselves it will be . . . after first having crushed the reformers."

In 1906 he wrote that he believed he must wait "until I am expelled from the Roman Church." That event occurred very swiftly after Tyrrell contributed to the London *Times* a two-part analysis of the encyclical *Pascendi*. The articles were bitter and biting. Tyrrell suggested that the synthetic and inaccurate picture of Modernism (compared with orthodoxy) was still so seductive to the educated mind as to further the cause of those anathematized. He remarked, in passing, that the condemnation was noteworthy as the first such in which the offenders were not accused of personal vice. His friends pointed out that to answer a pope was bad enough. To answer him "in a Protestant newspaper" was much worse. It was, they said, an act of "ecclesiastical suicide." Tyrrell agreed. He admitted that he had written in haste and anger, adding that there was nothing for him to do but "await decapitation." He was excommunicated on October 22, 1907.[47]

IV

TYRRELL'S OFFICIAL MODERNIST WRITINGS were discursive, repetitious, and often marred by polemic. In them he said again—more elaborately, and more openly—much of what he had been saying since 1899 and even earlier. *Through Scylla and Charybdis* (1907), *Medievalism* (1909), and *Christianity at the Crossroads* (published after his death) all developed parallel themes. The last book, however, struck out in directions which Tyrrell had long been discussing in his letters with von Hügel and Maud Petre, but which he had not previously set down for publication. Nevertheless, Tyrrell's acceptance of the categorization of Modernism gave a unity and consistency to his thought (after his break with the Church) which it had not possessed before. The devotional and theological lines were merged in an attempt to express rationally a defense of an irrational or antirational approach to religion which was not merely an extension of the tradition of mysticism as an alternative to the tradition of the *via dogmatica* but an explanation of the way in which modern natural science, philosophy, and historical science had made all tra-

ditional religious categories subject to revision. The crisis
of modern religion focused on two issues: authority and
revelation. These were ideally inseparable, of course. The
very confusion of the Catholic Church in the modern age
came from the fact that it had failed to see that a change had
taken place in the nature of revelation. All this could not
help changing the structure of authority. Tyrrell's views on
both matters were always conditioned by the idea (for him,
it was a notion that could also be described as a *belief*)
that religion was simultaneously an individual and a social
experience, since it dealt fundamentally, not with questions
of morality, but with questions of transcendence.

Accepting the terms "Modernism" and "Modernist" meant
that Tyrrell had to approach the crisis in the Church negatively, at least at the beginning. From the *Times* article on,
he had first to point out what Modernism was *not* before he
could say what it was. And he had to point out what was the
matter with the Church's teaching on authority and revelation before he could sketch what teaching it had to adopt if
it was to weather the crisis and fulfill its vocation. Polemic
distorted both these undertakings, as did growing doubt that
his efforts or those of the more moderate apologists of the
left would have any results. In 1903 he had written to von
Hügel that he was beginning to doubt (as the Baron did not)
that "the ideal of Catholicism which we both would stand
for . . . is really incarnate and in process of development in
the Roman communion; that it is not violently read into it,
or out of it, by Hope that will not face barren facts." The
present form of the papacy, even then, appeared to him to
be inseparable from the "institutionizing process by which
the gospel was Catholicised" and, at the same time, no different, in its causes or effects from "Czardom or any other des-

potism." In 1899 he had sketched the liberals' task as to "destroy the notion that narrowness and orthodoxy go hand in hand; to show that the deeper we dig into Catholic truth and the closer we hold to her word, the broader we can afford to be." In 1903 he wondered "if any instruction so (it would seem) *essentially* the foe of liberty and the principles of the gospel can, by steady evolution, develop into that Catholicism of which we dream." Then, with appropriate Byzantine confusion, he likened Pius to the Czar—well-meaning men who were the prisoners of systems and servants—and the Curia to "that old fanatical Torquemada of a Pobydonostzeff." In 1909, in *Medievalism,* he gave citations from a contemporary French work, *De la Dévotion au Pape,* and commented:

I have seen one of the crosses sold to the faithful of Rome on which the figure of Christ is replaced by the figure of the Pope. I admit the logic of it all, but I ask myself: Where is it to end? Have we yet to learn of the immaculate conception of the Pope, or his real presence in the sacrament of the altar? May I not justly ask: was Pius crucified for you, or were you baptized in the name of Pius?[48]

In spite of such statements, Tyrrell maintained that he held no brief for "virulent anti-clericalism and scandal mongering" and that he felt, "with Lord Acton," that only the *"principle* of Ultramontanism is profoundly immoral and unchristian." Tyrrell's ostensibly more principled attack in his later writings went back to the distinction he had drawn in the debate over the Joint Pastoral between authority conceived as something above and outside the Church, as in the orthodox interpretation of infallibility after 1870, and authority understood as the organic principle of the life of the whole Church. He saw Döllinger, Acton, and Newman hold-

ing to what he called "the Catholic and traditional conception of the Church's institution": "the supremacy of the
orbis terrarum, of the totality of the Church, over even the
highest of her representatives and interpreters: over Bishops,
Councils, and Popes." Tyrrell denied the accusation of Cardinal Mercier of Belgium (in his Lenten Pastoral of 1908)
that this was a Modernist position, much less a liberal Protestant one. Mercier had argued that both Modernism and
Protestantism substituted the agreement of individual minds
for the direction by ecclesiastical authority. Tyrrell replied
that the greatest proof of the extent to which "Romanism"
had departed from the truly Catholic position was its inability to see that "to make the *agreement* of individual
minds a rule of belief [was] at once to set up an authority
over the separate individual minds." Thus he ignored the
Cardinal's real complaint, i.e., that the agreement of a number of individual (Modernist) minds had, on issues of criticism, authority, etc., set itself up as a doctrinal norm in
opposition to the magisterium, which was the true mind of
the *orbis terrarum.* This kind of argument was inevitably
tautological: to the orthodoxy of his day Tyrrell's criticisms
were *a priori* flawed. Nevertheless, he insisted that the pope
and the Curia and the theologians did not speak for the social
mind of the Church. To the Ultramontanes there was no
alternative between "the individualism of anarchy and that
of a dictatorship." They could not see that the papal dictatorship was itself as much of a rejection of community for
individualism as the Protestant extreme. Mercier wrote that
the Protestant nations were sick from too much individualism. Tyrrell replied that the Catholic Church was dying
from authoritarianism, bad scholarship, suspicion of science,
fear of democracy, and the self-seeking lust for power.[49]

Tyrrell had developed a more positive approach to the "Catholic" idea of authority in *Through Scylla and Charybdis*, a work which was overshadowed by his violent polemic with Cardinal Mercier. These ideas had also had a "private life" in his letters, and had their origins in the debates over Newman and with the Ward school. In 1904 he had described the forces of continuity and the forces of change in the Church in an image of two arms (in which length equaled intellectual depth): the short left arm, which was very heavy, was made up of the old theology, the papal monarchy, and the devotional security of the masses of Catholics; the right arm, which was very long but very light, was the liberal and progressive minority. The situation was clear: "It is numbers versus brains." The challenge was for the right arm somehow to redress the balance without harming the organism as a whole. The background of the dilemma also had been sketched in one of the essays of the nineties in which Tyrrell had called for the creation of a kind of Catholic apologetic writing which would close the gap between the intelligentsia and the masses of the faithful. In an early essay entitled "Tracts for the Millions" he had pointed out that "the paradoxes of one generation are the commonplaces of the next: what the savants of today whisper in the ear, the Hyde Park orators of tomorrow will bawl from their platforms." The difficulty lay in the fact that the masses often inherited the problem, and not the solution, since the learned men had passed onto some new quandary. The result was scandal. In the *Letter to a Professor* he had made more explicit the privileges of the intellectual (and automatically liberal) minority, especially their right to see the invisible church behind the visible, the symbol behind the sacrament, the dimly apprehended reality behind the dogma.[50]

His last statement on the constitution of the Church elaborated a sociology of Catholicism, which first distinguished the Church from Protestantism (this was the inevitable introduction to any explication of Modernist ideas). Protestantism was a rational and puritan religion limited to "a certain class, a certain temperament, and a certain culture," whereas Catholicism was, because of its complexity, the religion of the crowds and masses as well as the religion of "the intellectual, the cultivated, the mystical, the esthetic minority." In its "untrimmed luxuriance" Catholicism was not only true to the religious life which Christ knew in his own day, but true to the whole religious experience of mankind as well. Its historical pattern was that of civilization itself. It was an interweaving of labor, science, art, social and political institutions, by which it summed up the past, directed man into the future, and sustained him in the present. Generically speaking, Catholicism as a religion was older than Christ, as old as speech and language, and yet ever new. It had succeeded because the ancient world had been ripe for a "religion of humanity, a synthesis of all other religions."[51]

This description of Catholicism anticipated the discussion of its evolution in the context of world religions, and was an introduction to the role of the intellectual minority in a process of renewal which Tyrrell described in borrowed theological terminology. Christianity had "transubstantiated" paganism, keeping the accidents, but changing the substance; Catholicism continued in its universal vitality because it continued the transubstantiatory process in each successive age and culture. In terms which obviously owed a great deal to Lamennais, the Church lived through a perpetually renewed tension between reaction and revolution, between the stationary and progressive elements which,

Tyrrell said, were the inescapable characteristics of all living religions. The balance between the two elements was maintained by authority, which lay in the social and collective mind of the people. Tyrrell hastened to add that by "the people" he did not mean the "crowd" or the "masses"; for their faith was "a passively received impression from a common external influence—imitation, obedience, faith in the faith of others, and so forth." Rather, "what we mean by the voice of the people in Church or State is not the average opinion, but the best, the highest product, the ripest fruit of the whole social process." But the advanced cadre so described seldom coincided with the official ruling body. Tyrrell made a distinction between the "theoreticians" and the "theologians," and, in effect, subdivided the magisterium, giving the creative responsibility to the intellectual elite and leaving to theologians and theologism the job of general guardianship of the status quo.

Ideally, of course, there should be no conflict between the "theoretician" on the one hand, and the "theologian" and the *rest* of the crowd on the other. When it *appears* that a member of the intellectual and spiritual elite has made a discovery or a judgment contradictory to the social mind of the Church for which he speaks, then he has either misinterpreted it or simply erred. *Otherwise,* he has made a discovery or a judgment which is in fact a deeper and truer interpretation of the social mind than that of the "average and official interpreters." In the second case, "he differs from, but does not contradict them, in as much as his is only a stricter conformity to the same rule they profess to obey. He will be counted heterodox by the average, but he will have an intuitive certainty that he is nothing of the sort, and that where he stands today, they will stand tomorrow."

"From the nature of the case" he can understand the position of the "orthodox." But they cannot understand his. This was not to say that careful control will not be necessary to guard against "blameworthy revolt, and immoral self-seeking" which might grow out of violations of "liberty or error." "It is desirable that those who eventually do get the lead of the progressive movement and overcome the inertia of the average should be the very strongest and the very best; that mediocrity, eccentricity, and blatancy should never be able to seize the reins; that the pedant, the crank, the faddist, should have nothing to do with the process of social development." Perhaps the greatest responsibility of the theoreticians was never to forget that the religious life of the Church was "a corporate super-individual life," that they should always "gladly hold back help on the rest of our fellow-travelers."[52]

Aside from ignoring the tendency of the theologians of his day to regard theoreticians—or, at least, mystics—as "cranks and faddists," this analysis had the fault of disregarding the possibility of tension between the discoveries and judgments of the progressives and the devotional life of the masses, as well as the theologism of their mentors. Tyrrell recognized the point when he compared liberal Catholicism with the religion of the positivists as being "too academic, too philosophical for the average humanity." But, at least, the liberal Catholics recognized the limited attraction of their insights, and only asked the same freedom in their speculations that the masses were allowed in their devotional life. The more serious possibility was that their discoveries and judgments might make that freedom meaningless.

Tyrrell's discussion of how Catholicism was to be renewed in its universal variety and appeal and his study of the social character of authority in the Church were secondary to the issue of revelation. This was the problem to which he addressed himself in his last book, *Christianity at the Cross-roads*. Again it was necessary to begin with negative distinctions, clarifying the Modernist position from the positions of the liberal Protestants and liberal Catholics. Tyrrell, perhaps because he believed that he had once been too enthusiastic for the liberal Protestant argument, perhaps because the fever of search and disappointment was so strong at the end of his life, perhaps because he knew how effective the papal juxtaposition of the two movements had been in stifling Catholic thought, was extremely bitter toward the liberal Protestants. But he was no less hard on the Catholic progressives. The Protestant mistake was to see the Modernists as liberal Catholics of the type of Lamennais, Lacordaire, Montalembert, and Newman, "a little Goshen of Enlightenment amid the waste of Egyptian darkness," men who, "in spite of the Index and the vigilance of the terrible Inquisition, have dared to read and think for themselves, with the inevitable result of developing strong Protestant and rationalist sympathies." Tyrrell resented the patronizing attitude which pointed to the Modernists' inability to see papal history for what it was, predicted inevitable excommunication, marveled that the Modernists clung to their "childish dreams" of reform, and refused to come to the "only possible conclusion, which the world had discovered centuries ago," i.e., that the "Bark of Peter will pursue its course towards the rocks as before."[53]

The major distinction between liberal Protestantism and Modernism was drawn in a discussion of the consistent eschatology of Weiss, Schweitzer, and Loisy. Tyrrell found in this a conclusive refutation of the argument that Jesus, in his

central ethical ideas, was essentially modern "in so far as
our rediscovery of the equation Religion + Righteousness is
modern, not to say Western and Teutonic." Tyrrell exaggerated the moral aspects of Harnack's essence of Christianity, and commented:

For this almost miraculous modernity the first century was not
prepared. No sooner was the Light of the World kindled than
it was put under a bushel. The Pearl of Great Price fell into the
dustheap of Catholicism, not without the wise permission of
Providence, desirous to preserve it until the day when Germany
should rediscover it and separate it from its useful but deplorable
accretions. Thus between Christ and early Catholicism there is not
a bridge, but a chasm. Christianity did not cross the bridge; it fell
into the chasm and remained there, stunned, for nineteen
centuries.

Somewhat more sympathetically, Tyrrell rejected the liberal Protestant effort to bring Jesus into the nineteenth
century and make him meaningful to a generation that had
"lost faith in the miraculous and in any conception of another life that was not merely a compliment, sanction, and
justification of this life." Thus they had found "the German in the Jew; a moralist in a visionary; a professor in a
prophet; the nineteenth century in the first; the natural in
the supernatural. Christ was the ideal man: the kingdom
of heaven, the ideal humanity." But Tyrrell insisted that
"whatever Jesus was, He was in no sense a Liberal Protestant."[54]

The definition of Modernism, apart from the liberal
Catholicism with which it had been confused, was made on
the issues of history and development. Tyrrell insisted that
the fundamental Modernist challenge to orthodoxy was the-

ological, not social or political. The liberal Catholics of the old school believed that the categories of Catholicism "were elastic enough to accommodate themselves to the latest requirement of modern life—ethical, economical, and social." They argued for the "energetic development of those categories along the old lines without any change of direction," and they entertained the hope ("which no sane Modernist entertains for a day) that some spiritual-minded Pope might one day, in spite of the bureaucracy that exploits his primacy as a political asset, approve and give force to their ideas." The important point was that "any sort of revolution seemed to them incompatible with substantial continuity." The discoveries of biological evolution, scientific biblical study, and the comparative history of religions had made the liberal Catholic position untenable. The Modernist was convinced that Catholic Christianity could not live much longer on the old lines, that it had come to a stone wall which it must surmount "unless it be content to dwindle away as it is even now doing."

Tyrrell's introductory statement of the Modernist's religious philosophy was uncompromising. Admitting that the approach of *L'Evangile et l'Eglise* was no longer possible, Tyrrell said that the time had come for a criticism of all religious categories, not merely those of Catholicism. There was some confusion—or mystification—still lurking in the call for revolution: on the one hand, the "very ideas of religion, of revelation, of institutionalism, etc.," were being called into question; on the other hand, it was only the "current expression" of those ideas which was "provisional." The Modernist believed that "the Catholic Christian Idea contains, within itself, the power continually to revise its categories, and to shape its embodiment to its growth." He also held that "such a transformation or revolution" for the modern period "would be within the orderly process of its life—merely a step forwards from a confused and instinctive, to a fuller and better, self-consciousness." The element of paradox, always strong in Tyrrell's thought, had now come to mastery:

The Modernist's confidence in Christianity may be misplaced, but it cannot be dispatched in a smart article or encyclical. We may be sure that religion, the deepest and most universal exigency of man's nature, will survive. We cannot be so sure that any particular expression of the religious idea will survive. Nay, we may be sure that all must perish, that none can ever be perpetual and universal save that which shall at last recognize and conform to the laws of the religious process, as they come to be established by reflection on wider experience.[55]

The problem was "not Catholicism, but Christ and Christianity." And "should Christianity be unable, or unwilling, to conform to these laws, it must perish, like every other attempt to discover a universal religion as catholic as science." Clearly the Modernist was far in advance of the liberal Catholic with whom he was confused—and, of course, was utterly opposed to traditional orthodoxy. The different views the Modernist held on the process of growth in religion established the central direction of Modernist proposals for moving Christianity and the Church beyond the crossroads onto the true path. Tyrrell admitted that, from the orthodox static point of view, Modernism was indeed the compendium of all heresies as the pope had claimed. "Former heresies . . . questioned this or that dogma, this or that ecclesiastical institution. Modernism criticizes the very idea of dogma, of . . . revelation." If some defense could be made for theological

Modernism, its "milder forms"—social and political—would become "defensible *a fortiori*."[56]

As a way of setting the Modernist position in clear opposition to that of the liberals, Tyrrell reviewed the various official and unofficial "hypotheses" which had been used to explain the development of Catholicism. The *disciplina arcani* he identified with the explicatory school of Bossuet. Tyrrell called it "the old orthodoxy." This teaching, defended by the Fathers and the councils, according to Tyrrell, held that the doctrines and essential institutions of the Catholic Chuch have been "always and identically the same." "The whole dogmatic sacramental, and hierarchic system, as it now stands, was delivered in detail by Christ to His apostles and their successors"—if not the very words, then the very substance of the decrees of Trent and Vatican I, as well as the earlier institutions of sacraments and hierarchy. On the basis of this view, Pius X taught in one of his early encyclicals that the dogma of the Immaculate Conception was familiar to the primitive Christians, if not to the patriarchs. In this view, the sole function of the Holy Ghost was to stimulate the Christian memory from time to time. Nothing new had ever been introduced: definitions have always been of revealed truths themselves or of other truths necessarily connected with revealed truths.

Tyrrell once more gave as his example the Immaculate Conception as having been the faith of the Church "always as well as everywhere." This doctrine was opposed by a minority of innovators which included Augustine, Bernard, Thomas Aquinas, and Anselm—"heretics in good faith, but none the less heretics." When images of development were admitted to this orthodox view, they were complementary, since they were all based on a preepigenetic view of organic

growth. Namely, they assumed that the seed or germ or
embryo was a complete miniature of the mature organism.
The true metaphor for the orthodox school was that of the
Council of Florence, which compared efflorescent Catholicism with primitive Christianity as in the same relationship, as the same cloak now folded up, now spread out.[57]

Tyrrell felt that, with all its weaknesses, the "old orthodoxy" of Bossuet had some advantages over its modern successor, the dialectical approach, which deduced the implicit
contents of belief from elements already explicit. "In the old
view revelation was guarded by the infallible memory of
the faithful collectively. To know what was of faith was not
a question of speculation and argument, but of observation."
According to the newer dialectical view, "revelation is
guarded by the infallible understanding of the episcopate in
ecumenical debate—infallible in deducing the logical consequences of the faith of past generations, and adding them
to the ever-growing body of explicit and actual beliefs." As
Tyrrell read the dialectical approach, its ultimate conclusion
was that "the body of actual beliefs . . . is susceptible of indefinite increase." But how was this view to be squared with
the facts of church history? Clearly the Fathers and the
councils had no such idea of logical development in mind.
If drawing one premise from another was what they had
meant by *semper, ubique, ab omnibus,* why didn't they say
as much? For surely the idea of dialectical development was
as old as civilization. The only result of this approach was a
"torturing of texts and documents incompatible with any
sort of historical sincerity."[58]

Tyrrell admitted that there was another approach to doctrinal and institutional growth: that of Newman, who was
mistakenly accounted the father of Modernism by those who

did not see that his notion of development was not at all evolutionary. Tyrrell, who had deeply resented the attempt of the progressives and moderate liberals to clear Newman of any connection with the ideas condemned in *Pascendi,* and had spoken in the *Times* articles of the "modern and Newmanistic" theory as over against the Scholastic view, which saw Christian faith "packed up in a single portman-teau-idea rather than as vitally evolved from a single germ," was still ambiguous in assessing the connection between New-man and Modernism. He described Newman's definition of revelation as an idea, not in the sense of an intellectual concept, but as a "spiritual force or impetus." He said that Newman knew that the dialectical idea was inadequate to the growing knowledge of church history, and argued that Newman himself must have known that when the Fathers spoke of the unbroken identity of the faith, they were not thinking of an "idea," but of "a dogmatic system" which neither had been nor could be developed. At the same time, Tyrrell classed Newman with the (conservative) liberals who sought to preserve the integrity of the Catholic tradition "from the corrosive atmosphere of rationalism and liberal-ism." He also said that the "Roman Church" was right in being suspicious of Newman's theory of development, since "so far—and it is now very far—as the Roman system has been created by Scholasticism, it can only be maintained and defended by Scholasticism."[59]

As he had outlined more clearly in *Through Scylla and Charybdis* and the debate with Ward, there were in fact *two* readings of Newman. One, taken by the Modernists, followed lines set down by Newman in the *University Sermons,* and argued that "the subject matter of develop-ment is not a formulation of the object revealed, but the object itself ever present to experience. . . . So, the Church of today speaks from *vision* of revealed truth, not from a *memory* of it." The second, taken by the orthodox dialecticians as a complement to their Scholastic approach, followed lines set out in the *Essay on the Development of Christian Doctrine*. It saw the deposit of faith as "an unchanging dogmatic nucleus around which 'additional' propositions ever group themselves into a doctrinal system, ever the 'same' because the central beliefs are *actually* (its subsidiary beliefs are virtually) Apostolical—i.e., identical with the deposit of faith." Whether this second interpretation was true to Newman or not (the same might be said of the first), Newman so presented did appear as little more than a footnote to the logical argument. From the Modernist point of view, Newman's theory had several weaknessess. The least important of these was that it was an argument *ad hominem* created in the circumstances of the Tractarian movement and more concerned with the "idea" of Catholicism than with that of Christianity, which was admitted as a premise by Evangelicals, Anglicans, and Roman Catholics. The real weakness of Newman's theory, however, was that it was constructed with little or no knowledge of the discoveries of modern criticism. New issues scarcely broached in Newman's generation (and, at that time, mainly by German rationalists not read in England) had now reached "the street and the railway bookstall." The problem before present-day Catholicism was no longer to reconcile itself with the Catholicism of earlier centuries (to find in itself and in earlier "Catholicisms" a common "idea" of ecclesiasticism), but to find ecclesiasticism of any sort in Jesus Christ as he is given to us by historical criticism. The modern critic might be willing to agree with Newman (in his earlier and more radical days) that one idea governed the Catholic tradition from Paul to Pius X. But the problem was no longer what it had been for Newman: What has the Church been; what has it taught? Rather, here was the problem: Who was Jesus Christ? What did he teach? Was he a theologian? Did he found a church?[60]

The *positive* argument of *Christianity at the Crossroads* was twofold. Tyrrell first set out to prove that Catholicism, even with its Roman accretions and perversions, and in spite of the fact that its development had not been determined by any fixed and unalterable deposit of faith, was the only true form of Christianity. Then he attempted to prove that Catholic Christianity was the form of world religion best suited to further development in keeping with the principles or "laws" of religion as they were emerging from historical study and from man's deepening grasp of his own social and psychological nature.

In a letter of 1902 Tyrrell had set himself the task of reconciling "the Weiss and Harnack (i.e., outward-future and inward-timeless) views of the kingdom of God." He was then convinced that the two were correlative and not contradictory when properly understood. The future kingdom, which was described and announced in the gospel, in apocalyptic clothing, was the "natural development, not merely extension, continuation, deepening, of that inner kingdom of love which Christ describes *in its own terms.*" In other words, Christ's teaching of the life of love in place of the life of law was teaching preparation for the future development of the spirit "into something over-human in an over-natural environment." Only the historian's question stood as a challenge to this synthesis. The "evidence," as Weiss and Loisy had examined it, left no room for an interpretation of the king-

dom as the long-postponed fulfillment of a process of evolution whereby the spirit in man was perfected in, and out of,
its nature. But Tyrrell was not a full-fledged historicist, any
more than was Loisy, though the latter, for a variety of reasons, foreswore the deliberate theological effort. Tyrrell
resolved the historical question (raised by consistent eschatology in tension with Catholicism) by admitting that Jesus
was indeed entirely limited by the categories of his time, but
that his followers need not be. On the first point Tyrrell
was never so frank in print, even in *Christianity at the Crossroads,* as he was in his letters, in which he spoke frequently
of Jesus' "mistake about the *parousia.*" Regarding Jesus' belief that the end was near and that he was the messiah, Tyrrell
said: "The first we know was a mistake; the second may
have been." The second was indeed his major concern in the
last book, so much so that Christology overwhelmed science—
at the last possible moment.[61]

The unbridgeable gap was bridged by an immanentist and
symbolical reading of the gospel and Christian history. What
mattered was not "the mortal life and thought of the
Galilean carpenter," but Christ who had eternal life in the
lives of his followers. At the same time, Tyrrell did not dismiss the categories of late messianic Judaism as merely the
integument, the body, which was needed for what Loisy
called "the impulse of will" to make its entrance into history. Tyrrell rather insisted on "the abiding value of the
apocalyptic idea" for its own sake, as a symbol of the fact
that true religion was concerned, not with morality, but
with transcendence. His survey of the historical picture of
the gospel and of primitive Christianity followed Loisy in
many respects, especially in its anti-Protestantism. From the
start he insisted that the original "idea" of Christ was funda-

mentally and inescapably apocalyptic. Transcendence was the content of his teaching and the purpose of his life and death. His messianic convictions as well as his consciousness of his unique relationship to God his Father were not inventions attributed to him by his followers. "Righteousness"—ethical exhortations, moral patterns—was in no way the substance of the kingdom which he preached. "Eternal life was not moral life." It was true that the kingdom was to be "stormed and harried by prayer and repentance," but this anticipatory struggle would soon end. "It would be rewarded by rest in glory, not by the glory of going on." The idea of Christ did not contain the notion of "a reign of morality here upon earth to be brought about by the gradual spread of Christ's teaching and example." Morality in this life was "the passing condition [for,] not the abiding substance of blessedness." Christ believed that he had seen two of the traditional apocalyptic preludes to the kingdom: John the Baptist as the type of Elijah; his own preaching as "the Outpouring of the Spirit." He believed that the third sign, the "fiery tribulations," was imminent, as is shown by the pleas for protection which end the Lord's Prayer. John's baptism was for him no mere symbolic act "as we Modernists take for granted." Christ, possessed by the Holy Spirit, was driven into conflict with the spirit of evil in the desert. Contrary to the pseudo-Modernism of the followers of Harnack, the forty-days struggle "was no mere moral parable, but a visionary experience: and visions in those days were not hallucinations but revelations of hidden realities."[62]

The disciples of Jesus were not missionaries, but heralds of the end. When they returned, his predictions unfulfilled, Christ realized that he must storm the kingdom even more violently. He went up to Jerusalem, not to preach or teach,

but to provoke, meanwhile having made Peter and the
apostles (who had already apprehended the secret of his
messiahship) the chief and the judges of the elect. Now his
life became "a quest of that death which was to open the
kingdom of heaven to all believers." With the crucifixion—
probably brought on by the revelation of Judas, but confirmed only by Christ's witness—he achieved his goal. The
apostles expected Christ's resurrection, having been told of it
by him. "There is no reason to doubt that they had visions
of the risen Jesus." Tyrrell argued that "if the value of a
hypothesis is to be rated by the number of phenomena that
it unifies and puts in their places," then this "hypothetical"
reconstruction of the gospel can stand as history. Transcendence, not righteousness, was the "idea" of Jesus. Liberal
Protestantism, therefore, was refuted. But the liberal error
had its historical basis. For as the predicted and hoped for
kingdom delayed in coming, the expectant Church became
itself the kingdom. The result was that this tendency "to
transform what was at most an ethical religion into a religious ethic" was accentuated by an age which "repudiates
the miraculous and distrusts the transcendent."[63]

After first introducing a theory of ideas to replace the
various notions of the *depositum fidei* which he had rejected,
Tyrrell now turned to the Christ of Catholicism in order to
prove that in Catholicism the eschatological consciousness of
the original gospel was maintained and the transcendental
goal upheld, in dogma, ritual, and sacraments. Tyrrell re-
versed the traditional understanding of Christian sources by
outlining a theory of religious ideas "akin to that Augustinian
notio (or *ratio*) *seminalis,* with which every living germ seems
to be animated, and which works itself out to full expression
through a process of growth and development." The reli-

gious idea was properly understood on the model of modern, not preepigenetic, biological science. For modern sciences, in the "realm of organic life" and also in the life of human activity, an idea was something which directed and controlled growth. It was the good or end to be realized, as much as, if not more than, it was the point of departure. And in both realms the factor of will preceded intellect, so that in its origins the creative idea was more "a volition than a concept," present in the agent, but "not necessarily given to the clear consciousness of the person who wills." Again the biological parallel was drawn, and now referred to the animal world: "animals obey instincts without any knowledge of the ends with which they are pregnant. The meaning of many of man's spiritual and rational instincts is revealed to him only gradually, as he follows them step by step." Man has "instincts" for civilization, education, society, liberty, justice; but he does not begin to create them with a clear conception of what they are or are to be. Put another way, "the form of the idea was contained within its substance." The religious idea, "soul of the lowest and the highest forms of religion," was nothing more than man's will to come to terms with the "invisible and mysterious world." The multitudinous expressions of this urge were in every case "determined by the idea and its environment—the intellectual, moral, and social condition of man." Paradoxically, these expressions could only be corrected by the idea: there was "no practical corrective, since man only apprehends it in the very form that needs correction." This tautology was an admission of the weakness of reason and an exaltation of the ability of the idea, "like Nature," to heal itself and "assert itself triumphantly over all obstacles."

The force of the idea, its drive to triumph over the his-

torical forms of its expression, broke down the biological
analogy, for Tyrrell argued that there was no single "series
of embodiments" for the idea as there were in the stages of
organic growth. Even when the student of the religious idea
found in a certain culture or historical period an "unbroken
series of ever fuller expressions of the same idea," he could
not dismiss the possibility or even the actuality of "other
quite different series" of expressions in the same context.
Tyrrell cited the idea of liberty and the religious idea as two
such volitions which had multiple processes of self-embodi-
ment with nothing in common "but their many-sided and
inexhaustible idea."[64]

The residue of this mélange of neo-idealist, voluntarist,
and pragmatist epistemology (for which sources could be
found in Tyrrell's philosophical reading, from Schopenhauer
to James and Blondel) was the conclusion that the idea embodied in the eschatology of the gospel was to be defined,
not by its origins, but by its end. Tyrrell now argued (a)
that Catholicism had continued the "series" of evolution of
the religious idea initiated in the gospel teaching of the
transcendent kingdom, and (b) that the idea itself still had
meaning in the modern context. The equation of the gospel
of eschatology with Catholicism was something of a tour de
force, similar in outline to Loisy's defense of the Church,
but more inventive and impassioned. "No doubt the expression or form" of the apocalyptic idea was "more ample and
complex in Catholicism than the gospel, but its main and
central features" were the same. Tyrrell's apologetic, like
Loisy's, bifurcated between "Romanism" and true Catholicism as he moved into the modern period. He insisted, for
instance, that the irreconcilable opposition of good and evil,
the kingdom of God and the reign of Satan, was "common to

the idea of Jesus and the idea of Catholicism." To prove this point, he alluded to the repudiation of the devil in the sacrament of baptism and the rite of exorcism.

> . . . a host of mental, moral and physical evils, which science now deals with—not to speak of storms, plagues, and other destructive phenomena of nature—have, till quite recent times, been ascribed to the Devil by the Church, and treated by prayer and exorcism. Even so modern a pope as Leo XIII accepted the fables of Leo Taxil and his mythical Diana Vaughan, and exorcised Rome daily; and the prevailing mind of uncritical Catholics is still quick to explain all the evils of the times by the Devil and his human agents—Jews, Freemasons, Protestants, and Modernists.

How could either a gospel encouraging such practices or a church faithful to such a gospel speak to the modern mind?[65]

To answer this question, Tyrrell now enlarged his theory of ideas, drawing especially on the notions of futurity and of parallel series, and sketched the evolution of the religious idea through stages which owed something to Comte and Frazer. In brief, from a magical stage (in which he sought to appease and control the unknown) man had moved through a moral stage (in which he began to conceive of God as a moral being and to love righteousness for its own sake) on to a spiritual stage (in which he achieved union with God). The great leap occurred in the second stage, when the initial sense of control was replaced by profound pessimism as man discovered the powers of his spiritual faculties, rebelled against his "relativity, finitude, and evanescence," and, finally, came to desire "some sort of union with and appropriation of the infinite and eternal." Relief from pessimism and progress to the third stage came when the religious idea expressed itself in the notion of immortality; the gloom of

Sheol was replaced, first by a false hope for reform of this life in the kingdom of Israel and then by the vision of the kingdom of God in the prophets and in Jesus. Somewhat anticlimactically, Tyrrell announced that the apocalyptic idea of the gospel was nothing more—or less—than a symbol of the goal of immortality. The mistake of Judaism, now being repeated by the Catholic Church, was that in its preoccupation with static theology it took the symbol for the reality.

Anti-Protestantism provided a much-needed cover for Tyrrell's treatment of Christology in the context of this future-oriented idea of the third stage. By repeatedly dismissing the notion that Jesus was in any way directly concerned with righteousness for its own sake, Tyrrell was able to blur the line dividing Jesus' apprehension of the kingdom from the understanding of it that he assigned to Christian history. Jesus' idea of the kingdom and modern Catholic teaching of transcendence were parallel series, developing the fundamental concept of immortality, quite as necessary to man in the modern period as it had ever been, though obscured in its primacy by the materialism and (false) optimism of the day.[66]

The "fact" most accentuated by the rational applications of consistent eschatology to history was the failure of the kingdom to materialize from the skies when Jesus challenged the gates of heaven with his death. Tyrrell de-emphasized this "fact" in favor of those aspects of Jesus' life and teaching which could be disengaged from the "symbols" and "hypotheses" of late Judaism. There was no question but that Jesus felt himself to be the mediator between the natural and supernatural (or "over-natural") orders, that he knew himself to be "set as a magnet for souls, which, magnetized through Him, should draw and magnetize others, till the whole of redeemable humanity in Him, with Him, and through Him, should be drawn back to God." Of the inward experience whereby Jesus "felt Himself identified immediately with the Divine Source of Redemption, we can say nothing," but "we may rest satisfied that, when He claimed to be one with the Father, it was in no mere sense of accordant wills: but had reference to some mystical experience, some intuition of sameness in otherness."[67]

Heinz Zahrnt has written that "we see again and again in discussions about the faith how theologians and non-theologians, believers and unbelievers, suddenly push aside everything that has been said and ask bluntly and briefly, 'Do you or do you not believe that Jesus Chirst is the Son of God?' " For Tyrrell, the dogma of the Incarnation was "the statement of the problem rather than its solution." Tyrrell's Christology was the zenith of the confrontation between the old and the new theology. Tyrrell was conscientious in searching for ways of describing the religion of Jesus which preserved the essence of traditional faith; he was equally conscientious in refusing to use the traditional formulas whereby that faith had been in fact preserved. Refusing to talk of *ousia* and *hypostasis,* he elaborated a modern theory of psychology which allowed for the phenomenon of "possession" to explain Jesus' messianic consciousness. He rejected out of hand the reading of the gospel which argued that when Jesus called himself the "Son of Man," he did so because he felt himself to be "entirely human—The Man *par excellence.*" Though eager to correct what he felt to be the excessive emphasis, in Catholic orthodoxy, on the divinity of Jesus at the expense of his full humanity, and although suggesting that Jesus might not have felt himself to be completely the Christ until he had been glorified by the Father, Tyrrell

dismissed the rationalist contention that Jesus' claims were
the manifestation of "a little touch of the megalomania so
frequently attendant on genius and on the realization of un-
usual influence and power."[68]

As had been the case for Loisy, these questions were for
Tyrrell fundamentally unimportant. What mattered was the
ability of the followers of Jesus to evolve new symbols and
sacraments and institutions which expressed the notion of
immortality taught by Jesus in the kingdom and dependent
entirely on the example of his life:

The faith in His own Christhood that Jesus, by the power of His
personality, was able to plant in His apostles, has been continually reinforced by the experience of those who have found
Him, in effect, their Redeemer, the Lord and Master of their
souls, their Hope, their Love, their rest—in short, all that they
mean by God. For them He had become the effectual symbol or
sacrament of the transcendent through which they can apprehend
the inapprehensible—the Eternal Spirit in human form.[69]

The relationship of man to God expressed in the teaching
of the kingdom, and even more fully in the life of Jesus, was
a relationship which could be stated in a variety of other
ways; and undoubtedly, if Christ's mind "had been stored
with our historical, scientific, philosophical, moral and religious beliefs," he would have given it some other expression
than that of the symbols of the kingdom and the messianic
initiation. Other religions, other stages of the development
of Catholicism, had produced other statements. The truth of
them all "is the same if they yield the same control over
experience. To say that they are but symbolic of the transcendent is not agnosticism, since symbols may be representative. Nor is it pure pragmatism, since the degree of their

practical utility is just that of their correspondence with reality." Jesus himself did not think that the kingdom was a symbol, and there was no point in trying either to make the kingdom a type of modern material progress or in trying to work out a nineteenth-century version of the apocalyptic symbolism, since this would in its turn be as unacceptable to future ages as the eschatological kingdom was for the nineteenth century.

The only remedy lies in a frank admission of symbolism. With this admission, we have no need to abolish the Apocalypse, which, as the form in which Jesus embodied his religious "idea," is classical and normative for all subsequent interpretations of the same. In the long series of translations the original sense may be easily perverted if the original text be lost. What each age has to do is to interpret the apocalyptic symbolism in terms of its own symbolism.[70]

In Tyrrell's view, the symbolism of the gospel was not merely an antiquarian totem to be carted through history by Western culture. This gospel symbolism had the unique virtue of expressing the real interpenetration of the natural and supernatural realms. Apocalyptic thought "knew of earthly bodies and spiritual bodies; bodies of flesh and bodies of glory. . . . Of a disembodied immortality it had no notion. The two orders were not wholly discontinuous; far less were they violently opposed. One language fitted them both." And elsewhere he remarked of Jesus: "For Him, spirit is not the negation, but the refinement of matter."[71]

Tyrrell made his final defense of Christ and Christianity in terms of scientific history. To "apologize" for Catholicism, it had been enough to show that the essence of the gospel was the teaching of a transcendent kingdom behind the symbol

of which was the mature religious idea of immortality: union
of man with God. Next, one pointed out that the idea of
immortality had evolved in Catholicism new symbolic forms
appropriate to each successive age and culture with which it
came in contact. And, finally, the life and example of Jesus
Christ provided for his followers the faith in the full transformation of nature into "over-nature" of which he himself
was the living example.

Tyrrell, at the time he had begun the task of reconciling
the inward and outward versions of the kingdom, had reacted
to another set of influences and seen another set of problems
with which the modern apologist had to deal. If Harnack and
Weiss had presented challenges to Catholicism from within
the Christian world, comparative religious history and the
modern secular sciences had questioned, not Catholicism, but
Christianity itself. Tyrrell's concern for the faith of the millions, for the faith of the intellectual minority, for the shape
of the Church to come, had been stimulated by discoveries
in science which seemed to confirm his personal search for
theism. In 1903 he had written to von Hügel: "The question
of the relationship of Christianity to other religions is just
the *whole* question." Two years later von Hügel summed up
his reactions to the direction of Tyrrell's thought by saying
that the latter "made paganism, as a substance and a system,
swallow Christianity as a spirit and quality, and then undergo
a modification from this, so to speak, swallowed pill." Tyrrell
confirmed this reading a few months later when he told von
Hügel that he had made two great discoveries:

(1) that Catholicism is Christianized paganism or world religion,
and not the Christianized Judaism of the New Testament; (2)
that this is altogether a liberation and a spiritual gain—a change
from tight clothes to elastic.

The first discovery was Harnack's; the second was "an intuition that puts Harnack . . . out of court finally." In Tyrrell's last letters he juxtaposed a deepening faith in the "personality" of Jesus with a widening sense of the "pagan" in Catholicism, seeing virtues and defects not only in all religious systems but in all types of theism. Pantheism escaped the "humanesque" element which held back the religious idea as much as it advanced it; polytheism had the virtue of allowing for "a greater fullness and variety of human excellences than are compatible in the structure of a single character." In one note he wrote: "Polytheism a better expression of the divine than anthropomorphic deism. No room for *all* good qualities in one man. Jahweh cannot be at once Apollo and the Man of Sorrows, Minerva and St. Francis." These speculations marked a growing conviction that religion was primarily about *man*, not about God. What, then, would the religion of the future be?[72]

Tyrrell was now quite clear as to what this religion of the future should *not* be. It must not be intolerant and exclusive, as Catholicism had been preeminently. The jealousy of gods for worship and their priests for authority were marks of the first stage of development of the religious idea. The search for unity must not deteriorate into primitive insistence on uniformity, on Rousseau's return to savagery, on the peace of the desert. The religion of the future must have content, but it must be such as to produce the minimum of disagreement. Nor could it be built on sentiment. Modern "religiosity," a term in vogue to express "the one thing needful, when religion had been purified of all doctrinal and institutional accretions," was nothing more than the consciousness of a need which by definition cannot be answered: "We are to feel the significance of life; we must not dare to say what it signifies." Dogmatic literalism paradoxically generated this vague yearning for the ineffable and the indescribable. Religion must not be confused with the religious need.[73]

The movement away from literalism toward the understanding of doctrine as "symbolical and analogical truth" produced a worse evil: indifferentism (which argued that "one religion [was] as good, instead of bad, as another"), because it failed to understand "any sort of variation and development of the religious idea corresponding to these varieties of its expression." To this misunderstanding of the historical process of growth and development, Tyrrell answered that "the religious idea reveals itself more fully in some religions than others; but in all more than in any one." Even this response to indifferentism carried its own error: the idea of "a sort of syncretic Catholicism, embracing all religions as one integral expression of the religious idea." This proposal Tyrrell countered with a Spencerian argument: religions could no more be blended than genus and species. The varieties of the religious idea "do not converge towards, but diverge from, a point of sameness." The law of religions is the law of "rivalry and hostility," and "there is more reason for such rivalry in the more nearly allied branches of the family." Tyrrell was impatient with ecumenism: "The tendency towards reunion among the Christian sects of today is the result of weariness and decay; of skepticism as to the value of their several systems. The withered branches break off at their point of bifurcation. Union is restored by going backwards to an original state of indetermination." Every religion of the spiritual type has considered itself catholic. Each such system has been an attempt to express "the *whole* idea," not a part of it. A truly catholic religion, whether it was the development of one already in existence or a new type would not achive its position by "sinking differences" or issuing an appeal to "the generic idea," but by containing the main advantages of all other religions, thus becoming "first the principle, and, at last, the only religion in the world." "Such a Catholicism would be the result, not of any sort of reunion, or cessation of inevitable rivalry, but of a world-old conflict, ending in the survival of the fittest."[74]

Tyrrell was inclined to admit that history promised no such victory, or emergence, and that "dissension will ever be the law of the religious world." But a rapid survey of the advances of modern civilization suggested another possibility: a universal and permanent religion based on "a knowledge of the laws and uniformities revealed by a comparative study of religions and a study of religious psychology." Such a construction should not be confused with the attempt of the eighteenth century to rationalize religion. The religion of the Encyclopedists was not scientific, if "scientific" means suggested and controlled by experience. Rather, it was an "a priori construction of a philosophical intellectualism . . . Scholastic theodicy with the supernatural omitted. Hence its marble coldness, its inability to make any sort of appeal to religious feeling. It had not sprung from the heart and could not speak to the heart." The Evangelical and Catholic reactions in England were its results. "From rational theology and rational ethics men sought warmth and color and life in sentimentalism, mysticism, sacramentalism."[75]

Nevertheless, the attempt of *les philosophes* should be respected. And there were grounds for renewing such an attempt. The historical and comparative method and "a practically new psychology" had made possible a true "science of religious phenomena." Of course, science could no more create religion than it could create life; but it had developed amazing techniques for understanding what was normal, abnormal, progressive, decadent, in man and society. If medicine and social science enabled men "to diagnose and cure the ailments of the body or the ills of society, may we not hope to remedy those of religion?" "Why . . . should it be a profanity to suggest that science may come to the aid of religion? Is not science from God and for God?" The natural sciences had progressed from the subjective to the objective stage. Religions could do as well. Moreover, modern science had advanced over at least one sector of Enlightenment opinion in understanding that religion is a part of man's nature rather than a disease—or, at best, a normal expression—of his intellectual childhood. Researches like those of Frazer had shown how fruitful was the irrational in the development of primitive society. The whole history of medicine was an illustration of the way in which science passes from subjectivism, arbitrary authority, and chaos on ahead to "catholicism."

Though "the unity and catholicity of the science of religion" was "a very different thing from the unity and catholicity of religion," its tendency, like that of our Western civilization, to become "cosmopolitan and universal" suggested an imitable analogy for the future development of religion itself. The science of religion did indeed examine all three stages of the growth of the religious idea; but it concentrated on the third, or spiritual stage, seeking to discover "the unity that underlies its multiplicity." Religion had been the source of man's first scientific efforts in the magical stage, the guarantee of his morality in the next, the necessary answer to the pessimism it had generated in its higher forms. As Tyrrell presented his argument, the study of religion was almost inseparable from the thing studied, so that it seemed logical to sketch an influence of the methodology of the former on the latter. "What we cannot create, we can condition." Tyrrell had already presented his arguments for Catholic Christianity as the most "microcosmic" form of Christianity. The neo-scientific terms he had established had, clearly, a retroactive application to the earlier material. It only remained to indicate those which seemed to him "quite objective and impersonal reasons" for seeing Christianity, of all the religions of the world, as the highest spontaneous development of the religious "idea" and most capable of becoming "as catholic and perpetual" as the science of religions had become.[76]

At this point, when Tyrrell had expanded his argument to its widest and most "scientific" dimension, he contracted it suddenly into a narrow and intense range all the more startling for its Christological conclusion. Again the sequence of the three stages was rehearsed, but not merely as a statement of a general socio-religious law. The progressive revelation or discovery of God through the magical-propitiatory and social-moral stages was an impressive one. The religion of Israel presented man with an image of God as "heart-reading." But God was still external to man. The achievement of the third stage was man's discovery that he was "no longer a servant or imitator of the Divine Will, but a Son of God, a free and original co-operator in the Divine work. . . . Now it [was] no longer from without, but from within, that God reveals Himself as a mysterious, transcendent force," for man had come to understand that the Divine Spirit was to be understood as "the condition and foundation of personality. For what is personality if not that which is divine in man, that which makes him master of the determinism of nature of which he is at first the slave?" This was the discovery of

Jesus. Moses and the prophets had pointed to God. Jesus
knew that he could point to himself. "What Moses *had*, He
was." Tyrrell dissolved the distinction between the Second
and Third Persons of the Trinity. "Jesus and the Spirit became interchangeable terms" for Christianity, because "Jesus
himself was the Great Sacrament and effectual symbol of the
Divine Life and Spirit." Jesus, in whom God is fully revealed,
is therefore pure personality, and his personality works on
those of his followers to give birth to the spirit in their souls.
"The spirit of Jesus, uttered in the Church, in the Gospel, in
the Sacraments, is apprehended by his followers, not as a
doctrine but as a personal influence, fashioning the soul to
its own divine nature."[77]

Both the Spirit and Jesus were knowable only in the emergence of consciousness of personality. "The vehicles and sacramental symbols, through which the Spirit communicates itself, are no part of the Spirit." The "accidents" of the revelation of the Spirit in Jesus were unimportant: "the human
frame and mind of Jesus, His local and temporal limitations
of thought and knowledge, were but the sacramental elements
through which the influence of His divine spirit was medi-
ated." To our age he would have spoken differently, but the
spirit would have been the same. Unlike Mohammed, or St.
Francis, he did not teach *about* God, but appeared "as Himself the revelation of God, as communicating, not His ideas
or doctrines, but His very self." It followed that the discoveries of modern criticism made little difference to those
who lived, not by his human mind, but by his divine spirit.
The culture of no one age could contain him. "Had He
spoken the language of the twentieth century, would He be
intelligible to the fortieth, were it His language and not His
personality that He had to communicate and reveal?" Jesus

completed the process of the creation of the human conscience. This achievement made all the claims and all the complexity of Christianity tolerable. What mattered was not what he said, but who he was. Tyrrell had reached a point where he could sum up his apology for Christianity as the essence of religion by defining in a sentence its nature: "The idea of Jesus as the Divine Indwelling and saving Spirit seems to me the very essence of Christianity." From this essence the ecclesiology of Catholicism followed naturally. The Church was the body of Christ: "not merely a society or a school, but a mystery and a sacrament," just as Christ was the sacrament of God. The great error was in understanding the Church as the kingdom of God in a monarchical sense, in failing to see that a truly "Catholic religion will lead the soul through externalism to internalism" and will be able to hold the rational and the mystical elements of faith together.[78]

Because of Christ, Catholicism would not entirely disappear into the science of religion. The science of religion "would, in some sense, be a science of Catholicism . . . a microcosm in which the whole religious process of the world is represented." Of course, to fulfill this role, Catholicism would have to be freed from the vested temporal interests of its present rulers; but "it is not of Catholicism in the grip of the exploiter, but of Catholicism as a living and lived religion, as a school of souls, that Modernists are thinking." Repeatedly, Tyrrell anticipated accusations of "Utopian dreaming" and "delusive hopes." But the "deliverance" of the Church "from the hands of her oppressors within and without" could no longer be resisted. The knowledge that made for reform or revolution was no longer in the hands of an easily oppressed few. Modern scientific knowledge was the means God had chosen to "inaugurate a new epoch in man's

intellectual life" and to extend his "lordship over Nature."
Tyrrell rested at the crossroads with a question:

Shall He do less for man's spiritual life when the times are
ripe? and are they not ripening? Are we not hastening to an
impasse—to one of those extremities which are God's opportuni-
ties?[79]

V

Christianity at the Crossroads satisfied neither Roman Catholic nor Anglo-Catholic. *Etudes* devoted thirty-eight pages to it and concluded: "The Christ of Tyrrell is no longer our Christ." Though preferable in many respects to Loisy, Tyrrell was "quasi-Nestorian"; a "disquieting vagueness" had replaced the traditional formulas of Catholicism, "so plain, so precise, so clear in their unfathomable profundity." The Roman Catholic Church taught the revelation of God *in* Jesus; Tyrrell taught God's revelation *through* Jesus and fell into error. The reviewer was not insensitive to Tyrrell's good will and the honesty of his attempts to be at one with the Catholic mind, and noted that "many pages in the work ring with a knell of agony." Dean Inge, writing in the *Hibbert Journal*, rejected Tyrrell's wholesale adoption of the consistent-eschatological reading and insisted that modern criticism did not make Jesus so subject to the ideas and institutions of his time as Tyrrell believed. The *Church Times* proclaimed that here Tyrrell's "mordant and searching criticism, though still in full evidence, gives way to constructive

243

work." The *Daily News* said that "never had it been more
clearly shown in what sense religious development is possible
at all." All these were the responses of friends of the kind
Modernism did not need. Neither the Roman nor the Anglican reviewer gave serious attention to the social-scientific
speculations of the second part of the book.[80]

An assessment of Tyrrell's Modernist apologetic must work
backward from the scientism of the second part of *Christianity at the Crossroads.* Tyrrell's enthusiasm for the Weiss-
Loisy interpretation of the New Testament and the "original"
gospel of Jesus was balanced by his strong conviction that
the personality of Jesus made the apocalyptic symbolism
normative for the subsequent evolution of the religious idea.
Mankind moved closer to its perfection and constantly re-
vamped the forms whereby transcendence was brought into
consciousness and was enabled to transform consciousness.
No age and no culture had yet evolved an expression, as
perfect for its own time as was Jesus' for his, of the hope
and conviction of immortality, both individual and collective,
personal and racial. There was no such counterbalancing idea
to control the enthusiasm for a "science of religion" which
Tyrrell brought to his speculations about the Church of the
future. His deep despair at the scandal of Ultramontanism,
his conviction that nothing could be salvaged from static
Scholastic theology, and his fear that Catholicism was in the
process of losing its claims to universality made him uncritical in his adoption of modern science as a solution. But
Tyrrell's cultural relativism was consistent: Paganism had
swallowed Christianity and been transformed by it; medieval
Catholicism had swallowed Aristotelianism and been transformed by it; now science would swallow Christianity, and
the cycle would begin again. Tyrrell's was not in any case

a naïve positivism. If there were to be laws of religious growth and development, they were to come from observation (primarily psychological and sociological), not from hypotheses on the physical or biological model. The Church was the mystical body of Christ, and would survive no matter how thoroughly science revised the categories of revelation and worship, no matter how unrecognizable it might appear to the historical mind.

Tyrrell's positivistic approach to the evolution of religion leads to the question of orthodoxy. This was never a serious problem in the discussion of Loisy's religious thought: once the hope of an inward transformation of Catholicism into an evolutionary religion of humanity, uncontrolled by any revelation, had failed, Loisy abandoned even the fragmentary aspects of traditional belief which had lasted through the crisis of 1882–83 and 1893. Loisy remarked that *Christianity at the Crossroads* was a call for revolution, "Christian, but hardly Catholic." A few hours with Tyrrell's works will confuse even the most disinterested student. Proponents of propositional orthodoxy will come away clutching enough citations to satisfy the old Holy Office. Enthusiasts for religionless Christianity, the secular city, or the reign of the Noosphere will all emerge with plenty of grist for their mills. At times Tyrrell wrote in agreement with Harnack and Sabatier; at times, violently against them. His early confession of faith to Bremond owed more to Matthew Arnold than to St. Matthew. But in 1909 he wrote: "If we cannot save huge chunks of transcendentalism, Christianity must go. Civilization can do (and has done) all that the purely immanental Christ of Matthew Arnold is credited with." At one point he almost described the gospel away in terms of symbolism, visions "intercalated into the physical order." But he also wrote: "The value of the gospel is not that it gives us an ideal life, but that life was actually lived. The historicity of [Christ's] passion is all important. The factualness of His resurrection equally so. But the mode, not equally so. What imports is the triumph of the Gospel through His death." Tyrrell inevitably has the best of any argument about his orthodoxy, since the issue upon which he was exerting all his strength was precisely that credal definitions and confessional abstracts of whatever sort were not what Christianity was all about. Christianity was a life, not a belief. Yet he wrote: "In the sense of survival and immortality, the Resurrection is our critical and central dogma: 'If Christ be not risen,' etc." Perhaps Tyrrell's "last word" on the question—words written three years before his excommunication—might be interpreted in the following:

The thoughtful Catholic no longer regards [the Church] as a sharp-edged sphere of light walled round with abrupt and impenetrable darkness, but rather as a centre and focus from which the light of religion, spread over all ages and nations, shades away indefinitely and is mingled in varying degrees of darkness which can never wholly conquer it. . . . He cannot stand so far from the focus as not to share some measure of its influence, however qualified; in a word, he cannot suffer complete, inward, spiritual excommunication.[81]

But the personal dimension of Tyrrell's orthodoxy is less important than the implications of his symbolic Christianity for the faith of the intellectuals and the "masses" of whom he wrote in *Through Scylla and Charybdis*. What was to be the impact on the people of Ely Place, whom he had followed down into the crypt of St. Ethelreda's—those who asked "for blind, not open-eyed adherence"—when they were confronted with a religion of symbols? Perhaps the greatest

flaw of Tyrrell's apologetic was that the best he could offer
was a doubtful truth, like the Averroism of Siger de Brabant:
devotional life for the masses, and evolutionary hope for the
elite. It must quickly be added that, in Tyrrell's view, this
was precisely what Catholicism had always done, and only
failed to do properly in the modern age because the man-
darins of faith had lost touch with the fabricators of modernity, the theologian with the theoretician. In the reply to the
minister of the Comtian religion quoted above, he remarked
that the liberal Catholics (read "Modernists") only asked of
the Church the same freedom for their "reading" of Catholicism as was allowed to the masses in their devotional life.
The positivist wanted to force "meat for the strong" on everyone. Rome "would diet the strong on what is milk for babes."
Both were equally guilty of an "unCatholic sectarianism."
But in *Christianity at the Crossroads*, if not long before,
Tyrrell had made the masses subject to an eventual reform.[82]

Tyrrell was fond of insisting that the Modernist was the
true conservative: it was the Modernist who wished to maintain the richness of Catholicism in the face of Protestant
reductionism, who insisted on full adherence to the original
formulation of traditional beliefs when the so-called liberal
[Catholic] attempted to minimize or reinterpret doctrine in
the light of modern science. A long discussion with von
Hügel over various approaches to the doctrine of the Virgin
Birth produced a less ambiguous statement than any published. Denying the doctrine outright was not in question;
such a denial would not only undo "centuries of developing
mariology" but would challenge Christology as well. The
"plain man" (that is, ninety-nine percent of the Church)
could never believe "that she has not blundered in a way to
forfeit all credit as a doctrinal guide and as a director of
worship and devotion." Denial of the Virgin Birth would

open up the way to revolution. But even mild "explaining" was potentially disastrous; retailing how a belief could have "naturally" developed (as the liberals proposed to do) did not necessarily prove it false, but it did stimulate the critical faculty. "And where the alleged fact is miraculous or violently improbable we have so much reason for saying it is false. I have no reason to assert or deny that you had mutton for dinner yesterday: but I am sure you had not roast bear." (Von Hügel had a delicate appetite.)[83]

Tyrrell but reflected the orthodoxy he criticized. He had been attracted to Catholicism, "the *whole* religion"; and his all-or-nothing attitude toward belief, which admitted of no distinction for the masses between fundamental and non-fundamental articles, was simply a symbolist version of the kind of theological positivism he derided. Tyrrell argued, in writing to von Hügel, that the whole ensemble of primitive Christian belief could not be tampered with at all. It was "an inspired construction of things in the interest of religion" which could not be developed or changed. All its elements, including apostolic faith in the Virgin Birth, "conspire to express one thing—the Kingdom of God." The curious fact was that Tyrrell admitted that matters such as the Virgin Birth were, for the "theoretician," "dogmas in a secondary sense" (in a phrase he attributed to Dilthey). But he did not consider the impact of the above distinction for the "ninety-nine percent." Nor did he consider the effect on them of the following explanation: "When we say 'consubstantial with the Father' is a revealed truth we certainly do not mean that the *expression* is inspired or revealed as is 'Thou art the Son of God.' We can only mean that it is a rational or philosophical equivalent of a revealed prophetic truth. Our *faith* is in the revealed truth, not in the translation." The Church was the "guardian of revelation" and could not add to it in any way; and yet, the meaning of revelation was accessible only to a good deal of scholarship.[84]

But one must quickly add: not entirely. In the *Times* article (and as a theme developed in his letters) he had criticized the inability of Catholic thought to distinguish between "reason and the higher spiritual powers" on the one hand, and "the scientific faculty" on the other—"the *Verstand* of Kant" versus the *"ratio* and *intellectus* of the schoolmen." Presumably, what reinvigorated and sustained the faith of the masses was that they "understood" revelation in the sense of *Verstand* rather than *Vernunft*. This was not a point the "theologians could take": it was as much as saying that the only real way for all Christians was the *via negativa,* the path of the mystic. With an insight which did not inform his last book, Tyrrell wrote to von Hügel in 1908: "Our whole aim is to return to the simple faith of the masses, as against sacerdotalism and esoteric theology." However, the "modern syntheses and solutions" devised to this end "have raised *theological* difficulties in solving *historical* [questions]; and they, the officials, have fastened on the former and ignored the latter." But no clear criticism of Tyrrell on this point can be made. In acute conviction that his search for security had been frustrated, not fulfilled, in Roman Catholicism, he wrote eight months before his death that he was thankful he had not been *born* a Roman Catholic, for "to have had the primary religious and moral beliefs amalgamated with so much that is secondary and disputable is a calamity for those Catholics who are forced to dispute these secondary matters. The baby and the bath are thrown out together."[85]

"Hope, rather than faith" was Tyrrell's personal answer to the quest. "Our best God is but an idol, a temple made with hands in which the Divine will is as little to be confined as in our Hell-Purgatory-Heaven (*rez-de-chaussée; entresol; premier étage*) schematization."[86]

Tyrrell died after a brief illness in July 1909. Controversy did not end with his death; nor did persecution. In the absence of a clear retraction of his errors, he was refused burial in consecrated ground. He, on his part, had left a statement in his will explaining that if he died without the sacraments, it was because he wished to make it clear that he had not recognized "the Vatican heresy." In fact, though somewhat delirious, he was twice shriven. His friend Henri Bremond spoke at the grave, and with a gesture reminded friends and family that Tyrrell lay halfway between the Anglican and Catholic churches of the village. Bremond insisted that "no greater mistake could have been committed about him than the mistake of those well-meaning opponents who looked upon him as the modern apologist of private judgment and individualism in religion." The key to his faith, Bremond said, was the phrase *credo in communionem sanctorum.*

When he was stricken, Tyrrell left the revolution unborn. He could no longer think in terms of reform. In one of his last notes he sketched the need of the time as he felt it by recalling, after Tocqueville, that in 1789 even the names of the months had had to go. He was not unaware how hard a saying he offered to modern man in search of a faith and to the Catholic beginning to wonder what his profession of faith meant. The fever of fanaticism, on the far left and on the far right, would have to burn itself out before reconstruction could begin. "From the ashes a new phoenix will arise"; man would move "from the prison of theology into the liberty of faith." But the immediate prospect was grim; there lay ahead a *"religio depopulata,"* since "for the man in the street God and the idol fall together."[87]

Even in its most consistent and positive form, Tyrrell's

apologetic was not a faith for the millions. But at least it had the virtue of freeing one man from "Gaud" as Ugly Jane with her tongue stuck out. At least it pulled down the kingdom of heaven as "Mrs. Heaven . . . with a huge cap tied under her chin and a red plaid shawl folded across her capacious bosom." At least it let George Tyrrell go.

NOTES

1 George Tyrrell, *The Autobiography and Life of George Tyrrell*, ed. M. D. Petre, 2 vols. (London, 1912), Vol. II (*1884–1902*), p. 92.

2 Even when he was writing with the greatest confidence and originality, Tyrrell assessed himself a rank below the "scholars" of liberalism and Modernism. George Tyrrell, *Medievalism: A Reply to Cardinal Mercier* (London, 1909), p. 105; *Autobiography* II, p. 176. Vidler emphasizes that, as a "thinker" rather than a scholar, point of view mattered more with Tyrrell than special sources. He adds that William James and Arthur James (later Lord) Balfour (acknowledged in the correspondence) were probably major influences, and also Bergson. "Pragmatism, voluntarism, intuitionism, were 'in the air.' " Bremond, as has been mentioned earlier, told Loisy that "a third" of Tyrrell came from Arnold. Miss Petre obscured the connection, if there was one. A friend of Tyrrell's youth said the influence of Arnold was great. Alec Vidler, *The Modernist Movement in the Roman Catholic Church* (Cambridge, England, 1934), pp. 158–159; Alfred Loisy, *Mémoires pour Servir à l'Histoire Religieuse de Notre Temps*, 3 vols. (Paris, 1930–31), Vol. III, p. 268; J. Lewis May, *Father Tyrrell and the Modernist Movement* (London, 1932), p. 272; Charles E. Osborne, "George Tyrrell: A Friend's Impressions," *Hibbert Journal*, Vol. VIII (1910), pp. 253–263.

3 Von Hügel suggested the characterization; Tyrrell accepted it. Even in jest, Tyrrell's estimate of von Hügel was high ("Bremond and I have decided that the Baron is God. The attribute of omniscience is beyond dispute, and the others must be entailed." Tyrrell to A. L. Lilley, n.d., British Museum Ad. Mss. 52368). Mrs. Wilfrid Ward maintained that the friendship of the two men was Tyrrell's undoing (Maisie Ward, *Insurrection versus Resurrection* [London, 1937], p. 187). Tyrrell's friend and executor, Maud Petre, was also critical of an influence which lacked direction and responsibility (cf. M. D. Petre, *My Way of Faith* [London, 1937)], pp. 289–291).

4 George Tyrrell, *Christianity at the Crossroads* (London, 1910; reprinted New York, 1966), p. 270.

5 *Autobiography* II, pp. 414–416.

6 Wilfrid Ward, *Last Lectures* (London, 1918), pp. 207–221, 210–211; Tyrrell *Autobiography*, Vol. I *(1861–1884)*, pp. 133–134, 45, 111.

7 *Autobiography* I, pp. 32–34, 45, 67, 71, 92–94.

8 *Ibid.*, pp. 98–99.

9 *Ibid.*, pp. 104–105, 109, 7–9, 114–116, 119–123.

10 *Ibid.*, pp. 126, 128–132, 133.

11 *Ibid.*, pp. 139, 153.

12 *Ibid.*, pp. 155–158.

13 *Ibid.*, pp. 180–193, 206, 215.

14 *Ibid.*, pp. 223, 231.

15 *Ibid.*, pp. 242–244; *Autobiography* II, pp. 40–47.

16 *Autobiography* II, p. 347, I, pp. 85–98. The course of their friendship is charted in more detail in M. D. Petre, ed., *Von Hügel and Tyrrell, The Story of a Friendship* (London, 1937). Estimates of the effect of the long association vary. Cf. M. Ward, *Insurrection*, p. 187; Petre, *Way of Faith*, pp. 288–289. Tyrrell was always frank and open in exposing his ideas; the Baron was usually cautious and circumspect in criticizing them. It seems likely that Tyrrell never grasped how fundamentally severe were von Hügel's objections. On the reasons for their original contact, cf. Friedrich von Hügel, *Selected Letters, 1896–1924*, ed. Bernard Holland (New York, 1927), pp. 7–12.

17 Some of the *Month* articles were pseudonymous (cf. *Index to The Month, 1864–1908* [London, 1909], p. 97 ff.; *Autobiography* II, pp. 163, 47–70.

18 *Autobiography* II, p. 164. The "French student" was the Abbé Ernest Dimnet, who argued, incorrectly, that "no one had assimilated more profoundly" than Tyrrell "the teaching, or rather, the spirit, of the teaching of Newman" (*La Pensée Catholique dans l'Angleterre Contemporaine* [Paris, 1906], p. 131 n. 1). *The Dictionary of National Biography*, Second Supplement (New York, 1912), Vol. III, p. 545, makes an even more extravagant claim: "much as he [Tyrrell] owed to Newman's inspiration, in learning, critical acumen, and mystical depth, the disciple far surpassed the master." George Tyrrell, "SS Peter and Paul," in *Nova et Vetera* (London, 1897), cited in *Autobiography* II, p. 66; Tyrrell, "A Great Mystery," in *Hard Sayings* (London, 1898), cited in *Autobiography* II, p. 68. Miss Petre could have selected worse passages from the latter work to illustrate the young Tyrrell's adamancy. Cf. *Nova et Vetera: Informal Meditations*, 4th ed. (London, 1905), pp. iv, xxv, 27–28, or better, to show his growing tolerance, p. 97 ff.

19 Tyrrell to Henri Bremond, October 2, 1898, and September 20, 1899. *Autobiography* II, pp. 72–73. On his conviction of his own disinterestedness on theological questions, see Tyrrell to M. D. Petre, November 1900, *Autobiography* II, p. 78 (cf. p. 133); Friedrich von Hügel, "Father Tyrrell," *Hibbert Journal*, Vol. VIII (1910), p. 240. (Tyrrell to von Hügel, December 5, 1902). Henri Bremond, editor of *Etudes* from 1899 to 1906, author of the *Histoire Littéraire du Sentiment Religieux en France depuis la Fin des Guerres de Religion jusqu'à Nos Jours*, was himself under a cloud when the *Autobiography and Life* were published, and not solely for his friendship with

Tyrrell. Miss Petre suppressed a long chapter based on their correspondence (von Hügel, *Letters,* p. 199; Petre, *Way of Faith,* pp. 260–269). For a recent assessment of Bremond, see A. Blanchet, "L'Abbé Bremond, Quelques Traits pour un Portrait Futur," *Etudes,* January 1966, pp. 59–71.

20 *Autobiography* II, pp. 72–73.

21 George Tyrrell, "The Relation of Theology and Devotion," *Month,* Vol. 94 (November 1899), pp. 461–473; reprinted in George Tyrrell, *Through Scylla and Charybdis, or The Old Theology and the New* (London, 1907), pp. 88–105. The new title *"Lex Orandi, Lex Credendi"* was meant to prove that the article was "fundamental" to the essays collected in Tyrrell's two earlier volumes, *Lex Orandi, or Prayer and Creed* (London, 1903) and *Lex Credendi, A Sequel to Lex Orandi* (London, 1906).

22 George Tyrrell, "A Perverted Devotion," *Weekly Register,* December 16, 1899; reprinted in George Tyrrell, *Essays on Faith and Immortality,* ed. M. D. Petre (London, 1914), pp. 158–171. Mivart, a biologist and a convert with a deep commitment to the Church, whose work had been praised in the 1880's, fell afoul of the authorities for a series of articles in the *Nineteenth Century Magazine* in 1892–93. Tyrrell had been recommended to him as a suitable confessor by Cardinal Vaughan (*Autobiography* II, p. 169). A later series of articles by Mivart led to his excommunication in 1900. (See J. W. Gruber, *A Conscience in Conflict* [New York, 1960], pp. 176–187, and J. Derek Holmes, "Newman and Mivart: Two Attitudes to a 19th Century Problem," *Clergy Review,* November 1965, pp. 852–867.)

23 *Autobiography* II, pp. 118, 122–124. Tyrrell's departure from Farm Street merely brought into the open a dissatisfaction with the Society of Jesus which antedated his very frank correspondence with Bremond.

24 He wrote to Loisy (to whom he had been introduced, in correspondence, by von Hügel [Loisy, *Mémoires* I, p. 480]) linking the two works, and claiming the exegete's book was the only satisfactory answer to Harnack (Tyrrell to Loisy, November 20, 1902, *Autobiography* II, p. 394). In this as in subsequent letters, Tyrrell took pains to display his familiarity with German and French critical scholarship lest he be thought "a wholly unprepared and *naif* reader" of Loisy's work (*Autobiography* II, p. 395). On his initial reaction to Harnack, see George Tyrrell, *Letters,* selected and edited by M. D. Petre (London, 1920), p. 78; also, von Hügel, "Father Tyrrell," *Hibbert Journal,* Vol. VIII (1910), p. 240 (Tyrrell to von Hügel, December 5, 1902). The autobiography and the letters are full of references to the changing image he had of his vocation; he was especially frank to Miss Petre, at whose request he wrote the autobiography) cf. Tyrrell to Petre, December 18, 1900, Ad. Mss. 52367; also, *Autobiography* I, pp. 133–134, II, pp. 142, 463.

25 *Autobiography* II, pp. 141, 144.

26 The *Tablet's* response was a sharp attack on liberalism (*Tablet,* January 5, 1901, pp. 5–6; *Autobiography* II, pp. 147–152). Wilfrid Ward felt that the Joint Pastoral marked Tyrrell's move to the radical position (M. Ward, *Insurrection,* p. 187).

27 M. Ward, *Insurrection*, pp. 153–160.

28 For a fuller exposition of Tyrrell's ideas on authority, see Tyrrell, *Letters*, pp. 91–93.

29 *Autobiography* II, p. 209. "The recent biography of Newman, by Père Bremond more nearly represents my conception of Newman than any other treatment I know."

30 *Ibid.*, pp. 111, 99–100.

31 *Ibid.*, pp. 101–102. The letters are to Wilfrid Ward and Maud Petre.

32 *Ibid.*, p. 102.

33 *Ibid.*, p. 210. The articles were reprinted in *Through Scylla*, pp. 106–154.

34 The technique was similar to that which Tyrrell had used in "A Perverted Devotion." *Autobiography* II, p. 212.

35 *Ibid.*, p. 216.

36 Tyrrell to Wilfrid Ward, December 11, 1903, *Autobiography* II, pp. 215–219.

37 M. Ward, *Insurrection*, pp. 165–168; J. H. Walgrave, *Newman the Theologian* (London, 1960), pp. 283–307.

38 George Tyrrell, *Oil and Wine*, printed "for private circulation only," n.d. (appearing 1900), p. 6; *Lex Orandi*, p. 210.

39 *Autobiography* II, pp. 167–175. Even devotional writings were not entirely safe. *Oil and Wine* (which Tyrrell later characterized as marked by a "voluntarism as crude as the intellectualism against which it revolts") had been passed initially by the censors of the Society. Subsequently it was refused the imprimatur by Cardinal Vaughan, who was troubled by Tyrrell's insistence on the "infinite inadequacy" of the teaching of the Church to approximate the divine reality. Tyrrell threatened to repudiate all his books, since he had evidently been misleading Anglicans as well as Roman Catholics into thinking that his apologetic represented at least part of the mind of the Church. In 1903 he wrote that he could get nothing past the censors, "not even the Pater Noster if it were in my own handwriting." But the apparent orthodoxy of the attacks on the Ward school reassured the authorities.

40 Tyrrell to Lilley, September 21, 1904, *Autobiography* II, pp. 184–185. Cf. Tyrrell, *Letters*, pp. 91–93, for a comparable statement on the problem of candor and authority.

41 *Lex Orandi*, pp. vii, viii, xxx–xxxi, 80–83, 86.

42 "Hilaire Bourdon," *The Church and the Future (L'Eglise et l'Avenir)*, printed "for private circulation only," n.d. (appearing 1903), pp. 194, 74–75, 83, 87, 62–67, 40.

43 *Autobiography* II, pp. 194, 297–331; George Tyrrell, *A Much Abused Letter* (London, 1908), pp. 51–52, 52–54, 57, 59, 72, 87–88, 89.

44 *Autobiography* II, pp. 268, 248.

45 The long, painful, and confused process of Tyrrell's separation from the Society is fully narrated and documented by Miss Petre (*Autobiography* II, pp. 224–331); Tyrrell's correspondence with the Society is reprinted in the Third Appendix (pp. 458–506).

46 *Ibid.*, pp. 292–293.

47 *Ibid.*, pp. 378–379, 408–409; Tyrrell, *Letters*, p. 139; *Autobiography* II, p. 339.

48 Tyrrell to von Hügel, January 25, 1903, Ad. Mss. 44929 (cf. Tyrrell, *Letters*, p. 110); Tyrrell, *Medievalism*, p. 70. See also, on forms of the devotion to the pope, M. D. Petre, *Modernism, Its Failures and Its Fruits* (London, 1918), pp. 188–198.

49 Von Hügel, "Father Tyrrell," *Hibbert Journal*, Vol. VIII (1910), p. 241 (May 2, 1904); *Medievalism*, pp. 19, 87, 93–94, 98–100.

50 Tyrrell, *Letters*, p. 95; George Tyrrell, *The Faith of the Millions: A Selection of Past Essays*, 3rd. ed. (London, 1904), Vol. 2, p. 136.

51 *Through Scylla*, pp. 35, 42, 45.

52 *Ibid.*, pp. 60–63, Cf. W. G. Roe, *Lamennais and England: The Reception of Lamennais's Religious Ideas in the Nineteenth Century* (Oxford, 1966), p. 145. Tyrrell had reviewed William Gibson's book on Lammenais (see *Faith of the Millions*, Vol. 2, pp. 80–95).

53 Tyrrell, *Crossroads*, pp. xviii-xix. Cf. Roe, *Lamennais*, pp. 145–148.

54 *Crossroads*, pp. 40–41, xxi; cf. p. 44: "The Christ that Harnack sees, looking back through nineteen centuries of Catholic darkness, is only the reflection of a Liberal Protestant face, seen at the bottom of a deep well."

55 *Ibid.*, pp. xix–xxi.

56 *Ibid.*, pp. xx, 10, 13.

57 *Ibid.*, pp. 15, 17; cf. especially p. 18 n. 1, in which Tyrrell sketches the distinction between the epigenetic and the older view of evolution.

58 *Ibid.*, pp. 22–25.

59 George Tyrrell, "The Pope and Modernism," London *Times*, September 30, 1907, p. 4, col. a. " 'Is it true,' wrote Tyrrell to a friend, 'that Wilfrid Ward is saying that if you read the Encyclical as it ought to be read, back before on a looking glass, it contains a very cautious approbation of Newman, and only condemns Loisy and me?' " (M. Ward, *Insurrection*, p. 268). Cf. *Crossroads*, pp. 29–34.

60 *Through Scylla*, pp. 139–154. Tyrrell was not alone in finding Newman's teaching ambiguous: "Catholic theology, as well as liberal and Modernist, was somewhat puzzled, even bewildered by Newman's psychological theories. They asked if he were speaking of logical or biological development, and failed to obtain a precise answer. Liberals and Modernists judged that he allowed logic too much play; Catholic theologians found biological ideas too much in the foreground" (Walgrave, *Newman*, p. 283). *Crossroads*, pp. 35–36.

61 *Autobiography* II, pp. 396, 400.

62 *Crossroads*, pp. 46–51. This marked an advance over Tyrrell's earlier (devotional) treatment of the Lord's Prayer, in which the eschatological element was ignored (see *Lex Credendi* [2nd ed., London, 1907], pp. 82–250, especially pp. 234–240).

63 *Crossroads*, pp. 60–61.

64 *Ibid.*, pp. 62–64.

65 *Ibid.*, pp. 66–90, 75.

66 *Ibid.*, pp. 115–119; cf. p. 157: "The Churches chatter progress, and the

secular and clerical arm are linked together in the interests of a sanctified worldliness."

[67] *Ibid.*, pp. 181–182.

[68] Heinz Zahrnt, *The Historical Jesus* (New York, 1963), p. 140; *Crossroads*, pp. 177–179, 186.

[69] *Crossroads*, pp. 183–184.

[70] *Ibid.*, pp. 210–218, 104; cf. p. 100: "Our symbolisms of the transcendent vary in value and truth. Like scientific hypotheses, those are the best that bring our life most fully into harmony with the world they symbolize . . . so far as a hypothesis gives a correct anticipation and control of experience it is true."

[71] *Ibid.*, pp. 204, 87.

[72] Von Hügel, "Father Tyrrell," *Hibbert Journal*, Vol. VIII (1910), p. 240; *Autobiography* II, p. 206; Tyrrell, *Letters*, pp. 33–34, 300.

[73] *Crossroads*, pp. 229–230. Miss Petre underestimated the degree to which Tyrrell had adopted liberal Protestant views earlier, as well as the force with which he rejected them at the end (cf. *Autobiography* II, p. 398).

[74] *Crossroads*, pp. 233–235.

[75] *Ibid.*, pp. 236–239.

[76] *Ibid.*, pp. 245–253, 256.

[77] *Ibid.*, pp. 262, 269–270.

[78] *Ibid.*, pp. 271, 278.

[79] *Ibid.*, pp. 274–282.

[80] *Etudes*, Vol. 123 (June 1910), pp. 737–775, 770, 774; *Hibbert Journal*, Vol. VIII (1910), pp. 434–438. The opinions of the other periodicals were quoted in publishers' advertisements for the book.

[81] Loisy, *Mémoires* III, p. 139; *Autobiography* II, p. 398; *Crossroads*, p. 146 (cf. p. 217); *Autobiography* II, p. 345.

[82] Tyrrell, *Letters*, p. 139.

[83] *Crossroads*, p. 4; Tyrrell to von Hügel, February 10, 1907, Ad. Mss. 44930.

[84] By the same token, Tyrrell paradoxically argued in support of the condemnation of Galileo because the confirmation of the Copernican view cast doubt on the cultural context in which the gospel made sense: "Thus when I say 'the sun goes around the earth' I mean 'the Scriptures are the word of God.'" Tyrrell to von Hügel, February 10, 1907, Ad. Mss. 44930.

[85] "The Pope and Modernism," London *Times*, September 30, 1907, p. 4, col. a (cf. Tyrrell to Petre, November 11, 1900, Ad. Mss. 52367: "*Vernunft*=pure reason=*intellectio* of the Scholastics; which Catholics translate as 'understanding' to the bewilderment of the Protestants. *Verstand*=ratio=the classifying, ordering, scientific faculty which Catholics translate as 'reason.' Hence, endless confusion."); *Autobiography* II, p. 349; Tyrrell, *Letters*, p. 96.

[86] *Autobiography* II, p. 416.

[87] *Ibid.*, p. 443; *Autobiography* I, p. 17.

Part Three - WILLIAM L. SULLIVAN

I

THE THEME which unified George Tyrrell's early and late work was the distinction between Modernism and liberal Protestantism. And Loisy's polemic with Harnack established the opposition between the two movements as central to an understanding of the implications of modern criticism and science for religion. Both men argued that biblical criticism was much more destructive of the simplicity of liberal Protestantism than it was of the complexity of Catholicism. Tyrrell remarked, apropos of the results of an application of a scientific theory of development, that all difficulties were resolved by it save that "involved in the admission of the initial miraculous intervention by which Christianity was created." Catholicism, of course, would have to put aside the notion of such a miraculous intervention; but it would not have to become liberal Protestantism to do so, nor would it inevitably develop along liberal Protestant lines once the process of demythologization was complete.

Loisy and Tyrrell were both accused of recapitulating several basic Christian heresies, and a late discoverer of the

more radical dimensions of Loisy's thought saw in him a
vague kind of Unitarianism. Tyrrell in his last years found it
very difficult to maintain the distinction of the divine Persons, and it is possible to cite passages both in the letters and
in the published works which seem to dissolve it altogether.
Both men have been accused of duplicating the religious as
well as the scientific development of Comte, and evidence
to illustrate that contention is also available. Tyrrell wrote in
the sense of this comment quite often: "It is manhood that
moves us, not supernatural humanity. If Christianity is more
than the perfect development of manhood, it is of no use to
us."

But neither Tyrrell nor Loisy followed a course which
would have confirmed the accusations of crypto-liberal Protestantism made by both Catholic and Protestant observers
of the movement. Loisy, who well before the break had written that he was "more positivist-pantheist-humanitarian"
than Christian, found the academy an adequate church. Tyrrell threatened to "pass over to Protestantism or Positivism
or Anglicanism or Socialism—most likely to Nothingism."
Given the strength of his personal faith and his impatience
with all institutions, the latter would probably have been
Tyrrell's choice had he lived—death found him on the doorstep.[1]

The third subject of this study, William Laurence Sullivan, did find a new vocation within the Church. As a Unitarian minister for twenty years after his resignation from
the Paulists, he achieved a personally and pastorally satisfying faith. For some of his contemporaries, his religious
development confirmed the orthodox interpretation of Modernism as a rite of passage to liberal Protestantism. But Sullivan was often as uncomfortable as a Unitarian as he had
been as a seminarian. He complained as mightily about the

defects of all forms of Protestantism as he did about those of his mother Church. He castigated both the dogmatism of the traditional reformed churches and the liberal humanism of the left wing of his own radical denomination. He insisted on the transcendent supernatural character of religious experience, and in his autobiography commented warmly on the unique virtues of Catholicism seen as a social and devotional system.[2]

In these and other particulars he fulfilled the peculiar vocation he had sketched for the Modernist who had to come to terms with the condemnation. In an unpublished essay written during the lean years between his departure from the Catholic Church in 1910 and his entry into the "liberal fellowship" a few years later, he characterized the "final phase of Modernism." It was clear, he wrote, that the Modernists were men of good faith—even the pope admitted that they were morally blameless. It was equally clear that they had failed in their mission "to reconcile the Church and the age, to prove that in the Roman communion was the purest expression of religion and the true house of human souls." The possibility of success for any effort like theirs was dim.

Never again in our generation will scholarship weary the Church with importunities nor democracy disturb the echoes with its robust and ringing call. The entire procession of modern ideas and modern men has gone another way, and over the schools and sanctuaries of Catholicism broods in Buddhistic calm the new Pax Romana.

But for the Modernists themselves, there was the hope of a new career, a "second spring." Its basis was to be found in the frank admission of Minocchi's contention that a

genuinely reformative Modernism within the Roman Catholic Church was "hopeless and impossible." The new phase
of Modernism would transcend "efforts like those of Tyrrell
at constructing a new philosophy of conformity to the traditional statements of the creed."[3]

In spite of this slighting reference to Tyrrell, Sullivan
described a Modernist future very similar to that sketched
in the second part of *Christianity at the Crossroads.* The
fault of the Modernist to date was that he had not gone far
enough in his application of science to belief. He must now
research the history of man's movement from magic to "a
worship which is in spirit and in truth," recognizing the
deposits of superstition for what they are, and purging them
without hesitation.

Religious criticism once begun is not worthy of itself if it stops
half way in its course. Its duty is to explore the basis of every belief, the natural history of whole religions as well as of individual
dogmas, the foundation of morals and the idea of God. It must
study not merely in what manner the Church is one with Christ,
but after what fashion we must conceive Christ himself both as a
figure in the history of religion, and in his relation to the eternal
idea of the Spirit.

For the Modernist, initially, but eventually for "the majority of men," the scientific study of religion will produce "a
change and enlargement in their conception of the world-
order comparable to that which opened infinite vistas to
human intelligence in passing from Ptolemaic to Copernican
astronomy." The work being published in *Rinnovamento*
and *Revue Moderniste Internationale* was proof that the
Modernists had progressed beyond trying to "coax a recal-
citrant Curia to smile pleasantly once in a while upon de-

mocracy and science"; from "serving a sect they are turning
to the ministry of the spirit of man." There was even a model
for this new career: Alfred Loisy, who from his chair at the
Collège de France delivered lectures that were "coldly critical and scrupulously scientific"; who was, "for the audience
of the elite that listens to him . . . a reverent believer in all
that is essential to religious faith—all perhaps that is legiti-
mately possible to it."

Sullivan did not realize in later life the scientific dimensions of the vocation he had sketched for the Modernist. His
talents were rhetorical and pastoral, and what time and en-
ergy were left from preaching he devoted to fiction, poetry,
and polemics. In fact, he was not an intellectual, either as
a Modernist or as a liberal Protestant, in the sense in which
the term can be applied even to Tyrrell, much less a scholar,
as was Loisy. One suspects that a good part of the optimism
of this piece was self-encouragement in a time of trial. Nevertheless, in certain particulars the essay sets guidelines for
understanding Sullivan's post-Modernist vocation. He persisted in seeing religion as in large part the product of the
history of religion, and wrote and lectured on the history
of the development of the faith as an integral part of the
training of the liberal Protestant. He rejected positivism and
atheist humanism, and tried "to apply [his] gifts and spiritual experience to the task of teaching an age that is threatened with materialism that there is something left to worship,
and that human life has transcendental values and august
responsibilities."[4]

But both as Modernist and as Unitarian, Sullivan added
to his religious philosophy elements which were distinctively Protestant and American. Tyrrell had written that
it was because "Catholic Modernism recognizes the iden-

tity of 'idea' of Jesus and Catholicism; because it acknowl-
edges that the apocalyptic elements of Christianity are
essential and not accidental, the moral elements subordi-
nate and not principal, that . . . it faces the conflict between
Christian and modern thought in its purest form." Even
when he admitted the irrelevance of the apocalyptic dimension, Tyrrell still insisted on the paradox of transcendence.
In contrast, Sullivan felt no need to polarize transcendence
and "the moral elements" in religion; on the contrary, he
insisted that it was only through the perfection of the moral
life—the cultivation of character and of an independent conscience—that man prepared himself for the experience of
the transcendent. This uncharacteristically liberal Protestant concern with religion as moral formation shaped Sullivan's major Modernist writings and made him appear as
much as echo of pre-Modernist currents of anti-Roman
thought as an American version of Tyrrell. In the long run,
the sins of the so-called "infallible" popes mattered more
than the critical insights of Weiss or Harnack; and Acton
and Martineau and Matthew Arnold were more influential
in his intellectual development than Houtin and Loisy.[5]

How significant was Modernism in America? Those most
intimately involved in the crisis in Europe did not know
that the movement had any repercussions in the United
States. Sullivan had been invited to attend an international
congress in honor of Père Hyacinthe in 1913, but he with-
drew at the last moment; and Loisy correctly denied that
he had met a William Sullivan, former Paulist priest and
presently a Unitarian minister, at that time. The statement
attributed to Tyrrell in Sullivan's *Letters to His Holiness
Pope Pius X, by a Modernist*—"Modernism has produced
there in America hardly an echo. The Church in America

is asleep; and I can conceive of nothing that will awaken it, but the production of some book native to the soil."— probably reflects Sullivan's hopes more than Tyrrell's opinion. Sullivan was only one of several Paulists to leave the order after the papal condemnations of Modernism; and there were other priests, secular and religious, who were affected. Sullivan alone of this group hoped for a new apologetic for the Church, worked toward it, and tried to transform it after the controversy had ended.[6]

The reasons for the weakness of the impact of the movement in America are not hard to find. In the first place, the American Catholic Church had already had its version of Modernism in the Americanist crisis of the nineties. The uproar over Walter Elliott's *Life of Father Hecker*, especially over Archbishop Ireland's enthusiastic introduction to the book, was greater in France than in America; and the polite-but-firm rebuke by Leo XIII in the Apostolic letter *Testem Benevolentiae* was clearly aimed at the transatlantic example which French liberal clergymen found so exciting. Ireland had praised the "pliability of will" which Hecker had applied to the reconciliation of Catholicism and American life, and which the Archbishop had evidenced by participating in the Congress of Religions at the Chicago World's Fair in 1893. Leo recognized that "the rule of life laid down for Catholics is not of such a nature that it cannot accommodate itself to the exigencies of various times and places," but denied that this adaptability meant license to "omit certain points of teaching which are of lesser importance" or "tone down the meaning which the Church has always attached to them."[7]

The condemnation of Americanism had a great effect on Sullivan, who, at the time, was finishing his training as a

Paulist. In his own personal case, the connection between the two movements was a strong one. For most of his contemporaries, the effect of the reprimand to the enthusiasms of a Hecker or an Ireland was to dampen any interest in other dangerous new ideas.[8]

But the Americanist crisis was not the major cause of the failure of Modernist ideas to stimulate a response in the United States. The principal reasons were more general: the low intellectual level of American Catholicism, and the barrier raised between the American Catholic subculture and the general cultural life of the country. Revolutions only appeal to men who know that they are suffering and think that they can do something about it. Moreover, there must be some contact between the impatient ones and revolutionary ideas. The American Catholic clergy was hardly oppressed at the turn of the century. The Church was growing, and there were never enough priests. A man who did not mind submitting to authority could find a full and happy life of service in the priesthood and, if he had any talent or ambition, position and power as well. The contrast with the French situation, or even with that of Catholicism in England, could not have been greater. In addition, it was unlikely that whatever discontent there was would come in contact with any stimulus to revolt. The insularity of Catholic life and the great gulf fixed between Catholic education (especially that of the seminary) and the intellectual tone of the Protestant world and secular universities made a confrontation with modern science, biblical criticism, and modern social ideas possible—or necessary— for only a minority. That minority included seminary teachers and the members of missionary orders. Sullivan was both, as well as a member of a society with a special concern for the reconciliation of Catholicism and American pluralism. His case proved the exception to the rule.

But Sullivan was prepared for the impact of European Modernism well before the controversy. In his autobiography he makes only passing references to the dissatisfactions of priestly training, but his diary of the seminary years reveals in more detail his early discoveries of the limitations of Catholic apologetics and gives added force to what otherwise might be regarded as the jaundiced remarks of the middle-aged Unitarian apostate.

II

WILLIAM LAURENCE SULLIVAN was the only son of an immigrant couple who arrived in Boston from County Cork only a year before his birth on November 15, 1872. He insisted in his autobiography on the simplicity and austerity of his parents' faith. "Do not offend God, perform your religious duty, and be true to the Church" were the family maxims. In a manuscript story, clearly of autobiographical character, Sullivan presents the figure of the father as a man of silent piety and endurance, who is driven one day from his work in a paralysis of preoccupation over the teaching of hell. His bench-mate fails to reassure him by admitting that he himself expects to die in drink, and adds: "Sure, all we hear ain't thrue—many a holy man has said things he knew nothin' about. 'Tis a way they have." The fictional parents subsequently challenge the authoritarian pastor, Maynooth trained, over the near-magical circumstances of their son's birth. In the autobiography the historical parents are praised for creating a religious atmosphere free from "fiddling and enfeebling devotional practices."

They reared me sternly, with true affection for me but with no extravagant display of it. . . . Their Catholicism had not a bit of sentimentality in it. . . . They interpreted their religion as a school of courage and decency.

This "parsimony of emotional religiousness" was reinforced by public rather than parochial education, and Sullivan recalled proudly that his lay teachers "had no St. Expedit, the intercessor of instantaneous speed in answering prayers, no Anthony of Padua for finding lost things, and no Little Flower to sugar the cake of our devotion."[9]

A few anecdotes suggest that his early schooling gave him an opportunity to follow this pattern. At thirteen he was shocked to read of the "sins of the bad Popes and certain excesses of the Inquisition." "I understood how heavy a reproach the Church suffered on these accounts, and was very angry at the . . . officials who had not destroyed the documentary evidence of these scandals but left them for hostile eyes to read." By the time he attended Boston College, his attitude had changed. There he wrote a course paper in which he expressed abhorrence of the cruelty of the Inquisition. His instructor asked: "Do you mean that the Church was wrong in punishing heretics?" Sullivan replied that he meant just that, and was sent back to his seat with a warning: "Look out for yourself, young man."[10]

The turning point came at age fifteen, when immersion in Alban Butler's *Lives of the Saints* produced decisions to take the name of the first martyr for confirmation and to enter the religious life. Sullivan went off to Brighton, with the family expectation that he would become a secular priest. The seminary was a joy and a discovery. The lack of "extravagant display" of affection in the family had taken its toll; much of Sullivan's diary for those years is a painful chronicle of adolescent infatuations in conflict with a typical fin-de-siècle emotional piety, in which vocational ambitions for a mission to "the dear children" are simultaneously generated by and in conflict with a most tactile devotion to the "dearest Child Jesus—so beautiful, so innocent, dear, sweet, mild-eyed child . . ." But the "Oh's" and "Ah's" with which he records his friendships with fellow seminarians, at age twenty-four (and with school children in earlier years), are soon displaced by more sober reflections. In spite of his intentions to keep his diary as a record of his soul's growth, intellectual matters soon intruded. The problem of vocation focused on books:

I hunger for wisdom, for eloquence, for all accomplishments, that I may use all for the One whom I wish to be the King and Monarch of my heart.

The outer world, on his brief visits to it, was dismaying:

Well! I am back in the world for a few days but from the depths of my soul I long for the seminary again. The hurry, the grasping, the hunger for self, the vileness, the callousness, the godlessness of the world sickens and disheartens me.

Brighton offered several examples of a vocation whereby the young man could change it all. Verbal portraits of distinguished visitors—Archbishop Ireland, Cardinal Gibbons, Bishop Keane—suggest the patterns competing in his mind. Of them all, that of Ireland was the most powerful. The young Sullivan summarized his talk: "Be in with the struggles and turmoils of the age, for Christ's sake; engage directly in the warfare of the times." The vision was one of action:

the "twentieth century's mighty struggles" could only be
fought by priests dedicated and prepared. This was far more
exciting than the injunction of Cardinal Gibbons: "Pupils,
love your masters."

In the next year a new maturity begins to emerge. "I do
not know how far from right I am, but it certainly seems
most strikingly true to me, that to *know* God and to *know*
ourselves should be the basis of the spiritual life." But the
search for friendship and affection persisted; and the inadequacy of family to answer it was expressed in the short
Christmas entry of 1895, "I was at home yesterday for an
hour."[11]

The tone of the diary alters with Sullivan's passage in
1896 from the "philosophy house" to the "theology house."
With this change came a diminution of piety comparable to
that which Loisy recorded when he arrived at Châlons. Sullivan now wrote:

The love of Jesus has largely become an unreal abstraction. I have
been living an easier but more imperfect life. The priesthood has
been but seldom in my thoughts, self-examination has become less
rigorous. A history that hardly tends to encouragement, certainly.
And here I am, almost half through my first year of theology.

Unlike Loisy, however, Sullivan was able to balance devotional fervor and theological development. The discovery
of the sterility of seminary training had no relevance to his
fervor for the priesthood. What could be termed the "uncharacteristically 'Protestant'" family experience of the
faith did not help him in dealing with the emotional dimension of his vocation. He continued to moon over his
need for love and for "rugged manhood and sturdy strength."

He worried repeatedly over the exact shape of his vocation, and admitted delight and fear in his discovery of a rhetorical power which emerged in a debate in which he defended "humanitarianism" against "super-naturalism." But his background did aid him in dealing with the dismaying theological particulars of his education. The conventional text, Adolf Tanqueray's *Synopsis Theologiae Dogmaticae Fundamentalis,* focused his awareness of the discrepancy between what Archbishop Ireland had demanded in the way of a new apologetic and what the official teaching Church seemed to offer. His negative response to seminary theology was intensified by his sympathetic reading of the anonymous work of Cassels, *Supernatural Religion,* which he read independently of his course of study. The author's "honest rationalism" and his apparently solid scholarship were impressive; even if the author was wrong—and Sullivan had no doubt that he was—it seemed clear that his sensibility demanded some serious response.[12] "Everywhere" in Tanqueray (and in his seminary explicators) Sullivan found "a violent perversion of proofs to give them a prop. Everywhere a detestable minimizing of the adversary's position." The young seminarian proposed another technique:

Give to the theological student the very strongest presentation of the unbeliever's position. Get them to work on it—give them to understand that the anti-Christian or rationalistic arguments are masterly, cogent, and learned.

This approach would be far better than the "personal pleading . . . niggardly one-sidedness . . . nauseating prejudice" and "cowardly unfairness" which made a man "blush for exponents so unworthy of God and of His Christ." Reflect-

ing the impact of Cassels, he added: "It is sad to have to go
to sceptics and rationalists for examples of candor and calm-
ness and passionless exposition." After cautioning any possible reader of his words that he was in no way speaking of
"things of faith—of that glorious, heavenly, effulgent truth
which God has designed to let me see," Sullivan let go:

*de necessitate religionis naturalis—de necessitate orationis et
petitionis—de miraculis,* etc.—his [Tanqueray's] flagrant assumptions, his ill-concealed sophistry—oh! I am sick of it—I am insult-
ing the reason God has given me by learning it. It is trash! Oh, if
thinking men were to read *Supernatural Religion* and Fr.
Tanqueray, I have no hesitation in saying that the latter would
drive more into infidelity than the former![13]

Sullivan apologized to his diary for these reflections: the
project had not been undertaken to chart his theological
growth. In fact, the idea of intellectual development was
meaningless to the author of the early entries. Religion was
for him entirely a matter of spiritual development through
moral struggle with a sinful nature. The conflict was carried on, hopefully to a glorious victory for God through
grace, in a propositionally fixed universe. But Cassels and
Tanqueray in juxtaposition altered even the devotional dimension. The "sweet child Jesus" began to grow up. "I
have been thinking of the strength of Our Lord's character.
It is so usual for us to look only on His humility, lowliness,
and self-abasement that we are likely to miss considering his
awful strength." The discovery of will and of human dynamism in the figure of Jesus had as its concomitant an implicit (and unorthodox) resolution of the problem of his
foreknowledge. Sullivan reflected on the disregard for death
Christ showed in pursuit of his mission among men, and com-

mented that even the realization that he would die "forgotten and unthanked" meant nothing to him in the face of "that for which he came down from heaven."[14]

Sullivan was far from seeing in these new apologetic or devotional directions any challenge to the mission or authority of the Church. If anything, his discovery of the irrelevance of seminary apologetics to the world of skepticism and materialism encouraged both his vocation and his conviction that ecclesiology was at the heart of religious studies. With a touch of condescension bred out of hindsight, Sullivan referred in his autobiography to the resolve of his Brighton days to become "an apologist up-to-date," to be "prepared to meet heretics and rationalists on their own premises, and refute them them for the honor of invincible Catholicism," in spite of the mood of the seminary—a place "for immature minds which were to be kept in immaturity." Sullivan's enthusiasm and loyalty to the Church were in fact so great at this time that his irritation with Tanqueray peaked when the class came to consider the manual *de ecclesia,* because style of argument weakened the impression of infallibility in the Church. Sullivan saw that "anyone with a head on his shoulders . . . can immediately perceive that no study in all theology" compared in importance with ecclesiology. Sacraments, grace, "the Bible itself—what are they as objects of belief without the authority of the Church?" So great was his conviction that he turned from Tanqueray to attack the professor for correcting a student who had affirmed that only on the authority of the Church can we be sure of the inspiration of scripture. "No, said [the professor] —poor man—it is too much to hold that—say, we cannot be altogether sure." Sullivan comments: "Oh! God help us and enlighten all of us. . . . I am sick and discouraged and weary of it all." It was a mood which justified the enthusiastic discovery of Orestes Brownson.[15]

The death of his mother in the spring of 1897 freed Sullivan to make a decision he had long entertained, and he resolved to enter the Paulists, encouraged in his missionary ambitions by a visit to the seminary by Father Elliott, the author of the life of Hecker. His last spring at Brighton was free of theological questionings; the diary becomes joyful. His reception of minor orders in June brought a spiritual visitation when he went to the chapel after the ceremonies were over:

Instantly, the very moment I fell upon my knees, without the slightest effort on my part, Jesus filled my soul with the Holy Ghost. It was as if He rushed from the tabernacle and embraced me. I felt, I tasted, the Divine Presence, and tears streamed from my eyes.

In a later notation on this page Sullivan added: "I still remember this vividly as the most extraordinary visitation of God I ever experienced." But what is most noteworthy in the entries of this period is the theistic simplicity of the "spiritual revolution" he was undergoing. Its Harnackian tone is best conveyed by this entry: "A conviction is filling my soul such as I never felt before but vaguely . . . that God is my loving father and Jesus my affectionate friend."[16]

But the problem of vocation within the priesthood remained. Sullivan's self-image, his frequent reflections on his mother's life, on the needs of the Church in modern America, are all couched in terms of heroism, dedication, and sacrifice. A career in the non-Catholic missions corresponded to the cast of mind which had been shaped by Butler's *Lives*.

But with self-accusation and depression ("Who can understand me? Who can take me in hand?"), he pondered ambitions of another sort. At Lake George he recalled his
ambition, conceived after reading *Supernatural Religion,*
of "producing a great apologetic work"; later he admitted
his conviction that he could do "study" and might have "at-
tained some eminence" in his chosen branch had he not felt
so drawn to the active life. He had ideas for books: one for
priests and seminarians, one for non-Catholics. He longed
to become "something more than the ordinary" and had
"the decidedly unpleasant feeling" that he was frustrating
"a great vocation." The tension between the missionary
career and inchoate intellectual aspirations was resolved in
Washington, first in the direction of scholarship, and then
away from it. In March 1898 Sullivan wrote that he was
"learning depths yet unsounded of the spiritual life" from
his course in dogmatic theology. "The trinity—predestina-
tion—creation—the supernatural order—*salus reparata*—
what a magnificent universe of thrilling truth in all these!"
But a little less than a year later his enthusiasm had evap-
orated: "I who once looked so longingly to a life of study,
who abandoned it [in leaving Brighton] with so many re-
grets, I now think that I should pine away in a year or two if
I had to enter upon it."[17]

The autobiography is sparse in its discussion of his Washington years. Looking back, Sullivan recalled the "joyous
fraternity" of the Paulists. In fact, he continued to suffer
from the need for strong and intimate friendships, and continued to worry over their implications for his "manhood"
and the selflessness of his priestly vocation. He found the
theology in Washington little better than that of Boston.
The professor of dogmatics traveled through the Trinity

"as if it were our backyard," and taught the entire year
"without reference to the Scriptural difficulties and with no
concern for any . . . difficulty which might not have dated
from the thirteenth century." Sullivan "marvelled how a
man could live with his body in the nineteenth century and
his mind in the twelfth, the tenth, or the fifth." Semi-favor-
able references were made to the scripture professor, who
had at least "dipped his fingers in the sea of criticism" and
argued openly that *Providentissimus Deus* was not an infallible utterance but "the private expression of Joachim
Pecci the theologian," and to a history course which gave
him valuable training in "estimating the value of sources
and coming to personal conclusions upon debatable points."[18]

The notes and fragments upon which Sullivan drew for
these memories and evaluations were more explicit; but
nothing in them challenges his estimate, thirty years later,
of the circumstances of his ordination in 1899:

I dare say it will be hard for some of my readers to understand,
but it is the truth nevertheless, that despite the sparse symptoms of
liberalism thus far mentioned, I was ordained as fervent in
orthodoxy as any man could be. . . . The sins of Popes and
prelates I knew from church history; the unwisdom of some of
their policies I recognized from present history; the inadequate
education of priests I had observed in my own experience, short
as it was. But all this touched no doctrine of the Church. . . . In
a flood of joy, and with a hunger of zeal, I entered upon the
ancient ministry.[19]

For two years after ordination Sullivan's career was ex-
ternally activist. He became a missionary in the south. He
was quickly overwhelmed by the "appalling revelation which
the confessional, in both great cities and country districts,"

flung upon him. Initial responses of confusion and pity were transformed into a moral absolutism. His preaching grew "sterner and sterner," his judgments "more swift and harsh." He saw himself in a fight to the finish which required him to hold "evil as evil everywhere and in whomsover, without respect of persons or station." But on long lonely "Nights in the South"—the title of fragment of a poem written during this period—Sullivan continued to worry about the "characteristics of the church's new apology." In his notebooks he copied out poems by Browning, Byron, and Wordsworth, and mused on topics like the priest's training and "the church and the age."[20]

If his confessional judgments were stern, his private reflections were liberal. On heresy he wrote:

Errors are not rightly treated in our theological courts. Most of them are simply the best guess that tortured, questioning, truth-loving souls could make. Students should be taught this—to see the *soul-question,* the pathos beneath the error—then be shown the glorious complement of the broken truth in Catholicity.

Clearly Sullivan's sympathies were going out to the non-Catholic, if not in the south, then at least in modern literature.

How little of *life* or *heart,* of *warm-bloodedness* in our classrooms! We refute Arius and Sabellius and construct syllogisms . . . and how many have ever felt their eyes wet because a Wordsworth, an Emerson, a Burke, a deQuincey found not the Church. These men are laying bare bleeding hearts. Why do we turn aside with our oil and wine to pour them upon skeletons bleached white five centuries ago? Oh! That Christ's dear evangel should whither up the hearts of those who know it best! *Life—heart*—there is none of it in seminaries.

A little scenario, called "Dialogue in a Cloister," makes the point. A brother comes to the abbot and tells him that the poets affect him more than Christ, that their ideals seem closer to his soul. The abbot gives him a book entitled *The Philosophy of the Soul*.

Sullivan's enthusiasm for the Church as it might be is only matched by his love for his country and democracy. The linking of the two was the theme of the articles he wrote during this period, but they lacked the fervor he allowed to his notebooks. Democracy in fact brought men nearer to religion, whether they knew it or not, by teaching them "new ideas of sublime nobility." Seminary logic did the rest: "Now the nobler a man's thought of himself and his race, the nearer he is to God and to Christ, for the grander will be his conception of the *consortium divinae naturae* which God offers him." In spite of his moral failings, man was great in his salvation. "The glory of redeemed man, it is impossible to extol too high. Insist on this—and you have a nation of noble men." Another theme of the articles, and of Modernism, was sketched. Protestantism was not a viable progress from patriotism, and it was dangerous in its false humility and its pusillanimity. "Man knows his humility best when he realizes his grandeur clearest." Among other projects was one for a series of sermons on the theme of "Fragments—i.e., truncated truths whose fair complement is Catholicism." Among those listed: "Agnosticism," "positivism and humanitarianism," "devout philosophicism," and "mysticism."

The strains of missionary work limited Sullivan's reflections. The notebook became an anthology of long quotations with very little comment added. But now a great discovery resolved the discontinuities of the active and the intellectual life. Sullivan read Lord Acton. In "the glorious scholar's moral inflexibility" he found a philosophy of history which validated the attitudes his missionary work had fostered: "where evil is, God is not." All other Catholic writers took second place. Newman was was flawed by his subtlety and "churchmanship." "But Acton, the unshaken oracle of right as the canon of historical judgment to which every institution and every lord have to submit," he took to his "inmost heart." From Acton, Sullivan took both the habit of uncompromising judgments and the data on which to make them. The two issues on which he focused were undoubtedly the ones he most frequently had to debate and preach: the infallibility of the pope, and the Inquisition. Histories of the church he judged by their treatment of the sixteenth century. Newman's worst offense was his argument, so similar in style to that of the seminary text, that the crimes of the Old Testament committed at God's command offered an example for the severities of the Inquisitors. To his audiences, Sullivan insisted that such things as "the granting of indulgences for fetching faggots to the fire that burned a heretic" were "a systematic debauching and brutalizing of the soul of a continent, and the worst apostasy from Christ that has even been committed." The history of "that damned Council" (Vatican Council I) was equally offensive, and increased his doubts as to the morality of his allegiance to the authority of the Church. The connection between the dilemma of the historical Church and his vocation focused once again on the conventions of theology:

We shuffle on Church and State—Inquisi[tion] and Inspir[ation] —difficulties as to dogma. It all means we are not living these things which are not held by the inner mind . . . [They] overshadow the imagination [they] live and twist our life to suit theirs. Theology inculcates and fashions a *lie-life*. I must live the truth-life and abandon the lie-life.[21]

In 1901 Sullivan suffered a general physical collapse. He returned to the Paulist house in Washington, where he was assigned courses in scripture and theology—and where he familiarized himself with continental liberal Catholic thought and with contemporary higher criticism. In what he later called his "hopeful" (and naïve) years, he wrote for the *Catholic World* a series of articles which elaborated ideas he had been entertaining since his first contact with the realities of seminary theology and the apostolate proposed by Ireland, Keane, and the Paulists. He had already contributed a review of a French study of the Anglican missions, in which he commended the enthusiasm of a French Catholic for Anglo-Catholic work as an attempt to "do away with national and sectarian feeling" in winning converts to Christianity, and contended that the example of English zeal for primitive peoples should spur American Catholics motivated by "a divine desire of bringing the land we love to the faith we worship." In other early articles he reported enthusiastically on a conference of missionaries in Tennessee, argued for increased missionary work in Japan, and surveyed the achievement of the American missionary program on its tenth anniversary.[22]

In the last of these articles, ultra-orthodoxy, patriotism, and criticism of liberal Protestantism were blended. Skepticism, Sullivan argued, was the reason for the tremendous change from dogmatic firmness to "watery credal consistency" in "the sects." "Skepticism, induced by biblical and scientific criticism, has eaten away the very foundations of the supernatural Church in modern Protestantism." As a church, Protestantism had become "little more than the code of conduct of a good man's conscience enhanced by the moral authority of a purely human Christ who lived without sin or imperfection." Americans needed to be reminded that, in the hearts of the people, their country was "tenaciously Christian" (if not Protestant). This could be done only by Catholics preaching and teaching with "intellectual independence as God's freemen." Catholics in America had to express, as well as feel, love for America by working for the spread of religion: without such involvement, a potentially Catholic America would go the way of a once gloriously Catholic France.[23]

In Washington the scientific element displaced the Americanist. In a review discussion of a book by his old seminary teacher, John Hogan, in which the latter had argued for greater intellectual activity in the Church, Sullivan defined two possible attitudes toward science for the Catholic. The zealous conservative, who allowed "pious traditions, remote deductions, and [private] points of view" to grow up around the truths of faith through "theological speculation," ended up mistaking the extraneous material for the essential. Science could and should uproot such nonessentials, and by indirection Sullivan sketched the aims and methods of this approach. It would include the reform of seminary training and the de-emphasizing of Scholastic thought. He confidently predicted that a "broad, honest scholarship" would be joined to "an uncompromising Catholicity" under the benevolent neutrality of the pope. The argument was that of the progressive, and its mood of hope was echoed in a 1903 article on Montalembert and Lamennais, in which Sullivan hinted at a parallel between the dilemma of French

liberal Catholics in 1830 and the problems of the "thinking
Catholic" of his own day. Surely, the editors of *L'Avenir,*
with its splendid motto "God and Liberty," would be "better appreciated" today. "We are approaching a happier period
when men with great spirit will achieve their successes without their sorrows."[24]

By 1906, on the eve of the condemnation of Modernism,
Sullivan had become depressed and disillusioned with the
prospects in the Church for modern thought and science.
In an article on "The Latest Word of Theology on Inspiration," he surveyed recent developments on the questions of
inspiration, the authorship of the Pentateuch, and the Johannine comma, and then suggested that the acrimonious debates on these issues should be regarded "with unexhausted
good nature, spiced, perhaps, with a quiet grain of cynicism,
while the learned reprisals pass from one camp to another."
He discounted the risk that the critic might end up with
that "attenuated liberalism" which accepts the bible "as an
ethical and spiritual book, but utterly rejects it as an historical document," and insisted that the theology rejected in
one age often comes into its own in the next. "Time, like
the mill of God, grinds slowly, but with exceeding sureness
it crushes men and systems at last into conformity with perfect and passionless truth." The skepticism of this article
contrasts with the hope and enthusiasm with which he first
had approached the intellectual apostolate. In 1903 he had
insisted that what had happened to Lamennais in 1830 could
not happen again. In 1906 the parallel had taken on a more
negative significance.[25]

Sullivan ended his periodical writing with two articles in
the *New York Review.* One, a survey of the state of scholarship on the problem of the Johannine comma, concluded

that the Catholic position was not scientifically defensible. The other article centered on the themes of Americanism, authority, and morality which were elaborated in Sullivan's Modernist philosophy of religion. In the Paulist tradition, Sullivan argued that religion had to bring national sentiment into account if it was to succeed in winning men. It was a typical Catholic error to think that intellect was "the sole element of human personality which religion must satisfy," and a Protestant-democratic error to think that the Catholic's "profound respect for authority" was as ramifying as was commonly held. Authoritarianism was not inevitable or permanent: it was clearly not a characteristic of the early Church. Sullivan sketched a process of historical development whereby the Church, originally ordered by the people, came under the control of the prince in the middle ages, and only subsequently passed to clerical rule. He suggested, as he had done in the Lamennais article, that the Church, especially in America, was passing through a period of transition which would return power to the popular voice. There was hope that the Church would "once more show herself amenable" to the people's "just petition," that "in questions wherein we are not, from the nature of the case, forbidden to speak, we should expect and welcome divergent views, and allow them fair and free expression in a fearless press."[26]

Surveying these articles, Sullivan later judged that, apart from "generalized liberal sympathies," he was as orthodox in his belief in this period as he had been in the seminary, though he also wrote that he was "fated, no doubt, to take a position with the Modernists." But that "did not occur at once, or easily." When the condemnation came, his response was focused on the issue of liberty and authority, not on questions of dogma and belief. But he soon discovered that many of his fellow priests had long been troubled by critical questions, though quite paradoxically very few could see the implications (clear to Sullivan) of their enthusiastic or regretful acceptance of the conclusions of criticism—"strokes of lightning" to them all. One exceptional priest confided that if he could not rationally hold the dogma of the Incarnation, he would leave the Church "as in honor bound." Sullivan admired the honesty, but advised caution. Another priest-professor remarked casually one evening, "The infallibility of the Church will have to go." "He spoke the words with no sign of agitation or sorrow, and no indication that they implied a concern of conscience for himself." Sullivan added, "He knew, of course, that if infallibility has to go, there is little or nothing of Catholicism that can stay." Another came to him for suggestions for a Holy Thursday sermon. Sullivan proposed the Real Presence as an appropriate topic. "Yes," said the priest, "that is just the trouble. How can one make anything intelligible out of it?" Another confessed (in a dramatic scene) his disgust at the baptismal service. "I have been driving devils out of babies for the last hour, and it has made me sick. Come up to my room and talk to me." A learned Dominican told him the foundation text for the doctrine of Petrine supremacy "was, in his judgment, never spoken by Christ at all." An old friend, settled into the routine of parish life, interrupted a veranda chat on the difficulties of finding any place for the idea of God in a universe ruled by mechanical necessity, to reassure a little girl, "Now dear, run into the Church and say a prayer to St. Joseph to find your bracelet for you." The child departed, comforted; and the priest turned to Sullivan and resumed his argument against the existence of God. The culmination came when Sullivan, now himself deeply disturbed, consulted the president of a theological seminary, who turned out to be "far worse infected than the patient he was to cure." "One after another of the Catholic dogmas he tore to shreds. Baptismal regeneration was absurd. The absolute Deity of Jesus no man could lay rational hold on. And as for the Trinity, 'Why,' he said, 'I could no more pray to the Trinity than I could to a triangle.' "[27]

What dismayed Sullivan in the confidences of these men was their failure to realize the moral implication of their new belief, or unbelief, and to take steps to resolve their problems. Even Tyrrell, whom Sullivan otherwise admired and whose books exerted a clear influence on his thought, failed morally in his insistence that there was no sin but schism. Sullivan admitted that Tyrrell's defense of Catholicism by condemning "Vaticanism" was eloquent and ingenious; "but it never appealed to me, and I dare say Tyrrell himself at last saw its hopelessness." Tyrrell's "policy," like the behavior of the priest on the porch peddling atheism with one hand and superstition with the other, was morally incomprehensible. Sullivan found Houtin the most appealing of the European Modernists because he had written of the scandals of church history and had little or no sympathy with those who sought to admit the radical application of criticism to traditional belief and yet remain within the Church. Loyalty like Tyrrell's, though conditional and critical, might strangle the moral sense as effectively as would "prostrate submisssion to Catholicism."[28]

Sullivan could not conceal his growing anxieties. His teaching altered: "Complaints were growing against the liberalism of my scripture classes." In 1908 he asked to be transferred to parish work. He went first to Chicago, then to

a parish in Texas; but it was in Chicago that the final challenge to his conscience struck. A priest-professor at a Catholic university who had heard that Sullivan was in great dis-
tress over the problems of doctrine came to advise him. He
revealed that he had suffered in the same way, but had now
found peace. He had pulled himself up short, closed the
critical studies of the New Testament and the church-his-
tory books, and made a resolution that nothing would ever
move him from the Church or his priesthood. He had resumed the daily recitation of the rosary. The result was that,
although he was pained at the severe repressions practiced
by the Roman authorities, he had kept the faith and was at
peace. "You may call me what you please," he said to Sullivan, "a coward, a hypocrite, a man unworthy of a scholar's
status. I care nothing for all that. Here I am today a priest
and a Catholic."[29]

The interview was scarcely designed to free Sullivan from
"the treadmill of . . . perpetual inquiries" he had begun to
walk in 1907. "Once more, in dreary repetition" of talks
with his fellow priests in Washington, "I had a counselor
into whose head it had not entered for a moment that the
essence of my difficulty was not academic, not emotional, but
moral." The internal dialogue between Sullivan the loyal
priest, dedicated to his work and to the Church, and Sullivan the moral man, dedicated to truth, continued after the
dishonest but happy professor left. Was there, the student
of Acton asked, "in the logic of institution, any place for the
major premise of conscience, any room for the axiom of personality?" The advice of the priest who submitted to "the
logic of institution" could only be rejected. "If that is what
he calls peace, I do not want it, I reject it." Writing of his
departure from the Church, Sullivan notes:

When my time came, I did not take the last decisive step because I discovered that a reform of Catholicism was a hopeless cause, but because a profession of fidelity to an ideal Catholicism, joined to a rejection of actual Catholicism, threatened a shipwreck of all that I regarded as sound and straightforward.[30]

Sullivan's "ideal Catholicism" remained a hope, but as he sketched it in *Letters to His Holiness Pius X, by a Modernist* and in his novel *The Priest,* it had nothing to do with Roman Catholicism and was Christian in only the most liberal sense. Like Tyrrell in *The Church and the Future, Medievalism,* and sections of *Christianity at the Crossroads,* Sullivan had first to undo the false Catholicism of the Ultramontanes. The claim that this could be done within the context of the Church, as it then existed, was superficial in the most literal sense. *Letters to Pius X* was got up very cleverly to catch the clerical eye. Its dark blue binding bore the papal seal, which appeared again on the title page facing a portrait of Pius X, very much in the official style. "By a Modernist" was in very small type; all that was lacking to complete the air of orthodoxy and piety was the imprimatur and the nihil obstat.[31]

Undoubtedly, Sullivan hoped to capitalize on the comparative ignorance in America of the Modernist movement. The anonymous introduction proclaimed the author to be a devout Christian and a good Catholic "in the broad sense of the word," but the tone of the book undid the effect created by its cover and the measured words of the preface. Sullivan lacked Acton's ability to make polemic appear the inevitable concomitant of historical study. His exposé of the Inquisition; his diatribes against the apologetics of del Rio, the Augustinian teaching on the damnation of un-

baptized infants, that of Thomas on the execution of heretics; and his long summaries of the papal scandals, dogmatic
confusions, and conciliar controversies and definitions disproving papal infallibility were passionate and heavy-handed.
In the same spirit, he linked the condemnations of liberal
Catholics with the sad history of clerical oppression. "If
Popes through a long space of centuries have officially taught
theft and bloodshed, it should be in no state of uncritical
and ox-like obedience that we receive their words today."
Tyrrell frequently made the point that the generation of Newman, and of Acton, could not be considered Modernist since
they had not even known of the existence of the critical
material which galvanized the themes of the crisis: inspiration, the nature of revelation and tradition, the meaning of
dogma. Sullivan's *Letters* are pre-Modernist by those standards: the American "Modernist" was still fighting the bat-
tles of the European liberals. Matters of scripture and *early*
church history were given short shrift. Sullivan's moral absolutism focused on the issues of the 1860's and 1870's—and
the 1830's—and revived these issues in terms of the more
recent condemnation. Yet, in this emphasis, Sullivan was
not unique. The Modernism of both Loisy and Tyrrell was
finally overwhelmed by polemic against authority.[32]

But there was a positive side to Sullivan's presentation of
what he considered to be Modernist ideas. If it could have
life anywhere, the ideal Catholicism of the future would
grow in America. There were seeds planted "in the very
air and soil of America" which were "favorable to Modernism," as to all other movements that make for intelligence,
strength, sincerity and independence. "We know," Sullivan
wrote, "what the American spirit is in the political and social order. Translate it into the religious order, and you have
Modernism at its best and purest."[33]

What America had, Rome—or, rather, the "curial perversion" of Catholicism—lacked. Freedom of conscience, the freedom of "developing personality," the separation of church and state, intellectual freedom, were all the bases as well as the finest products of American civilization. It followed that the American Catholic Church, as a part of that civilization, was alone qualified to rescue the rest of the Church from the immoral history, devotional superstition, and primitive (from a democratic point of view) institutions to which papal rule had bound it. It was the job of books like the *Letters* to remove the factors disqualifying the Catholic Church in America from doing its divinely appointed work. The Catholic clergy were poorly educated in the seminaries and, in the Catholic schools, carried on a tradition of inferior education. The Church had, to date, been concerned only with growth and with building. It lacked a native intellectual tradition which would make it receptive to Modernism, which was "not wholly" but "predominantly an intellectual movement." These failings could be remedied through education. What was more, the American non-Catholic was willing to help. He, like his fellow citizens in all the "enlightened nations," was indeed in opposition to Catholicism as the "irreconcilable enemy of progress and civilization," but he knew that this was not the true Church. The history of the papacy—"perhaps the foulest infamy recorded in the annals of the world"—created his aversion. In fact, the intelligent non-Catholic revered the sanctity which is to be found in Catholicism, spoke affectionately of the "sisters who sacrificed their lives for orphans," and bowed his head "in veneration at heroic names like that of Damien." He esteemed his Catholic neighbors as individuals in spite of the government of their Church and helped liberally in supporting Catholic charities.[34]

Yet, the non-Catholic's ability to help in the reform was vitiated by his inability to understand how his Catholic friend could revere as sacred the authority which sanctioned, with "putrid casuistry," autos-da-fé, informers, and "monk-butchers of old women," who failed to see that it was the papacy which "unrepentant and unreformed . . . stands before the modern world with the millstones of the Inquisition about its neck." How can the Catholic not perceive that "obedience *purchased by the sacrifice of* reason is immoral?"[35]

The reason was not hard to find, nor the cure hard to propose. Catholics accepted this brutal regime because they lacked "any adequate idea of personality, of initiative, of the laws of life-growth and character-growth": they were "untrained in the ways of freedom." "Life, growth, initiative, personality—these are not the words one hears in Catholic schools, or finds preached from Catholic pulpits; but only obedience, authority, faith, dumb submission, blind acceptance, the sin of doubt, the pride of intellect." What was needed—and what the non-Catholic world had to offer—was a principle of "developing personality" drawn from history. Through slavery, feudalism, and autocratic monarchy, the principle that "non-representative autocracies are tyrannies" had gradually grown; and, with the growth of this principle, the common man had found liberty in the consciousness of "his manhood received from God." "Thus rose to power that other philosophy, which is to prevail forever; that not only for religion but for governments, man has an immortal soul, a free spirit, and divine rights."

American "nationality" was called into being by the cry that "non-representative government is tyranny," and America was an embodiment of the "gospel" of democracy: free personalities should be governed under freedom. The modern world was being regenerated by the idea of Democracy, which it "worshipped." "There is no measuring the fervor of the loyalty with which we hold it. There is no bound or limit to the sacrifices we would make for it." Eventually even the papacy and the Curia (that "cabal of irresponsible Italians") must bow before "Liberty, the Mistress of the Modern World." The original democracy of the Church, which Sullivan had analyzed in one of his articles, must be restored; and the bishops must regain their freedom. Reform in the Church had always come from the people and would do so again: "a representative government, autonomous local synods, and home rule" generally, would supersede the present Italian and papal despotism.[36]

The second pillar-principle upon which American civilization rested was the separation of church and state. This principle, "another step forward in historic evolution, another achievement of triumphant democracy," could not be abandoned as long as a "handful of [presumably non-Catholic] Americans remained on the continent." The papal contention that a state not united with the Church was in germ atheistic, Sullivan dismissed with vigor. The United States was far from atheistic. Was it not naturally Christian, Sullivan asked,

when it promotes justice, cherishes peace, elevates its colonies, and leaves the human conscience free . . . when its rulers enter upon their office with a solemn recognition of Deity . . . when it invokes divine favor upon its Congresses and legislatures . . . when it provides its simple seamen and common soldiers with every facility for worship . . . when it recalls its people on one day in the year to the thought of their duty to the God of Nations?

Religion had nothing to do with the "harlotry of politics," but a great deal to do with American destiny.[37]

Individual freedom and the absolutism of the moral law

were the residue of the bombast and passion of the *Letters to Pius X*. Sullivan's sources were Acton, Lamennais, and the other nineteenth-century liberals, but, especially, the American tradition. Though pre-Modernist in much of their inspiration and argument, the *Letters* show Modernist marks. Sullivan made frequent references to the comparative study of religions, linked Frazer with Holtzmann and Harnack as a great religious thinker, and drew heavily on psychological and anthropological materials in a long analysis of the parallels between, on the one hand, Christian sacramentalism, clerical celibacy, Christology, etc., and, on the other, various primitive tribal religions. In his effort to present a purified, de-Romanized, and federal Catholicism, Sullivan echoed the major European themes. He found a virtue in syncretism, saw Catholicism as the only institution embodying the universality of the human condition, and insisted that the Church was itself the greatest expression of the evolutionary thrust which now demanded its reform.

But Sullivan did not come to terms in the *Letters* with the relationship of Christianity to Catholicism. There was plenty of material in the book to suggest that its author had come to the radical symbolist position in dogmatics, and in conventional terms the Christology of the book is vague. But there was no doctrinal content to the ideal Catholicism of the future. Loisy had saved his polemic against the magisterium until he realized that there was no possibility of an internal de-Christianization of the Catholic Church. Tyrrell had carried on his apologetic on two lines right to the end, and was able to present a most eloquent and convincing argument for the continuity of the gospel in Catholicism at the same time that he was raising larger questions about the relationship of Christianity to other religions. The kingdom of humanity under the immutable law of evolution, the inward Christ transforming the People of God, were clear, if theologically simplistic, substitutes for the faith of Nicaea, Chalcedon, Trent, and Vatican I; and, at least to Tyrrell, they were not at all the same thing as liberal Protestantism. But Sullivan did not progress, or evolve, from the liberal-progressive to a Modernist, or post-Modernist, or non-Catholic, position in the same intellectually coherent fashion as did Loisy and Tyrrell. There is a great gulf separating the hopeful liberalism articles in the *Catholic World* and *New York Review* from the historicism, moral sermonizing, and religious nationalism of the *Letters to Pius X.*

This is not to say that there was no period in which Modernism and "ideal Catholicism" were not for Sullivan something more than sticks to beat the Vatican. Sullivan did have a vision of the gospel, but it was a highly unconventional one, even by Modernist standards. It was adumbrated in the other of the two works which Sullivan published before accepting a public vocation as a Unitarian minister. The *Letters,* he admitted in a letter of 1910, had expressed rather too much of the "mood of indignation" in which he left the Church. But ill health, loneliness, and disappointment at his failure to publish his poems and stories had not discouraged him in his ambition to write a book describing his "pilgrim's progress from the Roman system to the religion of the spirit." An autobiographical novel, *The Priest, A Tale of Modernism in New England,* was the result.[38]

III

THE HERO of *The Priest* is Father Ambrose Hanlon. A product of Brighton, he is sent to Rome for graduate study and clearly destined for great things in the Church. He returns from polishing what he is soon to regard as a useless scholasticism ("Why had they kept him in ignorance of positive theological erudition . . . he knew the tenets of Valentinian and Theodore of Mopsuestia, but not those of Holtzmann and Harnack"), and is given the assignment of establishing a new parish in the town of Axton, a bastion of rural Unitarianism which has recently been invaded by the "car barns" and Catholics. The Protestants are led in politics by a last puritan, Squire Wakefield, and in religion by a young Unitarian minister, Josiah Danforth. Hanlon has the job of ministering to a handful of "old Catholics" from the Irish immigrations and the new "'talians and Poles" who, like the "Hebrews," are all regarded as anarchists.[39]

Hanlon pays a courtesy call on the minister. He is stunned by the contents of Danforth's library: there are, not only all the latest German critical works, but all the books a New

England Unitarian should *not* own—the *Summa* of Thomas,
papal bulls and decrees, canon law, John of the Cross, Tauler,
Ruysbroeck, à Kempis—and, most shocking of all to the
young priest, "an ivory crucifix hung against a mat of velvet
above Danforth's desk." The two men quickly become
friends. Danforth guides the Catholic into the secrets of
New Testament criticism, and Hanlon begins to realize the
hopeless discrepancy between the "true" Christ of history
and the theological and institutional accumulations of the
ages. The keen-eyed, sharp-skinned, pure-minded liberal has
something to put in the place of Hanlon's dissolving Romanism: a religion of personality and Americanism.

Danforth explains to Hanlon that he became a Unitarian
because he felt that "in that fellowship, whatever the faults
of Unitarianism, and they are many, the greatest thing was
held to be personality freely growing towards its God."
"Truth," Reverend Danforth proclaims, in a criticism of
the Roman system,

cannot thus be fastened upon us like a bridle on a horse. Truth
reaches us by way of reason and conscience, and until reason and
conscience approve a thing as true, no human dictate can possibly drive it into a free intelligence. Personality, Father Hanlon,
is the divinity within us. . . . Why, tears of indignation burn
my eyes to this day, when I think of seventy-year-old Galileo standing up before the Roman Inquisition and forced to speak a lie
against his own intelligence.[40]

Both the fictional Unitarian minister and his inventor held
the word "apostate" as a term of honor. "Jesus was an
apostate. And ignorant authority, brutal, hierarchic, con-
servatism killed him for His apostasy, His magnificent, His
divine, apostasy!" declaims Danforth; and Sullivan, describ-

ing the agony of his religious crisis in his autobiography, writes:

Morning after morning I turned the mind's searching eye upon Christ . . . more and more clearly I saw him as an unbefriended soldier of a vocation destitute of consolation . . . I saw him called a drunkard; ambitious for eminent state, and even for a crown; a questionable character with a low taste for dirty company . . . such to orthodoxy was Jesus of Nazareth . . ."[41]

Danforth treasures America as much as truth; in fact, the two are identical. Hanlon's patriotism is scarcely less intense. To a bigoted Irish priest who has refused to bury a war veteran under the flag, Hanlon announces: "To me, my country's flag is more than secular. It is Sacred." "Rank liberalism," growls the old priest, who laments the passing of "that grand old intolerant integrity of faith which has kept Catholics vigorous."

Hanlon begins to attend Quaker prayer meetings with Danforth's saintly mother. He speaks out boldly and uncon-ditionally against the Inquisition and the Index at a diocesan conference designed to brainwash integrism into the clergy. When Danforth is murdered by the anarchists (who have, of course, been driven to the desperate deed by the con-servatism and venom of Squire Wakefield), Hanlon shatters "that grand old intolerant integrity of faith" by preaching his friend's funeral eulogy in the Unitarian church. For this crime, he is suspended indefinitely by his bishop and ordered to exile in a Trappist monastery. At the eleventh hour the Squire's daughter, as fine as her father is foul, helpmeet of the martyred Danforth, argues with him in a raging blizzard on the platform of the railroad station; he

must honor conscience and country and leave the Church to
carry on Danforth's work:

"Truth"—the passionate words fell swiftly from her lips, her hand
tightened on his—"Truth demands your fidelity, your sacrifice
and your life."
    The last car rolled by; the wild wind rushed after it . . . and
on the platform, careless apparently of the tempest that would
soon be at the height of its fury, stood the man and the woman,
hand in hand.[42]

But more than Danforth's example and Miss Wakefield's
powers of persuasion were needed before Hanlon could make
the decision for "apostasy" which ends the novel.
    As the story unfolds, Hanlon soon discovered that Dan-
forth was as impatient with the excesses of individualism in
the Unitarian Fellowship as he was with authoritarianism in
Roman Catholicism. Young Ambrose could not simply "go
over" to Danforth's Church because, in Unitarian terms,
Danforth was also a reformer, paradoxically full of admiration for Catholicism. As Hanlon and the minister became
friends, and the former moved from a position of tutelage
to partnership in religious philosophizing, Danforth admitted his great admiration for the ritual, cohesiveness, and
historical continuity of Catholicism, as well as the limitations
of individualism:

The individual preaches an ideal; only a system, an organization
apparently can conserve it. The mighty strength of the Catholic
Church lies precisely in this. Its immemorial history, its vast size,
its wealth of saintly traditions, all form an incomparable protection for the spiritual treasure of the Gospel. Man may fall away;

prophets and saints may die; but there stands the ancient system. . . .[43]

Admiration for those aspects of the Catholic Church which so held the "Modernist" imagination that they endured the collapse of Christian faith did not mean movement toward Rome for Danforth, or for Miss Wakefield. She, too, was amazed by the "hardly human power and efficiency" of the Church; she, too, complained of the "coldness" of Unitarianism and admitted to Father Hanlon that Unitarianism was fundamentally inadequate because it could not satisfy "the human side of religion." "The sense of personal sin, the meaning of repentance, the warmer religious emotions, the impressiveness of liturgical forms, the closer contact with Christ, the more intimate dealings with God," appeared to her as admirable advantages in Roman Catholicism: "these your Church enforces upon her children with magnificent felicity." The difficulty for both lay in that word "enforce." Roman Catholicism negated freedom. It satisfied brilliantly the common religious needs of the common man, but it failed to adjust itself to "the ever-progressing rational side of our nature." Reverend Danforth and Miss Wakefield believed, and taught their disciple to believe, that the Church could not preserve its institutional and devotional achievements unless it incorporated into its spirit "that individual liberty, that hearty welcome of modern thought, that less rigid formulation of belief which are so dear to us Unitarians." Unitarianism, unfortunately, had become so much less rigid in its doctrines and creeds as to threaten to dissolve completely. Ministers of the Liberal Fellowship were to be heard "preaching pantheism, or any other sort of ethical paganism."[44]

The attraction of the two systems was mutual in the long exchanges between Hanlon-Sullivan and Danforth-Sullivan. So was the factor of disillusion. After he had been publicly disgraced by his bishop, but before his eulogy of Danforth brought the accusation of "heresy," Father Hanlon fled to the Big City for anonymity and forgetfulness, and sought comfort—in mufti—in a Unitarian service. He was deeply moved by the meditation (it "lifted him into the abode of the Eternities") and by the four-part rendition of the Lord's Prayer, with its "stirring" though "textually inauthentic" doxology. But he was scandalized by the sermon. A young man whose whole approach was symbolized by his pulpit stance—hands in trouser pockets—took for his text a quotation from Herbert Spencer which proved to his satisfaction that the universe was infinite and uncreated and that God was "the name we give to that unknowable hidden life that throbs in sea and sky and star." The narrator and the hero both realized that this was no better than the orthodoxy from which Hanlon was in flight. "The 'old' idea of God was flung out of court" by the cocky disciple of Spencer "with an infallibility of assurance that no pope could pretend to equal. Belligerence, scorn, intolerant finality—all of this there was in abundance; but for the soul, for piety, not a word."

By coincidence, on the same day that Ambrose Hanlon's growing conviction that Unitarianism or at least "some such form of religion was destined to be the final form of Christianity" received this humanistic blow, Miss Wakefield had a similar shock. Reverend Danforth's pulpit was occupied for the day by a Mr. Snodgrass, who argued that all gods were anthropomorphic idealizations and that modern science has conclusively proved that God is dead. Man, Mr. Snodgrass insisted, must cease to scan the sky. He must harness that "outgoing impulse of the soul" which has wasted itself in cosmic speculation and build for it, with it, a home on earth: he must learn to do unselfishly the daily task, "and for the rest try to be reconciled to darkness and unsolved mystery forever." Miss Wakefield reported Mr. Snodgrass to Reverend Danforth with indignation, and ended with a passionate outburst:

Must we admit that the Church we have so loved has no message for human souls except that we must be polite and kind and keep out of jail? . . . If so, let us become Catholics at once; for whatever else the Roman Church may be, she at least is a teacher of God and of a soul that was made for God.[45]

Hanlon had, as a Catholic, theism, the soul, and a social faith; above all else he had transcendence. What he lacked was freedom of conscience, a symbolical reading of traditional dogma—or, better, no dogma at all—and social service. Danforth and his followers had the much-envied freedom, but feared the loss of transcendence in their religion. They attributed that loss, not to Unitarianism's dogmatic vaporousness, but to the lack of social cohesiveness and the sense of community which Catholicism possessed. Yet, as they could see from the unhappy treatment of their friend Hanlon, the possibility of more community had been strangled by authoritarianism and an irrational rejection of the facts of modern life.

The Catholic and the Unitarian at last found the perfect combination of the social and the transcendental urges in a religion of patriotism and character, announced one day by Danforth to a group of astonished women as "the plan." To them, and later to Hanlon, he argued that the experience of the American Republic had transformed the idea of patriotism. The old notion of it was unspiritual and material, a simple "blind attachment of the animal to the herd, of the savage to his tribe, of the serf to his clan" *(sic)*. Such an idea clearly was not one around which a civilized man could organize his life, or for which he would willingly sacrifice it. But the American experience had transformed the idea of patriotism into one of transcendent significance and power. The society and institutions of the United States had been built up on the principle of the essential goodness of human nature, and were devoted to "the purpose of developing free personality to the utmost"; therefore, love of country for the American was not an unreasoning submission, but "the sublime devotion of ourselves to mankind, to liberty, to progress, to the immortal spirit of man." Since patriotism in the American vein was so spiritual, it followed that the only true and intelligent American patriot was the man who cultivated "the spiritual qualities of developed manhood which his country essentially represents." The next step in the syllogism, and its conclusion, were perfectly clear. "But the cultivation of spiritual qualities," Danforth concluded, "is necessarily religious. Let Americans understand that their patriotism is sacred and their religion patriotic, and what a glorious nation we should have!"[46]

Danforth then announced that he would strive for "a patriotism which will know how to pray, which will count violation of conscience as infidelity to country," through a new religious society to be named "The League of Conscience and Country." Its motto: "Obedience to God and loyalty to country are one and inseparable." Miss Wakefield, who had long cherished the idea of a "great, all conquering faith which should win men's minds by its simple and unpuzzling creed" and which would possess "the mystical depth of Catholicism and the rational, modern freedom of Unitarianism" immediately urged Father Hanlon to join in the work of developing the new faith. "Why not write a book together on the Church that is to be?" she asked. "At least why not here in Axton break down some of the walls of division that so shamefully disunite us, and bring us all together now and then in a brotherhood of common worship?" Though she could see no difference between Danforth's proposed league and Catholics and Unitarians coming together "now and then" for worship, she was aware that Ambrose was a priest of "the most exclusive form of Christianity," which had never taken too kindly to any form of syncretism. But might he not be one of that small band of "liberal Catholics" who are doing their utmost to "broaden Catholicism and make it the religious home for mankind," one of those men who "are hastening, perhaps more than any others in the world, the advent of the ideal church of the future?"[47]

Father Hanlon, impressed by Danforth's idea and moved by Miss Wakefield's plea, argued that the Church never could or would "abandon or radically change a single dogma of her creed," but admitted that in matters of scholarship and democracy ("concessions to the *Zeitgeist,* to use an almost consecrated expression") "the Church is certainly remiss." He could only conclude: "To this extent your ideal speaks a message to me. Whether it will ever speak a deeper one, I cannot say." Miss Wakefield left, and "Father Hanlon returned to his study to reflect for a long time on this wonderful Puritan girl, who had come to announce to him a new vocation and a new scheme for a united Christendom."[48]

Hanlon's contact with Modernism proper only came *after* the announcement of "the plan," just as Sullivan's "Modernist" writings came after he had rejected the possibility of

radical revolution in the Church. Hanlon now plunged into
a year's study of "Harnack and Robertson Smith and Loisy,
Tyrrell and Leroy," and made the conventional discoveries:
the gospels were a witness to faith in Jesus, not a proof of
that faith, reflecting ideas foreign to his own understanding
of his role; the apocalyptic teachings were the product of
late Judaism and were not normative for all of history; the
doctrines of the Trinity and of baptism had "grown beyond
what the authentic words of Christ warrant"; the dogma of
blood redemption is the work of Paul, not Christ. Reluctant
at first to accept what he has read, but unable to find, in
Catholic writings, an adequate answer to modern criticism
and modern psychology, Ambrose Hanlon tried to work out
his own compromise solution. He told himself that it was
"better to make the attempt at least, than to cut loose from
the Church, abandon her many helps to the interior life,"
and to throw himself "into a work of disintegration rather
than of reconstruction"; but he could not conceal the fact
that the Catholic Modernist writers "were far more widely
removed from the Church, as a teaching Church, than were
any of the Protestant sects at the time of the Reformation."[49]

As Hanlon progressed in Modernist wisdom, his reputation
for orthodoxy fell. A villainous priest, eager for advancement, made a show of interest in the new ideas and begged
to borrow some of Hanlon's Modernist books. He immediately betrayed Hanlon to the bishop (and was appropriately
rewarded with the purple). The bishop interviewed Ambrose.

"Your patron saint, I dare say, is Hermann Harnack?", sneered
the successor of the apostles.

"I have never heard of Hermann Harnack."

"Ho! Ho! Ho! You are a fine rationalist never to have heard
of the great high priest of infidel criticism."

"He is wholly unknown to me," said Ambrose; "though I have read several writings of a namesake of his called Adolf Harnack."

"Hmmm," said the bishop. "Now what about this Unitarian minister? Is he a friend of yours?"

"He is."

"Do you visit him?"

"I do!"

"You read his books?"

"Yes."

"Do you think that proper in a Catholic priest?"

"I can see no crime or impropriety in it."

"Then you must be given a few lessons in what constitutes priestly propriety."

Hanlon was prohibited from reading criticism for six months, suspended from offering his Mass for a week, and, of course, forbidden to see Josiah Danforth.[50]

During this same year Danforth had been tireless in touring the country founding new branches of the League for Conscience and Country, with some success: "His discourses, so lofty, so earnest, so mystical, so filled with a sacred love of country and humanity, were arousing an enthusiasm like that which attends some extraordinary revival of religious zeal." He still had time, during his brief stopovers at Axton, to direct the process of Hanlon's emancipation and to suggest in a variety of ways that the young priest was suffering as a preparation "for some diviner vocation than he had ever known." In another appropriate coincidence, Hanlon attended Danforth's lecture on "Some Higher Aspects of Patriotism" on the Sunday of his suspension. This speech was the Sermon on the Mount of the new religion, whose central principles were the Ideal, Conscience, and Spiritual Patriotism. With what Hanlon and the author regarded as vigor and eloquence, Danforth argued that though there was nothing wrong with American prosperity or American territorial expansion, the United States had a destiny greater than wealth and empire: it had been given a divine call to bring into being "the kingdom of character," through exaltation of the principle of conscience.

America . . . calls for, lives by, and consecrates the courage of conscience. If some future historian shall ever write the history of our decline and fall, it will not be because our boundless acres have refused to yield their harvests, or our opulent mines their treasures, but because we have abandoned the integrity of principle and forgotten how to strive and suffer in the sacred cause of conscience.

Conscience, the inner oracle and true revelation of God, demanded of all true Americans the "apostolate of conscientious patriotism." At home the apostolate meant a life of service to all, including "wise guidance for the immigrant" and resistance to "the spirit of disdainful aristocracy." (Squire Wakefield was getting ready to fire Danforth for running night schools for the anarchist-immigrant car-barn workers.) But the apostolate of conscientious patriotism has a universal dimension. A people disciplined to righteousness and impressed with its predestined high vocation, Americans will become the "exemplars of spiritual liberty who bend the knee but to Justice, Truth, and Love, and to God who is all in all"; it is they who will lead the rest of the world into the kingdom of character.[51]

Danforth was wildly cheered. "He had set his audience aglow with moral enthusiasms; he had broken down every sordid barrier that hid the Ideal from their eyes; he had given them a glimpse of the shining stars in the high heaven of the soul of man." Hundreds rushed up to the stage to congratulate him, "but he had gone. The words of almost religious veneration that were upon every lip he had not stayed to hear." (Danforth, who earlier had kissed his mother with the words "Blessed art thou among women," became a more elaborate, though hardly more obvious, Christ-figure as the novel moved toward its close.) Hanlon sought him out in his hotel room for a further disquisition on the new religion. Danforth saw its weaknesses; they were those of all such movements. God raised up a prophet, who preached and aroused the conscience and the hopes of men. The prophet always died, however, and "his message will die with him unless an organization incorporates it and enforces it." But if the organization did develop, the message was invariably obscured, transformed, or lost altogether. Thus the prophets of the Old Testament were replaced by the Pharisees. Then "Jesus rescued the pure truth of God from the mass ritual and law. His word in turn was incorporated in Catholicism. Catholicism in its turn was broken up by the reformers. This is the life cycle of religion."[52]

Danforth thought he saw an end to the cycle. "My hope is this," he explained to Hanlon, "that spiritual power shall become so strong and pure that humanity will some day enjoy such a succession of prophetic men as will dispense with the necessity of systems of conservation, which sooner or later become systems of destruction." Eventually vocation to prophethood would replace vocation to priesthood, "but the prospect of this is sorrowfully and dreadfully distant." In the meanwhile the priest-prophet was the best hope, and Danforth insisted that Hanlon was better prepared for the work, since he was the servant of a "mighty religious system" whose corporate power could reinforce his work as a prophet of the new faith and the new kingdom so long as he could keep his

liberal interpretation of its dogmas and could work from
within to adapt the old Church to modern needs. To Danforth it seemed most likely that it would be Catholicism,
"massively fraternal," which would produce the new race
of prophets; and Hanlon would be *primus inter pares.* The
principles of Unitarianism were eternally true, but they were
also "lonely and cold." They were a foundation, "but of what
good is a mere foundation if the structure of vitality is not
there?"

Miss Wakefield, in a second interview, picked up the same
themes. Now that Ambrose had been initiated into the modern learning, she could come out into the open: "Mr. Danforth has a mystical, shall I say a Catholic soul. You, of
course, possess that too; but, if I am not bold in saying so,
you have come to realize that you have a Unitarian mind."
The "inspiring religion that is to come" needed both elements.
"Prophets, teachers, and it may be martyrs, are needed to
combine Unitarian freedom and simplicity with Catholic
solidarity and spiritual richness. . . . I believe that the beginning of the divine work could hardly be committed to
better hands than Josiah Danforth's and yours."[53]

But before Hanlon could move from Modernism to the
League for Conscience and Country, he had to explore the
possibilities for the new ideas within the old Church. Only
when he was convinced that the old Church was spiritually
bankrupt could Miss Wakefield's eloquence and Danforth's
heroism work their full effect on him. Like Sullivan, Ambrose
went in search of learned men.

The first, a doctor of philosophy in a distant city, argued
that he saw God in the prophets who prepared the world for
Christ, in Christ, and in the history of the Church. Outside
these events and personalities of history, he could not see

God. It followed that, since he believed in God, he had to believe in the prophets, Christ, and Catholicism as God's supreme manifestations. Hanlon asked if belief in these divine
manifestations meant that one must also believe in Christ's
personal divinity, the Real Presence in the Eucharist, and
the doctrine of Redemption. Hanlon admitted that, for himself, he saw God wherever God-like lives were lived, and to
some measure in *every* religion, from Babylonian mythology
to the Salvation Army. How could such a belief bind him
to any definite theology?

To this the professor replied that Catholicism was the
highest and fullest revelation of God in the modern age,
as were the prophets in their day. The truth of Catholicism
as a whole, understood in terms of this growing revelation,
contained within it the eternal truth of each particular
dogma. To these Tyrrellian accents were added the argument from scandal: "If Catholicism be false, we are under a
colossal hallucination. It must be true or God would be guilty
of having led nineteen centuries into abomination and
idolatry." This would indeed be the case, Father Hanlon replied, *if* theologies were the core of religions. But he had
come to believe that theologies must change, that "dogmas
must die in old forms to be born in new and freer forms."
Had he been a contemporary of the Nicene theologians, he
would have had no difficulty in believing that the victim of
a Jewish mob was the Son of God. But since his outlook on
the universe differed from theirs, because he lived in a later
and vastly more intelligent age, he could not believe in a
Deity who thus "localizes and, as it were, parochializes himself."

Up to this point the argument had been based on an implicit distinction similar to the one which Tyrrell had made

between revelation and theology. The learned priest Hanlon
had consulted argued that the objectivity and historicity of
the first somehow guaranteed the truth of the second. Hanlon
insisted that revelation was inward and immanent, and
theology symbolic. Neither the "orthodox" professor nor the
Modernist priest made any distinction between dogma and
theology, though Sullivan had given the orthodox theologian
a view of the development of doctrine rather more evolutionary and less logical than would have been likely.

Such an argument had little chance of convincing Hanlon.
The professor admitted that any specifics of scriptural interpretation which he could give would be of no use: clearly,
Hanlon had gone beyond the issues of the authorship of the
Fourth Gospel and the Johannine comma. But the argument
did not alienate him. The professor erred when he shifted
the burden of his apologetic for Catholicism from revelation
to morality, and confided in the younger man that for him
the real value of the Church was the guarantee it gave of
control and restraint in social life. "So far as I am concerned,
if I were convinced that Catholicism were not true, I should
fling off the restraints of moral living, and indulge my
passions according to my fancy." He would cease to believe
in immorality, and there would be for him no basic religious
ideas.

This line of apologetic shocked Ambrose Hanlon to his
moral roots. Incredulous, he asked again if the other man
really believed that "the sacredness of duty, the dominion of
conscience, the high value of human life, the being of God,
all the 'eternal verities' graven in the soul of man" had no
life or meaning apart from the "accuracy of any bible or the
correctness of any system of theology." When the professor
replied, "If I thought Catholicism untrue, those things would

mean nothing to me," Hanlon left with pity and scorn mixed
in his heart for a religious philosophy "as crude as Bossuet's
theory of history." The theologian had a parting shot: the
young man would do well to see one of his colleagues, for
his difficulties were "mainly of a philosophical order."[54]

From the progressive-mediating theologian, whose apologetic was flawed by original sin, Hanlon went to visit the
ideal Modernist priest-scholar, a successful Loisy of the
New World. This Father Fleming's library shamed even
Josiah Danforth's. To German criticism was added works of
comparative religion, hundreds of volumes of oriental
philology, "with Assyrian and old Persian dominating." The
brilliant priest-scholar's position appeared at first to be, in
moral terms, identical with that of his visitor. He, too, was
adamant on the issue of intellectual honesty, unlike his
counterpart in real life, the theologian who had abandoned
reflections on revelation for the rosary. He assured the
troubled Hanlon that he would rather "go to Patagonia and
live on raw fish" than mumble with his lips ancient formulas
which he has not brought to the test of reasonableness and
truth in his own mind. And he saw clearly that the issue of
Hanlon's continuance in the priesthood without belief in
the literal truths of the dogmas of the Church was a matter
of conscience.

In explaining his position, Father Fleming spoke with the
accents of French philosophical Modernism. His dogmatism
was moral; he explained that when he spoke in his priestly
character of doctrines whose present formulations he could
not accept, he simply ignored their philosophical terminology
and concentrated on the value they had for "putting us into
the mood of kinship with spiritual realities and God." But
there was nothing specifically Christian in this moral dog-

matism or in the conception of his vocation as Fleming presented it. He remained a priest because he believed that he could forward "the processes of the diviner life of developing humanity" by using his office and the prestige of "a venerable religious system" to inculcate the "virtues of noble character" in his parishioners. "I am forever preaching conscience, love of truth, justice, benevolence, the spirit of service, responsibility, manliness, and character."

He clearly recognized, of course, that the problems he had faced and resolved, which were now troubling Hanlon, confronted the laity as well. The best he could do was to advise prayer and fidelity to conscience to those who came to him feeling that they must leave the Church, and to discourage vocations to the priesthood. He stood in no awe of the hierarchy: if "certain gentlemen" should take action which would threaten his integrity, or menace his peace of soul, he would immediately leave the Church. But until such a crisis arose, he would continue to contribute his mite toward "that coming kingdom wherein men will be able to distinguish between the vulgar disputes of theology and the eternal verities of religion."[55]

Father Fleming's moral dogmatism, his faith in the rule of conscience, and his hope for the evolutionary divinization of mankind were all flawed by disinterest and near skepticism. Father Hanlon's experiences, limited though they were to the tiny world of Axton, left him no reason to believe that there was anything in the "venerable religious system" which could advance what he had come to see as the essence of Christianity, and his passionate and idealistic temperament made such an urbane Modernism as insupportable as the casuistries of the mediating liberal. Ambrose Hanlon had to go.

"The people are not at fault; human nature has not lost its

God-ward impulse. But the school of prophets is vacant. . . .
All history tells me that humanity has grown better, and
gives me assurance that the progress will continue." Hanlon-
Danforth-Sullivan saw, like Tyrrell, "an era of desolation"
intervening between the decline of the old faith and the
great moment when the new religious spirit seized mankind.
But he did not lose hope. In fact, there is little in *The Priest*
but hope. Nothing approaching theology or philosophy re-
lieves the bombast of Danforth's sermons and the drone of
conversations which scarcely differ from character to character in style or tone. The League of Conscience and
Country is, even as a fiction, a particularly unhappy offspring
of the characteristic pre-World War marriage of the tradition
of the religion of humanity and patriotism. Nationalism as a
religion was a commonplace in more than a metaphorical
sense during the early twentieth century.[56]

The Catholicism imagined by the protagonists of *The
Priest* was vitiated in its symbolist dogmatics: it was nothing
more than a rite, a warmth, and a long history. Their Unitarianism was remarkable for its theocentricity, its fidelity to
the historical character Jesus, and its insistence (somewhat
clouded by love of country) that Christianity was somehow
the normative expression for the religious impulse in man.
Moral absolutism underlay both. There is never any question in the minds of Josiah Danforth, Ambrose Hanlon,
and Miss Wakefield that there is *one* moral law, that it can
be known, that it can be obeyed. Obstacles are admitted.
What Miss Wakefield calls "the Cause" will be opposed by
"the colossal power of unrighteousness" and the slow grind-
ing of God's mills; and, of course, there is the much-lamented
dearth of prophets and the (momentary) weakness of their
own appeal. They suffer "horrible temptations" to despair
of the perfectibility of man. But they do not succumb to

them. History proved human advance, and it is history which is in the last analysis the only reliable oracle, the only perfect revelation—especially history, as it has revealed both God and godliness, in America.

Accepting the new religion of the kingdom of character did not mean a moral conversion for Ambrose Hanlon—or William L. Sullivan. The fictional character Hanlon was much more of a "Modernist" than Sullivan had been: Hanlon went through a symbolist period, and he attempted to liberalize and reform from within. But on the essential point, the moral question, he appears as resolved for reform before he meets the Modernists, and even before he hears of the League for Conscience and Country, as was his inventor. Ambrose Hanlon comes to Axton without a belief in radical evil, a devotee of moral and social progress by virtue of being a child of his time. He has most of his "Unitarian mind" before he meets Reverend Danforth, probably because what Miss Wakefield so named was nothing more than an American mind, confident, optimistic, full of the social gospel, marching with history; a mind *positive* in the tradition of both Auguste Comte and Norman Vincent Peale. Such a mind could entertain without pause the exchange of priesthood for prophecy, the transformation of the kingdom of heaven into the kingdom of character, and the substitution of the Apostolate of Conscientious Patriotism for the Good News of Christ Crucified. Christianity as a moral system, simultaneously expressing and guarding the evolutionary advance of men and nations, was the outcome of Modernism in New England. It would seem that "Hermann Harnack" had won.

IV

WILLIAM LAURENCE SULLIVAN chose a more outwardly conventional path than Ambrose Hanlon. In going from the priesthood and the Roman Catholic Church to marriage and the Unitarian Association, he did what no other Modernist had done. But Unitarianism made more sense than Josiah Danforth's League. More significantly, Sullivan argued throughout his life for the kind of catholicization of Unitarianism that Danforth had preached. Sullivan had been known as the "priest of the Blessed Sacrament" to his fellow novices at the Paulist house in Washington, and this reputation for a devotional and mystical faith continued. He gave retreats as an Unitarian minister, and was known in the Association, as well as in his parishes, for his "Catholicism." His sermons and pamphlets were (often apologetically) traditional in their devotional Christology, even if the traditional problems of theological definition were rejected.[57]

In his "Baltimore sermon," a speech called "The Ultimate Principles of Unitarian Christianity" given in 1917, he echoed the hope for a distinctively American religion which he had first stated in the *Catholic World* articles twenty-five years earlier, as well as the fundamental character of morality to religious truth. "The highest test, the ultimate standard of any religious doctrine or institution or scripture is to be found in the moral faculties of man. . . . Nothing can be good in God which would be base, revengeful, in man. . . . Whatever the unspoiled conscience of good men agree upon as fundamentally, ultimately, good, is God Almighty's will." A catechetical presentation of Unitarian Christianity described it as "a religion that puts the essential elements of the life of the spirit foremost, and leaves the nonessentials to the free choice of the individual." In another sermon on ecumenism he explained that the "liberal" Church was excluded from the reunion movement because reunion was based on dogmatic adjustments, but the liberal Christian rejected *all* dogma in favor of "simplicity and inwardness" and "the open road of the spirit." Repeatedly his text was that "the most odious term is sect," whether the sect be Protestant or Catholic.[58]

A disquisition on "The Limitations and Failures of the Protestant Principle" and other sermons made it clear that Sullivan did not believe that he had rejected Catholicism for Protestantism. The Protestant theory of the atonement was for the modern mind as unacceptable as the Catholic teaching on limbo; the Protestant reliance was as confining as the Catholic dependence on the *ecclesia docens*. Sullivan's peroration was "Live unto God in liberty! Worship him in the simplicity of freedom!" In his autobiography he took pains to distinguish his own case from those of other priests who, disillusioned by the failure of Modernism, became Anglicans or Protestants.

Whether Sullivan's Unitarianism was or was not the kind

of apostasy both liberal Protestants and orthodox Catholic critics of the movement had predicted as its inevitable conclusion is a moot point. What is significant is the way in which Catholic elements transformed the conventional liberal stance. Injunctions against the worship of modern science, fulminations against the temptations presented to youth by "a most disillusioning collapse of moral standards," and cautions against the growing dominance of secular subjects in Unitarian pulpits were conservative touches, but not theological. In an Easter sermon Dr. Sullivan, after warning his parishioners that they might be shocked, declared his own personal belief in the historicity of the resurrection. In "The Meaning of Jesus for This Age and for All Ages," he argued that creeds, churches, schools, and systems could make no claim to universality; but the message of Christ could: it was needed by all ages, not only because it was a message of beauty, but because it was the message of the cross, of "hard sayings" without compromise. Jesus' achievement was that he taught God independent of history, race, and culture. Sullivan was more concerned with evil than the autobiographical hero of *The Priest*, and more insistent on the objectivity and otherness of God than the majority of liberal ministers of his time. He insisted that God was "something out there" as well as something immanent in the individual conscience. Experience of the latter depended on the fact of the former. Union with God was possible for the human race; for the human race was, in its essence, "glorious"; yet there was a "willfulness" in men which prevented them from achieving full contact with Him. This willfulness, however, was left unexplained; what mattered was that mankind would "go forward to indescribable destinies." As pastor of All Souls Church in New York, Sullivan insisted that the liberal Church needed a greater development of personal spirituality. He denied the historical idea of original sin and insisted that God was the only fit subject for preaching, but again he admitted that curious willfulness, and again insisted on the primacy of Christ and the "sunlight" and "joy" of his teaching as means to a true understanding of Deity.[59]

Sullivan spoke of his decision to leave the Catholic Church as an event which broke his life into two distinct parts. The language of his autobiography and of *The Priest* conveys the momentousness of the break: images of loneliness, darkness, and coldness recur. Yet his sermons and tracts, his autobiography, and a statement of personal theology which he wrote shortly before his death in 1935 all emphasize continuity as much as change. And he did not hesitate to extend his own experience into generalizations about the effect of Catholic belief and life on the individual.

He argued that Catholicism had three characteristics which became "dispositions of mind and heart" in the ex-Catholic. First, there was the objectivity of God and the individual soul, and of salvation, impressed on heart and imagination, mind and will, by the "pedagogical apparatus" of the Church. "Whatever else may or may not be, God exists and your soul exists." "There is nothing aerial in Catholicism. If you knock your head against it, you know that you have hit something, and if you knock your heart against it, you know that something has hit you." The man who has once been presented by the "Given" of the Catholic Church will always demand a "Given" in his personal faith. "He will require a fact." Even if he is forced to admit agnosticism about God, he will never let go objective belief in the dignity and divinity of his soul; he will not allow "absolutism or psychologism" to reduce it "to the marionette-play of an emo-

tion-focus which is only a queer function of the organism."
To the man who has had an experience of Catholicism, the
ideas of modern naturalistic and materialistic psychology will
be unsatisfactory. To him they "smell of the academic mor-
tuary. They cannot withstand the test of life. They are
pompous phantoms from a world of no-where. They have no
history, and cannot be fitted into history as man has lived
it." The modern psychologist who claimed that he was ex-
plicating a deeper understanding of man's nature based on
love would be found to be "completely unacquainted with
psyche, and engaged in heavy dalliance with eros—and not
Plato's eros, but Freud's."[60]

Sullivan fulminated against the "behaviorists" who were
out to destroy all the ideals of his boyhood and of the adult
career of Sullivan-Hanlon-Danforth: "aspiration, heroism,
pity, and self-obliterating love." He warned them with the
example of Comte, another man who had made "metaphysics
and religion his devil [,] and fact his God," who was saved
from complete dehumanization by "crashing" into love with
that "charming grass-widow" Clothilde de Vaux, and by the
job of drawing up the creed, worship, hierarchy, and sacraments of the religion of Positivism. In contrast to "our
American naturalists and materialists" who worship the
fact and never get behind it, Comte grew "warm and fervent"
as he reached "above leaden facts to imagination and aspiration"; even his style improved, for "his spiritual system—
travestied copy of Catholicism though it is—partook somewhat of its majesty and tenderness." (There seemed little
chance that such a happy redemption would come to the un-
named American villains.)[61]

Modern philosophy was no better at recognizing the first
of the "lasting marks . . . or signatures" of Catholic faith: it

was a *"Schreibtisch-ideologie"* as incomprehensible as the "polysyllabic suicide-scheme of the scholastic," a "fashionable absurdity" which needed to be countered by the Catholic gesture of "putting into the universe a moral as well as a physical teleology." Worse even than the failure of modern psychology and philosophy was that of liberal religion. Here Sullivan echoed Josiah Danforth, attacking the excesses of the theological faculty of "nearby H——— University." The new breed of Unitarians who sat "on the left wing of the religious Parliament" admitted that they believed in God, but when pressed, announced that "Man is God." "Quite insane," Sullivan called them and their conviction that this statement was the logical conclusion of the liberal position. To him their lapse from the "free mind" made them no better than the Catholic theologian who sacrificed infants to hell to preserve a consistent orthodoxy. He was at a loss to understand how they could continue in a church "whose historic claim has been not only that it is Christian but that its mission is to recover Christianity in its purest form."[62]

The second lasting mark which the Church left on its members was "legality," by which Sullivan meant a concern for institution, for order, and for definition. "Catholicism is articulate. It is more than organization, it is organism. It has a voice and behind the voice a logic of speech. Logic indeed, if not its soul, is the habitation of its soul. To be inaccurate is to be heretical and to be heretical is most likely to be damned." The Church's "majestic length of history," its "magnificence of corporate life quite beyond the reach of rivalry," must impress any imagination not "injured by theological prejudice." The man which has experienced them firsthand will feel as their residue that his faith must have quite as determined a structure as does his body. He will have a creed, even if it is a creed of atheism: he will not use the word God "to designate a memory, a sign, or a romance."

The reality of the soul remains the "Given" for the former Catholic, who continues to see a struggle for its salvation and resurrection carried on between the forces of the Ideal and the forces of "willfullness" even though he rejects traditional formulations such as the doctrine of original sin and the atonement. Similarly, he transmutes within himself the experience of Catholic organization and definition, typified by the insistence on creeds, into a consistency and articulateness of "personality." His creed becomes a moral life. "For a moral person existence is and must be a vocation: the *Leben* is merely the raw material of the *Geist*. As sharp in outline, therefore, as ever an institution was, as definite in articulation as ever a system of thought has been, it is his calling to become." The positivist argued that "given the right conditions again, alcohol, bicarbonate of soda and the enzyme that hydrolizes protein can write the Divine Comedy" and challenged all uniqueness and all fixity, all personal responsibility, with his doctrine of "a life stream or a consciousness stream." This was arrant nonsense. "To be is to be defined. To live is to have a form." The religious man— every man—had to build his character and personality in a manner analogous to that proposed in the formal structure of the Catholic Church. He had to admit the logic and authority of the past. He had to receive, with a "disposition of docility," the lessons of the men and books of the past, and then impress upon this inherited material the clear stamp of his own "moral personality."[63]

The third characteristic of the man who has experienced Catholicism is that he "will find it hard to lose the sense of the transcendent" he has acquired through the Church's "rich cultivation of the devout and mystical life." Moreover, he will maintain the dual understanding of transcendence which is characteristic of the Church: he will continue to hope for personal salvation, and to believe that his salvation depends on that of his fellow men. "Because a man has to save his soul, that does not destroy the fact that he must save it in a commonwealth of souls, nor the further fact that his salvation precisely depends on how he has worked with and for these souls."[64]

Sullivan's tone was apologetic on this difficult issue. He had to admit great admiration for the teaching of the Catholic Church on salvation and judgment, even though he recognized the historical difficulties. The idea of "accounting, review, and sentence" which had been impressed upon him in childhood still had force. Whether the "liberals" liked it or not, life was a struggle; and "at the heart of the preoccupation with sin and its penalties" which marked and somewhat marred Catholicism, "there was a sense of reality, of man's earthly warfare, of soldierly responsibility," which he had come to recognize as "sturdy and robustly true and wholesome." (It had disgusted the author of *Letters to Pius X.*) The "liberals" might castigate concern with the salvation of one's soul as "selfish, individualistic, anti-humanitarian, anti-social," but the moral life of most men was based on it. Sin and hell and God as Judge might be harsh thoughts to put into the mind of a child, but they were "no harsher than the world he had been brought into nor the life-long conflict that awaits him there."[65]

This aspect of Catholicism had been presented to Sullivan in his own childhood without morbidity, as a heroic venture; and struggle, war, soldierly responsibility, martyrdom, crucifixion, death, the banners of clashing armies, were recurrent themes in his sermons and in the autobiography. His view of evil—"willfullness"—was dramatic and simplistic. God is the judge, Christ is the captain, man has a role to play, and triumph is assured. But, in the discussion of the "three marks," Sullivan insisted that they were not simply aspects of his own spirituality which he had brought from Catholicism into Unitarianism. They were permanent and universal aspects of all religious life, imperfectly expressed in Catholicism, but better expressed in it than in Protestantism or (excessively) liberal Unitarianism. They were much more important to him in later life than during his Modernist years. Then the enemy had been Romanism, and every admiring remark for the Catholic Church made by Josiah Danforth or Miss Wakefield had to be immediately countered with a criticism of its authoritarianism. In the twenty years which followed Sullivan's break with the Church, he came to see secular modernism—behaviorism in psychology, neopositivism in philosophy, socialism and syndicalism in place of theology in religion—as more dangerous to the free Christian life than the perversions of the papacy.[66]

At the end Sullivan came to speak in the prophetic accents Miss Wakefield had hoped to hear from Ambrose Hanlon. In unpublished novels and in a tract on *Evolution,* the echo of doom muffled the trumpet call of progress. Sullivan had attempted to find a balance between the optimism and belief in progress characteristic of early-twentieth-century America and the older ideas, not merely of moral responsibility, but of judgment and retribution. In place of a balance, he had produced a paradox. On the one hand, he believed that man could eventually triumph over his "inveterate materialism and scepticism." He foresaw some kind

of salvation *within* history, a salvation which would be collective; and thus he continued to dilate on the perverted
teaching of the Church on hell, etc., in apparent rejection
of the kind of individualistic supernaturalism which dis-
tracted man from that hope. On the other hand, he wrote
that "retribution is a correlate of responsibility. A divine
Vindicator is inherently implied in moral personality and
righteous law." And Sullivan spoke in apocalyptic tones of the
"abomination of desolation" which had come upon modern
man because he had ceased to take seriously "a moral personality, a spiritual universe, a righteous God." "These immense and besetting realities we relegate to rhetoric and
dreams. We leave them to churches, and the churches have
left them to oblivion." As a result, "our philosophy is sterile,
our culture invertebrate, our politics staggering on the rim
of the precipice, our religion without resonance, without
glory, without adoration." No wonder Nietzsche had called
for the Superman. His philosophy was an expression of the
"decadence and ghastly dangers that now threaten us."[67]

Sullivan's Christology was also an attempt to blend traditional and modern, Catholic and liberal, ideas; and like his
view of transcendence and judgment, it tended to oscillate
between mysticism and moralism, naturalism and super-
naturalism. "Logos-speculations and Trinity-Godheads" he
could not understand, though he respected those who did.
The "gospel fragments" were obviously interpertations as
well as descriptions, "justifiable and inevitable interpretations
indeed, but giving me the interpreter, not Christ," who was
misunderstood during his life and, more than likely, after
his death. Each Christian had to be his own interpreter, and
"from priceless data that the four biographies give us . . .
reconstruct the mind and heart and soul of the Son of Man."
There was no question of denying the gospels all utility or

of maintaining that the historical Jesus could not be known. Interpretation was difficult, but the dangers decreased as "we carry forward toward substantial certainty our analysis of the documents."

Two different Christs seemed to emerge from his independent, but "scientific," study of the Christian documents. First there is Christ "the Captain of the eager host of aspiring souls":

Sure of Himself, sure of His Universe, sure of His God, He asks men to "be defined!" do something! do something utterly real and radically true. . . . To the utmost, be true, He said . . . commit yourself! Get the "once for all" quality in your heart and will! Strike the plow in the furrow and look back no more.

But, side by side with this bully Jesus, there is another picture. Though Christ is not our redeemer in the sense taught by Catholic and Protestant theology, he does somehow "involve the temporal in the eternal without compromising the eternal by the temporal." If man's spirit has been lifted up in the Christian era, it is because Christ added an "indestructible reality" to its "imperishable life": his cross is "the guarantee of a new age for the world. . . . In His life and death the mystery of our existence passes over into the mystery of God's existence, a mystery not in the sense of a bewilderment but as the unfolding of a consummation beyond our capacity to comprehend but [not by] our own capacity to aspire, to trust, to adore." Just as surely as men are sent to the earth to "carry on a strife toward immortal issues," so Jesus of Nazareth was "sent" to be the leader of mankind in the "transfiguration of the world."[68]

William Sullivan's death (he was stricken with a fatal attack of pneumonia while on vacation in Maine in the fall of 1935)

was noted and mourned in several Unitarian journals and by
memorial services at the various churches he had served. The
power of his preaching and the strength of the hold which
his personality exerted over his parishioners was witnessed
by plaques, busts, and chapels. The memorial in All Souls
Church, New York, reads: "He forsook the shelter of authority in the perilous search for truth." Though Sullivan pros-
pered as a man, in marriage, in financial security, in personal recognition, in a limited range of literary activity,
he remained dissatisfied theologically with all churches. As a
seminarian and as a young priest, he had showed some insight into the contradictions of Roman Catholicism in a
democratic and pluralist setting, and had also responded,
though with little originality, to the European discovery of
the vast distance between Catholicism and the secular epoch.
As a mature minister and preacher, he reacted strongly
against the extensions of the political and scientific directions
with which Modernism had hoped to reconcile the traditional
Church. Patriotism, militant theism, and an ultimately dull-
ing rhetorical enthusiasm bridged the two careers. Shortly
before his death he wrote:

If this life of mine will add its mite to the centuries of testimony
of the existence, the nobility, and . . . the wonder and glory of
the Kingdom, I shall, with heightened expectancy, await the day-
break.[69]

Sullivan's religious philosophy remained personal in spite
of his attempts to generalize it. He considered himself as
"under orders" to his personal faith, and described it as "for
one human being at least . . . a creed that exalts life and
speaks of the promise of life immortal." In essence it was as

illogical a creed as Josiah Danforth's "apostolate of conscientious patriotism," though far less bizarre. But what is of importance is not the degree to which Sullivan's neo-Catholicism-cum-Unitarianism differed from the norm of orthodoxy, or even the norm of common sense, but the fact that he attempted to sketch, first in *The Priest* and then in his later life and writings, an ecclesiology which would embody the best elements of the two kinds of Christianity he knew. Equally significant was the fact that he did not consider any other Christian communion as a viable alternative. Christianity may have become moralism and a faith in transcendence in uneasy alliance. But Sullivan insisted that he had not left Roman Catholicism behind only to move to a less historical, less communal, and less mystical form of dogmatic religion, but rather in order to move onward to a catholicism which would recognize man in his dignity and liberty and, at the same time, preserve God in his power and transcendence.

NOTES

1 George Tyrrell, *Through Scylla and Charybdis, or The Old Theology and the New* (London, 1907), p. 110; Tyrrell *Letters*, selected and edited by M. D. Petre (London, 1920), pp. 115, 103; Maud Petre, *Alfred Loisy, His Religious Significance* (Cambridge, England, 1944), pp. 118–119. Cf. Alfred Loisy, *Mémoires pour Servir à l'Histoire Religieuse de Notre Temps*, 3 vols. (Paris, 1930–31), Vol. III, p. 303: Comte "had only missed the point that humanity still awaits its fulfillment."

2 Catholic opinion of Sullivan was expressed principally during the years of the crisis through critical reviews of his books. Sullivan's forebearance in the matter of polemics with his former Church was not matched by a Catholic paper which said, in its obituary notice, that he had begged for a priest when he was dying but that "one was denied entrance at the door." See John Clarence Petrie, in *The Churchman*, October 15, 1945.

[3] " 'The Final Phase of Modernism,' by the Author of 'Letters to Pope Pius X,' " William L. Sullivan Papers, Archives of the Harvard Divinity School Library. The typescript is not signed, but instructs the reader to return it to W. L. Sullivan in Kansas City.

[4] The references corroborate the statement in an anonymous biographical sketch, probably of the 1920's, that Sullivan was the American correspondent for the *Revue Moderniste Internationale,* published at Geneva. Sullivan Papers.

[5] The influence of Acton was generously acknowledged in the autobiography, but Sullivan made no mention of his reading of Cassels or Martineau. In a letter of September 1910 Sullivan wrote: "Years ago I made the discovery of James Martineau, and I doubt whether any other single writer did so much to prepare me spiritually and intellectually—but spiritually above all—for the great readjustment which I have been forced to make." Notebooks on his reading, probably dating from as early as the late nineties, contain quotations and comments on Martineau, Huxley, and Arnold, as well as Browning, Macaulay, and other poets and historians. Sullivan Papers.

[6] Jean Rivière, *Le Modernisme dans l'Eglise, Etude d'Histoire Religieuse Contemporaine* (Paris, 1929), pp. 400 n. 2, 53 n. 3; Loisy, *Mémoires,* Vol. II, p. 353, III, p. 271; William L. Sullivan, *Under Orders, The Autobiography of William L. Sullivan* (New York, 1944), pp. 198–200, 106–109, 213; Alec Vidler, *The Modernist Movement in the Roman Catholic Church* (Cambridge, England, 1934), p. 213; R. D. Cross, *The Emergence of Liberal Catholicism in America* (Cambridge, Mass., 1958), p. 215. The *Converted Catholic Magazine,* March 1945, pp. 68, prefaced a review of *Under Orders* with the note that Sullivan was one of five New York Paulists who resigned in 1909. The others were Thomas Healy, Daniel Carey, Thomas Walsh, and William Walsh. It seems likely that Sullivan kept in touch with some of these men. There are a few letters from "Tom" (Healy? Walsh?) in the Kansas City correspondence (Sullivan Papers).

One periodical in America reflected the range of the European crisis. The *New York Review,* which after a few years of publication was closed down by Archbishop Farley "probably for prudential, not financial reasons" (Cross, *Emergence of Liberal Catholicism*). In it appeared such articles as "Divorce in the New Testament," "Theological Method in Ethics," and "Assyro-Babylonian Elements in the Biblical Account of the Fall," all somewhat in contrast to the usual fare in Catholic periodicals of the time. Sullivan contributed several pieces to it; Tyrrell, one. Cf. also J. W. Dailey, "The Causes of Modernism," *Catholic World,* Vol. 86, pp. 645–650; T. F. Burke, "The Errors Condemned," *Catholic World,* Vol. 86, pp. 524–531; F. Woodlock, "English and American Modernism," *Gregorianum,* Vol. VIII (March 1927), pp. 23–40 (fasc. 1), 183–203 (fasc. 2).

[7] See Thomas T. McAvoy, *The Great Crisis in American Catholic History, 1895–1900* (Chicago, 1957), pp. 155–302. The text of the apostolic letter is given in the Appendix, pp. 379–391.

8 The intensity of anti–Roman and anticurial sentiment, which focused on the visit of Cardinal Satolli, the opponent of Archbishop Keane and of the liberalization of Catholic University, is suggested by the letters signed "Presbyter Vindex" and "Stet Veritas" in the New York *Sun,* November 4, 1903, and March 29, 1904. Sullivan clipped these, but there is no other evidence for his authorship.

9 *Under Orders,* pp. 55, 46.

10 *Ibid.,* p. 39.

11 Diary for 1895, passim, Sullivan Papers. One entry, a reflection after benediction, typifies the early devotional intensity: "Jesus—my papa—fold me closer to Thy breast, I am a wayward child, my sweet one, and I have long wandered through the darkness of hideous and awful night. Am I not safe now, Jesus? Surely nothing can harm me since I hold fast to Thee. O call me, Jesus, call me to Thyself! Heart of Jesus! Love-Love-Love!"

12 Sullivan did not cite the author of *Supernatural Religion* because the book remained anonymous until 1903. Cf. "Walter Richard Cassels," *The Dictionary of National Biography,* Second Supplement (New York, 1912), Vol. 1, p. 322. The Tanqueray volumes were published in the years 1894–96 and marked the latest style in apologetics.

13 Diary for 1897, January 15, Sullivan Papers.

14 *Ibid.,* January 24.

15 *Ibid.,* February 19. The one hope at Brighton was John Baptist Hogan, who offered an example comparable to those of Ireland and Keane. Hogan was a Paris-trained Sulpician who had taught in France. After five years at Brighton he became president of the School of Theology at Catholic University and then returned to Brighton. He was a liberal, interested in problems of education, and an enthusiast for the historical method. He may be the figure later consulted by Sullivan and the model for the seminary president in *The Priest.* Cross, *Emergence of Liberal Catholicism,* pp. 42, 148; *Under Orders,* p. 174.

16 Diary for 1897, March 8, May 24, June 14, June 8, Sullivan Papers.

17 *Ibid.,* September 3, December 22; 1898, January 1, February 7, March 7; 1899, February 22.

18 *Under Orders,* pp. 59–60. The professor was Charles P. Grannan. Cross cites this anecdote and adds, "it perhaps should be noted that Sullivan had left the Church before he published this recollection" (*Emergence of Liberal Catholicism,* pp. 155, 273). Of course, the great offense of Joachim Pecci was the letter *Testem Benevolentiae,* which Sullivan described as a "bombshell" which inaugurated a "regime of intellectual terror" and directly anticipated the Modernist condemnation of 1907. It was "a direct hit at the Paulists . . . an abominable document, sufficiently shaky and insinuating to bring lasting reproach upon my beloved Paulists." It was clearly "the revenge of Latin ecclesiastics for our country's recent defeat of Catholic Spain."

19 *Under Orders,* pp. 59–60.

20 Notebook headed "Characteristics of the Church's New Apology,"

Sullivan Papers. The manuscript is undated and unpaginated, and appears to be torn from a larger notebook.

21 *Under Orders*, pp. 63, 64, 66, 67, 83–86, 133. The last quotation is from a folder of undated and unpaginated notes; the context of the other material suggests that it was written before Sullivan returned to Washington (Sullivan Papers).

An important influence during these years was Bishop Shyrne of Atlanta, who introduced Sullivan to the post-conciliar correspondence of Acton with Bishop Kenrick of St. Louis. Cf. Raymond J. Clancy, "American Prelates in the Vatican Council," *Historical Records and Studies*, Vol. XXVIII (New York, 1937); F. E. Lally, *As Lord Acton Says* (Newport, Rhode Island, 1942).

22 William L. Sullivan, "The Missionary Movement in the Anglican Church," *Catholic World*, Vol. 72, pp. 315–325; "The Winchester Conference of Missionaries to Non-Catholics," *Catholic World*, Vol. 74, pp. 90–96; "Non-Catholic Missions, The Tenth Anniversary," *Catholic World*, Vol. 78, pp. 223–233. According to an article in the Washington *Times* announcing Sullivan's marriage in 1913 (June 25), he was "one of the best known of the younger instructors at the Catholic University."

23 "Non-Catholic Missions . . . ," *Catholic World*, Vol. 78, pp. 226–227. The need for such work was also emphasized in Sullivan's "Intellectual Apostolate in Japan," *Catholic World*, Vol. 80, pp. 283–293.

24 William L. Sullivan, "Fr. Hogan and the Intellectual Apostolate," *Catholic World*, Vol. 74, pp. 783–792; "Montalembert and Lamennais," *Catholic World*, Vol. 76, p. 475.

25 William L. Sullivan, "The Latest Word of Theology on Inspiration," *Catholic World*, Vol. 84, pp. 327, 333.

26 William L. Sullivan, "The 'Three Heavenly Witnesses,'" *New York Review*, Vol. II, No. 2, pp. 175–188; "Catholicity and Some Elements in Our National Life," *New York Review*, Vol. I, No. 3, pp. 259–268, 266.

27 *Under Orders*, pp. 80, 109, 110–144, 111. Of the "president of a theological seminary" Sullivan wrote: "I was no stranger to him, nor was he to me." Presumably this was John Hogan of Brighton.

28 *Ibid.*, p. 104.

29 *Ibid.*, pp. 115–116.

30 *Ibid.*, pp. 198–99, vii.

31 William L. Sullivan, *Letters to His Holiness Pope Piux X, by a Modernist* (Chicago, 1910). There is no question about the attribution of this work, although the Library of Congress card gives it anonymous authorship.

There are very few details for Sullivan's personal history in this period. From Kansas City, where he wrote the *Letters* and *The Priest* and met his future wife, Estelle Throckmorton, he went to New York, where he taught for a short time at the Ethical Culture Society. After ordination and a short stay in Schenectady he became successively assistant and pastor at All Souls Unitarian Church in New York, and then pastor until his death of the Unitarian Church in Germantown, Pa. For a brief discussion of the materials for his Unitarian career, see the Bibliographical Note in this volume.

The reviewer for the Jesuit magazine *America*, Henry Woods, wrote: "It [*Letters*] carries its effrontery on its cover, on which, whether by author or publisher we cannot say, have been emblazoned the arms of Pius X! Who ever heard of an attacking army marching under colors of the army to be attacked?" Father Woods found the technique representative of the whole movement: "External submission and internal rebellion, the profession of the Catholic faith for the purpose of undermining it, belongs to [Modernism's] essence." *America*, Vol. III, No. 8 (June 4, 1910), p. 212.

32 *Letters*, p. 44. Sullivan dealt in more detail and in less polemical fashion with the history of the Church in several sermons and in a handbook published by the Unitarian Association, *From the Gospels to the Creeds* (Boston, 1919). The attack on infallibility was recapitulated in *Under Orders*, Chapter VII, "A Twelvefold Challenge to the Council of the Vatican," pp. 117–134.

33 *Letters*, p. xviii.

34 *Ibid.*, pp. xvi-xviii, 15.

35 *Ibid.*, pp. 57, 43.

36 *Ibid.*, pp. 59, 60, 188, 84.

37 *Ibid.*, p. 131.

38 Within a year of leaving Texas, Sullivan regarded himself as a Unitarian, though he was not making the fact public. He had also established contact with the Unitarian Association in Boston and impressed some of its members with his abilities as a speaker. Sullivan to Dr. Wendte, September 4, 1910, Sullivan Papers.

39 William L. Sullivan, *The Priest: A Tale of Modernisim in New England*, 3rd ed. (Boston, 1914), p. 77.

40 *Ibid.*, pp. 58, 137.

41 *Under Orders*, p. 137. The points of resemblance in character are emphasized in Mrs. Sullivan's copy of the novel by underlinings and the notation "WLS" in the margins.

42 *The Priest*, pp. 268–269. The novel made some impact. Sullivan clipped more than a dozen favorable reviews. The writer in the diocesan Salt Lake City *Tribune* (March 26, 1911), who was implicitly sympathetic to the movement, wrote that "the story, as an ingenious account of the fall of a priest, is not without interest, but as a study of Modernism, ecclesiastically considered, it is absurd." Alluding to Hanlon's defection, he added: "Those who are held to be Modernists do not do these things. They hold fast to their Catholic faith and to their vows. They are not led away by any outside search for 'the truth' in religious matters." The Unitarian *Christian Register* (June 8, 1911), on the other hand, hoped that every Roman Catholic would behave as well "when the light of higher reason and conscience first dawns upon his soul" and identified Sullivan as "a brilliant and scholarly young Catholic cleric and professor." Several reviews pointed to the imbalance be-

tween plot and intellectual discourse, but Albert Houtin, the doyen of the
French radicals, could not limit his enthusiasm in a letter to the author
dated April 7, 1911: "If you produce a few other novels as good—I do not
say better—you will without doubt rank with the number of the great
writers of your country." Houtin's hopes for Sullivan as a writer were
matched by his discouragement about Modernism: "The movement in Europe
seems to me completely crushed."

In fact, the novel holds up badly under comparison with Fogazzaro's
Il Santo, which may have offered Sullivan some inspiration (cf. *Under Orders*,
pp. 189, 80), or Mrs. Ward's *Out of Due Time*, two major novels of the
crisis. All three are works of the type which Acton described as good for the
historian, bad for the critic (*Essays on Church and State*, ed. Douglas Wood-
ruff [London, 1952], pp. 421–422).

43 *The Priest*, p. 146.

44 *Ibid.*, pp. 102, 104.

45 *Ibid.*, p. 166.

46 *Ibid.*, p. 90.

47 *Ibid.*, pp. 105–106.

48 *Ibid.*, p. 107.

49 *Ibid.*, p. 113.

50 *Ibid.*, pp. 136–138.

51 *Ibid.*, pp. 144–145.

52 *Ibid.*, p. 148.

53 *Ibid.*, p. 167.

54 *Ibid.*, pp. 213–216.

55 *Ibid.*, pp. 226–227.

56 Sullivan's passionate merger of religion and nationalism remained a constant from the Kansas City period, when he wrote, under the pseudonym
"Hubert Haines," poems like "Columbia, Thou Ailest" and short plays like
"Atonement to the Flag" to later years when he wrote a full-scale novel
called *Downfall*, a liberal Christian anticipation of *Atlas Shrugged*, in which
the United States is saved from anarchists, communists, humanists (and oriental governments planning to annex the Panama Canal and parts of the
mainland), by an army officer named John Alden and a Right-thinking anti-
academic New England sage named Adam (Sullivan Papers). Cf. C. J. H.
Hayes' discussion of the flowing of religion and nationalism in this period in
Essays on Nationalism (New York, 1928); Dorothy Dohen, *Nationalism and
American Catholicism* (New York, 1967).

57 "Something of the mysticism of his Catholic background and training
touches and transfigures his wide-ranging liberal thought—a union of qualities rare enough and still more rarely blended" (Joseph Fort Newton, in a
memorial service for Sullivan held in 1935). John Clarence Petrie, another
former Catholic priest who became a Unitarian minister, commented in an
obituary notice on the conservative and nonpolitical character of Sullivan's
Unitarianism which others who knew him had remarked in conversation
with the author. Petrie wrote: "Unitarianism was a deep disappointment

to him. He never left it, but it was only because he could see no other denomination with enough attractions to lure him away. . . . He refused to resort to any of the proselytizing tricks of official Unitarianism" (*The Churchman,* October 15, 1945). Sullivan's only official polemics as a Unitarian were against the humanists, principally John Dietrich and John Dieffenbach (who was probably the model for "Rossignol Morwind," the self-dramatizing pulpit-pounder of *Downfall*). In a letter of 1925 he comments on an article he has written for the *Register*: "I don't know whether Dieffenbach will print it; for he despises me and all my opinions." Elsewhere he wrote: "Unitarian prospects, with a crude, illiterate aetheism spreading amongst our ill-educated sophomore ministers do not reassure me . . . I do not want to lie merely in order to tickle a lot of people at a banquet table. . . . Liberalism is a disease with a vulgar mania for publicity." Folder marked "Voigt Letters, 1912–1935," Sullivan Papers. Cf. the more formal attack in "Our Spiritual Destitution," *Atlantic Monthly* (March 1929), Vol. 143, pp. 373–382.

58 "The Ultimate Principles of Unitarian Christianity" (an address delivered at the Unitarian mass meeting in Symphony Hall, Boston, February 4, 1917); "Unitarian Christianity," Unitarian Laymen's League, Boston, 1922; "Christian Unity," All Souls Church, New York, 1915; "The Limitations and Failures of the Protestant Principle," All Souls', 1917. Sullivan Papers.

59 "A Religion for Modern Man," All Souls', 1914; "The Meaning for Youth of Unitarian Religion after the War," May 12, 1918; "Political and Social Radicalism in the American Churches," All Souls', 1921; "The Meaning for Jesus for This Age and for All Ages," All Souls', 1915; "A Sermon," First Unitarian Church, Worcester, Mass., May 18, 1924; "The Spiritual Ideal of a Liberal Church," All Souls', 1914. Sullivan Papers.

60 *Under Orders,* pp. 147, 19, 20. Sullivan was so eager to take a positive view of Catholicism in later years that he took a private advertisement in the Philadelphia *Inquirer* to dissassociate himself from the group around the *Converted Catholic Magazine.* An early sermon ("The Gain and the Loss in Joining Catholicism," All Souls', March 10, 1918) set out some of the same themes. Roman Catholicism did not suffer from that "twilight zone of semi-observance or of semi-denial that is hanging over every Protestant body in Christendom." He has the Church address puzzled and rootless modern man in tones reminiscent of Macaulay: "All the assurance of centuries gone I can give you today! When all this spawn of sects was not, I was! And after they have been carried to their deserved death, I shall be! Speaking with the ineffable security of Divine Authority, I give you the word of Salvation and the very Truth of God!" And Sullivan added: "Why, this thing is irresistible to thousands—absolutely irresistible!" But "if you carry a certain independence of mind with you, you are going to find misery," and lose your character as well. Here, as in the later writings, the only hope is that Christendom will come to transcend orthodoxy entirely. Sullivan Papers.

61 *Under Orders,* pp. 21–22.

62 *Ibid.*, pp. 125, 143.

63 *Ibid.*, p. 150.

64 *Ibid.*, p. 153.

65 *Ibid.*, p. 32.

66 *Ibid.*, pp. 29, 147, 19–20. Cf. Sullivan's "Anti-Religious Front," *Atlantic Monthly*, Vol. 145 (January 1930), p. 99: "Though they [the enemies of religion] reach for the whip if I say that I believe in God, I am favored with their approval if I say that when an infant sucks its thumb it is unconsciously pursuing a sexual adventure. Freud says this, so it is all right. Again, it is all right if, observing the same infant falling asleep after feeding at its mother's breast, I declare that the child sinks into the slumber of sexual satiety. No censure for that! No offense in it for the most antiseptic minds!" After more examples of Freudian analysis Sullivan concludes: "And if we inquire what then in heaven's name shall be kept out of the mind if these preposterous things are let in, we seem to be answered: Practically nothing except God!"

Sullivan tried to give his antipositivist bias a scientific foundation in a long manuscript refuting the theory of evolution. His conclusion was that "organic wholes come into being as wholes and could not exist except as whole"; his theme, that "evolutionary theory has profaned the sanctuary" of pure science, "bedevilling" scientific men, making "ducks and drakes of evidence." "It has pushed sooth-saying into the cold ritual of exact observance and beguiled a rigorous priesthood into fanatic prophesying." Signed typescript entitled *Evolution*, Sullivan Papers. Sullivan's Germantown disciples regarded the work as a sign of their "Dominie's" erudition. Cf. William L. Sullivan, *The Flaming Spirit, Meditations and Prayers of William L. Sullivan*, ed. Max F. Daskam (New York–Nashville, 1961), p. 18.

67 *Under Orders*, p. 165.

68 *Ibid.*, pp. 166, 168–169.

69 *Flaming Spirit*, p. 21.

Conclusion -
MODERNISM AND MODERNIZATION

THE IDENTITY OF *Romanità* with Catholic Christianity and the conviction that the shape and form of the Catholic Church was administratively, liturgically, and theologically unalterable were notions so strongly held at the turn of the century that the changes in Church polity and theology which have occurred since the pontificate of John XXIII were not imagined by the most radical critics of that period, in or out of the Church. One of Loisy's critics dismissed all talk of innovation with the simple statement *"On est catholique ou l'on ne l'est pas."*[1] What he meant, of course, was that one could not claim to believe as a Catholic unless one believed in the way Roman theology taught, as well as what it taught; that one had no right to make any distinction between "fundamental" and "nonfundamental" articles of belief; and that the content of sure belief, in practice if not in strict teaching, often included matters of the most doubtful and culturally attenuated tradition. He had in mind the kind of faith defined by the Irish actress who, when asked in an interview in what sense she was a Catholic, replied:

339

"Oh, I believe the whole goddam thing." Actresses, poets, peasants (we have been told), and perhaps really great theologians can believe that way; in the year 1900 it was becoming difficult for intellectuals to do so.

The apparent impregnability of Roman Catholicism to even the mildest suggestions for reform, such as those put forward by men like Wilfrid Ward, who wanted "not less, but more, and better theology," was as much responsible for the radical character of the Modernist critique as were the apparently incontrovertible results of "higher criticism" and the personal experiences of men like Loisy, Tyrrell, Sullivan, Houtin, Turmel, and Hébert. Even though the inner motivation for a reform of *orthodoxy* had rapidly faded for these men, they continued to ask questions that were quite significant for the development of theology. Their abandonment of anything but the most immanentist or symbolic kind of personal religion did nothing to impair the intellectual force of their criticisms, though, of course, as the debate was conducted, this crucial distinction was honored mainly in the breach. They were sufficiently convinced, if not of the truth of the Church, at least of the laws of institutional and intellectual evolution to insist that the Roman Catholic Church simply could not hope to survive if it tried to continue as "unchangeable" in its theology as it had been since the middle ages. "Theological speculation can never stop at any point in the subject it covers." And in spite of his own experience, Loisy dared to hope that "the theology of the next centuries will be more reserved than the theology of the past centuries, that it will have less confidence in the permanent validity of its formulas, that it will find its light in the obscurity of the faith more than in the fragile constructions of reason." Troeltsch defined in a sentence the history of religion in the modern period: "Divine infallibility and ecclesiastical intolerance necessarily give place to human relativity and toleration." The Modernists expected Catholicism to share in this history, whether its priests or its people wanted it to or not. Theology would eventually make the momentous discovery of Montesquieu: all knowledge is the knowledge of relations. Troeltsch had announced aloud to the Protestant world the vision that the Modernists wished to whisper to Catholicism, a vision of the power of history as it moved and changed every dimension of life.

... we see everything in the process of becoming, in an unlimited and ever new individualization, determined by the past and directed towards an unknown future. The state, law, morals, religion and art dissolve in the course of the growth of history and are comprehensible to us only as constituent parts of an historical development.[2]

The problem for the intellectual lay in the fact that the scientific dimension of this enthusiasm for history and evolution made the origins of that direction in the past seem as unknowable as the shape of the future. In fact, the peculiar characteristic of much of the thought of this period was that the future, at least in its broad outlines, seemed *more* knowable than the past, especially in matters of religion and morals. Anthropological research and the evidence of atavisms in modern man, the scanty records of the roots of civilization and the development of religious systems, seemed to indicate that there was little material with which to construct the kind of prehistory that was normative for positivism, namely, that of the modern nation-state as Ranke and his students had portrayed it. But scientific extrapolation from the progressive and optimistic (pre-World War) present into the future seemed both reasonable and necessary.

The three subjects of this essay were seized, in varying ways, and only for a time, with great confidence in the historical evolution of man toward a perfect civilization. Latecomers to the Enlightenment, to democracy, to that process of "individualization" which had seemed so dangerous to Catholicism since the experiences of Port Royal, they adopted wholeheartedly the idea of progress. Like their liberal forebears in the generations of Lamennais, Lacordaire, Montalembert, like Catholic liberals since, they sought to bring Catholicism to the modern world. What distinguished them from both their predecessors and their successors was their scientism—though on this point Sullivan's position was, at least superficially, more conservative. In this, and more particularly in their enthusiasm for what they considered scientific history, and what we would perhaps call historicism, they were paradoxically behind the times: at the moment when they saw salvation in science, the drift of Western intellectuals was away from positivism toward the poetry of hypothesis, *als obs,* and "ideal types." They mistook the bare beginnings of the scientific study of the bible for a mature and infallible discipline.

An even more crucial distinction between these three reformers and the progressives in the Modernist decades lies in the attitude toward the future sketched above. Christianity taken as a whole seemed to them to be the culmination of the evolutionary process as it could be observed at work in religion. But unlike other Christian enthusiasts for the modern world, they were sufficiently secularized to see the Church as a *possible,* but not the inevitable, vehicle of progressive civilization. If Roman Catholicism, or Christianity as a whole, did not assume the role of leading man into the future, science or nationalism or democracy—or, more likely, a combination of these and other forces at work in the modern world—would fulfill the task for the religious masses, even as they had for several generations of humanists. In contrast, their progressive contemporaries, like Blondel and Ward, believed that it was inevitable that Christian faith and Christian hope should shape the world toward its completion in the Parousia, whether Rome was apparently set against such a development or not. Once excluded from the Church, or once convinced that neither delicate persuasion like *L'Evangile et l'Eglise* nor frontal attacks like *Medievalism* or the *Letters to Pius X* had any hope of success, these men became as uncompromising in their opposition, as bitter in their polemic, and as intolerant of any "halfway" approach as their orthodox enemies. There was, of course, a logical contradiction between their evolutionary view of religious ideas and institutions and their final conviction that Rome had missed its opportunity to lead. But this contradiction was no more difficult for them to maintain than it was for orthodoxy to insist that the Church was universal in its appeal—and, potentially, in its membership—and at the same time to exalt a premodern polity and psychology of religion.

"Modernism" may have died with the condemnation, but the problems to which the Modernists spoke, and which they raised, remain. Since Vatican II, new connections have been made between the ferment in the Catholic Church today and the past controversy:

The most illuminating approach to the present crisis within the Roman Catholic body . . . is to treat it as one more, somewhat belated, frenzied and messy attempt to negotiate the hazardous

perspectives opened by the Romantic movement and the new
historicism on the traditional idea of dogma and history. But this
particular crisis, released perhaps unintentionally by the late
Pope John, is clearly the resurgence, at an apparently more
propitious moment, of the Modernist controversy.[3]

Admitting that this estimate ignores the developments of
the intervening sixty years, it is clear that much of what is
being written and said in the Church today goes far beyond
the tendencies of the theology of the interwar period, far
beyond the intentions of the Fathers of the Council. The
Council and the renewal and ferment of the early sixties
seemed at the time to take direction from the biblical revival of the previous fifty years, and to express itself in terms
of a return to Christian origins which would release, in
liturgy and theology, a vitality assumed to lie obscured beneath several centuries of propositionalism and immobility.
The lead for this development came from Protestantism, as
reformed theologians wrestled with criticism and the various
forms of liberalism from Strauss to Harnack. But since the
Council has ended, the historian can notice a new direction in
Catholic thought. The idea of the Church reforming itself
no longer seems adequate: and once again, following (in
sequence, if not in example) developments in Protestant
thought, Catholic thinkers are turning their attention from
the Church to the secular city. In the past—at the time of
the Modernist crisis especially, but also in 1860 and in 1848—
the discovery of the world has produced a clear and confident response. Admission of the facts of modern atheism,
secularism, and materialism always implied their condemnation and a renewed effort to call mankind back to the teaching of the Church and to the political and cultural styles

with which that teaching was impacted. Today the "grand old intolerant integrity of faith" (of which one of Sullivan's characters boasted) is being dissipated. In the crisis of cultural self-confidence which takes its place, some Catholic intellecuals have discovered that, like the internal combustion engine, atheism, secularism, and materialism are here to stay, and that there is very little weeping and gnashing of teeth going on in the darkness outside the Church. Some find that they are children of the Enlightenment, and are glad of the fact.[4]

Seeing modern history as a heritage rather than a heresy is a challenge. Since the French Revolution, Catholic orthodoxy has tended to treat the modern world as a providential testing, a time of trial through which the Church would inevitably move, possibly to triumph in a new age of faith and order. But the providential reading of history is a double blade: if one argues from the assumption that history has a meaning, one has to admit that its meaning may be positive or at least tolerable. The accents of fulmination and contempt have been drained away from words like materialism and atheism; the movement of modern thought toward history and phenomenology has come to be seen, not as something to be derided or rationalized in terms of the demonic, but as something to be accepted critically as what it is, namely, the manifestation of the real nature of mind.[5]

If, in this context of openness to modernity, historical comparisons between the present thrust of Catholic theology and the ideas of the Modernists are unavoidable, they should be made cautiously, not out of any desire to protect the new generation of Catholic liberals (for the conservative will persist in using the Modernist crisis as a whip, regardless of the facts), but out of a desire to understand what has happened in the last several generations. What is perhaps most inter-

esting is the fact that the contemporary modernizer is vastly
more radical, from an ecclesiological point of view, than the
generation of the Modernists, but, at the same time, more
conservative Christologically.

Evaluated independently, the three subjects of this study
illustrate several aspects of the change between their generation's crisis of belief and that through which the Church
is passing today.

Loisy did not hold to Jesus as Lord. On the one hand, detailed historical criticism convinced him that Jesus, insofar
as he could be limned through (and often in spite of) the
gospels, was a time-bound, historically relative figure; a man
of extraordinary dynamism utterly seized by the messianic
concept, convinced of the imminent coming of the kingdom,
a product of "late Judaism" whose charisma was so great
that it triumphed over the failure of his eschatological expectations. On the other hand, historical philosophizing in
the positivist and evolutionary tradition led him to interpret
the development of Catholic Christianity out of the witness
to that charisma as the culmination of a long process of self-
discovery and growth in consciousness which society had acted
out through religion. Organized religion—the Church—advanced (or should advance) the ongoing evolution of man's
consciousness by maintaining cultural continuity and, more
significantly, by providing him with a moral education.
There is no Christological problem here: Loisy, as a Modernist, was not a Christian. By his own standards, Socrates might
even be preferable as a model figure, but more logically, a
whole Comtian pantheon—or pan-*anthropon*—would be best.
The historian finds it difficult to evaluate Loisy in terms of
Christian faith, even though from a comparative point of
view it appears that much of the superstructure of his Chris-

tology (the problem of Jesus' knowledge, the problem of the foundation of the Church, etc.) now could be approached more sympathetically.

The fundamental principle of Loisy's ecclesiology was the utility of the Church as a sociocultural tool. Western history offered proof of its utility in the past. The doctrine of evolution and relativism which Loisy found implicit in the development of tradition from the very pages of the gospel on to nineteenth-century piety appeared to offer the means whereby Christian teaching of the kingdom could be frozen in its symbolic representation, corrected in the view of its historical origins, and adapted to the further advance of the consciousness which had produced it. Loisy soon realized the limitations of this proposal. Secular society, perhaps as organized in the nation-state, seemed to offer a more reasonable vehicle for man's moral education. Loisy abandoned the idea of the Church as educator and civilizer of men. Paradoxically, Catholic liberals in the succeeding decades, continuing the tradition of Archbishop Ketteler and Albert de Mun, tried to create specifically Christian and Catholic institutions whereby the gospel might be extended into the world. Today the direction of radical criticism of the Church as a civilizing force is away from the institutional; or rather, the gospel is seen as being of its nature so concerned with the world that the establishment of specifically Catholic or Christian organizations is understood as potentially destructive of its power, since they seem to imply that the Christian goes about living this life in a special way and for reasons which are not intrinsic to it. In abandoning what might be called the "vale of tears" syndrome, the contemporary Catholic theologian is finding the values of secularization. And if he does not mount an historical attack on dogma, as did Loisy, or work out sym-

bolic systems or theories of action in its defense, it is because
he tends to see the development (or evolution) of Christian
doctrine as a living tradition, "the collective memory of a
continuing community."

Finally, in terms of theism, it would be incorrect to see
Loisy as an anticipator of any modern current. His pattern
of intellectual discovery followed an older model, moving
from piety (superstition) to mystical humanism. In the end,
Loisy believed that humanity sought itself in seeking the
image of God: Jesus was only part of the search.

In this comparison with contemporary trends, Sullivan's
theological significance is limited. His main argument was
with authoritarianism and legalism in the Church. Sullivan
protested against dogmas as well as dogmatism, but largely
because there was in his day no alternative to the view which
saw Catholic teaching as a Newtonian physics of faith. He
was in no whit tempted by radical naturalism; religion was
indeed the expression of all that was best and most noble in
man, but its topic remained God. His confusion of nationalism with religion has no contemporary parallel, but his
conviction that freedom is a prerequisite for religious growth,
once it is released from his rhetoric, seems so simplistic that
one forgets how difficult a struggle the idea has had in its
growth in the Church. Sullivan, even in comparison with
Loisy and Tyrrell, seems an old-fashioned figure. But it is
important to note again that he was able to effect both a personally and a pastorally satisfying resolution of the crisis of
faith he experienced as a hopeful liberal.

Of the three, Tyrrell is clearly the most relevant today.
The reason for this is not hard to state. Tyrrell asked questions, found few answers, and forced in himself the hard
growth of a tolerance for ambiguity in faith which was

something more than the sum of a series of historical and logical contradictions. Tyrrell's essential genius was mystical and pastoral. Theology, especially theology done in tension with the search for the historical Jesus, was his undoing. Yet his personal struggle was heroic. Neurasthenic, intemperate, inconsistent, irreverent, he had an intensely acute vision of the crisis through which the Church was passing. The fact that a man of his spiritual insight and passion was shipwrecked trying to pass between the old theology dying and the new theology coming to life ironically confirmed his vision.

The central concern of contemporary Catholic radicals has changed: to paraphrase Tyrrell, it is not Christ, but Catholicism and Christianity, which exercise the theologians of today. But many of the "Modernist problems" remain. What is the relationship between theology and devotion, between the "theoreticians" and the "masses of the faithful"? How does the believer keep his heritage, knowing, not that freedom and faith must be reconciled, but that they are an identity? How does he escape from "the tendency of religious institutions to ignore the identification of God's magnificence with the welfare of man"?[6]

In the last analysis, the three men studied here (and the other Modernists) must be understood, not as precursors, nor as parallels, nor as flawed, nor as useful paradigms of how *not* to proceed in the reform of Christian teaching, but as individuals subject to, and to a degree shaping, the evolution of religious opinion in their own time. That time was the heyday of religious as well as political nationalism, when the opposition of state and church in much of the world was only surpassed in its bitterness by the conflict between sects. It was an age when the ecumenical idea was as strange to

Christians as the idea of world peace and order was to states-
men. As recently as 1950, Loisy's Modernism could be described as the *hydre venimeuse* striking at the bosom of the
Church. That kind of language was once commonplace.
Both Loisy's and Tyrrell's clashes with authority were characterized, in a conscious parallel with the cause célèbre of
the nineties, as *affaires*: *L'Affaire Loisy, L'Affaire Tyrrell*.
France was split into two warring camps; and, in the eyes of
Rome, the division between monarchist-clerical and repub-
lican-liberal was a universal one, even in countries where
the Church was in the minority. Anyone who challenged
authority, administrative or doctrinal, had to be lumped
unambiguously with the forces of evil. In the opinion of a
contemporary student of church history, the clergy had "become marginal to the society it wished to evangelize." Still
it persisted in attitudes, policies, and programs guaranteed
to advance, rather than halt, the de-Christianization of Europe.[7]

In the mid-nineteenth century Renan had predicted that
Christianity would be dead in a generation. In fact, the tide
of ideas was turning: to unreason—*and* religion. Europe
was moving toward a terrible demonstration of those limitations of the human will and intellect to which Christianity
addressed itself. Even before the war, the limits, not of reason, but of an overconfident and simplistic rationalism, had
been recognized in a variety of intellectual disciplines. Péguy
was calling for a mystique in politics and life, and he and
others were finding, in an imprecise Catholicism (or neo-
Catholicism), an answer to the questions which perpetual
social progress seemed unable to solve.

To that generation, paralyzed by the dilemma of either-
or, the Modernists wished to speak. To it they said, in Loisy's

words, "we do not believe in the Church because we believe in the Bible, but rather, we believe in the Bible because we believe in the Church." They saw in Catholic tradition a symbol of man's progress which, once freed from the literalism which a prescientific historiography and theology had laid upon it, could still provide that element of transcendence which the secular and material world of the nineteenth century had lost. The ethical Christ of Protestantism was inadequate, as well as historically incorrect. Only Catholicism had preserved the transcendent kindgom *and,* through the development of tradition, created a variety of ways to its achievement. Catholicism would live if it could adapt, die if it could not. The crisis character of their message, more and more radically stated as opposition to their ideas formed in Rome, corresponded in each case to an intense personal experience of what they believed to be the inadequacies of Catholic teaching for the modern world.

NOTES

1 Emile Poulat, *Histoire, Dogme et Critique dans la Crise Moderniste* (Paris, 1962), p. 140.

2 Alfred Loisy, *Mémoires pour Servir à l'Histoire Religieuse de Notre Temps,* 3 vols. (Paris, 1930–31), Vol. I, p. 463; Ernst Troeltsch, *Protestantism and Progress* (Boston, 1958), p. 19; Heinz Zahrnt, *The Historical Jesus* (New York, 1963), p. 26.

3 *Times Literary Supplement,* August 26, 1966, p. 746. Perhaps the most troubling accusation of a revival of Modernism is that of Jacques Maritain in *Le Paysan de la Garonne* (Paris, 1966). Maritain "bursts out with the forbidden word Modernism and says that the current neo-Modernist effervescence represents a fever alongside which the Modernist crisis of the time of Pope St. Pius X (1903–1914) was 'simply a case of hay fever.'" Maritain summarizes the neo-Modernist view as follows: ". . . the objective content of faith to which our ancestors were so attached—all that is mythology, like original sin, for example . . . or like the infancy gospel, the resurrection of

the body, creation, and of course the Christ of history. The phenomenologists and the form school have changed all that. The distinction between nature and grace is a scholastic invention, like transubstantiation. As for hell, why take the trouble to deny it, since it is easier to forget it?—and probably we should do the same with the Incarnation and the Trinity." Cf. *America*, Vol. 116, No. 10, p. 349; *Le Paysan de la Garonne*, p. 17.

One might compare Magdalen Goffin: "To believe in eternal punishment is superstitious" (*Objections to Roman Catholicism*, ed. Michael de la Bedoyere [New York, 1965]). Cf. also "Philosopher under Fire," New York *Times*, March 24, 1967; Claud D. Nelson, "The Modernist Movement and Catholic Renewal Today," *Christian Century*, Vol. 81, No. 38 (September 1964), pp. 1139–1141; John Ratté, "The Specter of Modernism," *Commonweal*, Vol. 82, No. 17 (July 1965), pp. 530–533, and "Crisis and Comparison," *America*, Vol. 117, No. 2 (July 8, 1967), pp. 35-37.

4 Michael Novak, *Belief and Unbelief* (New York, 1966), pp. 9–13, 35–54.

5 Christianity, according to Dewart, has received "immediate confirmation of its religious experience" (*The Future of Belief: Theism in a World Come of Age* [New York, 1966], p. 79).

6 W. H. Dubay, *The Human Church* (New York, 1966), p. 20.

7 Lucio da Veiga Continho, *Tradition et Histoire dans la Controverse Moderniste, 1898–1910* (Rome, 1954), p. 19; Georges Weill, *Histoire du Catholicisme Liberal en France, 1828–1908* (Paris, 1909), p. 255.

Bibliographical Note

I THE MEN

The Alfred Loisy Papers in the Bibliotheque Nationale will be made available in two installments in 1971 and 1981. A complete bibliography supplements Emile Poulat's edition of the memoir of Albert Houtin and Felix Sartiaux, *Alfred Loisy, Sa Vie, Son Oeuvre* (Paris: 1960), pp. 303–324. I have drawn primarily on the following: Alfred Loisy, *Autour d'un Petit Livre*, 2nd ed. (Paris: 1903); *Autres Mythes à propos de la Religion* (Paris: 1938); *The Birth of the Christian Religion* (*La Naissance du Christianisme*), tr. L. P. Jacks (London: 1948); *Choses Passées* (Paris: 1913), English edition, *My Duel with the Vatican: The Autobiography of a Catholic Modernist*, tr. R. W. Boynton (New York: 1924); *Etudes Bibliques*, 3rd ed. (Paris: 1903); *George Tyrrell et Henri Bremond* (Paris: 1936); *Le Mandéisme et les Origines Chrétiennes* (Paris: 1934); *La Religion* (Paris: 1917); *L'Evangile et l'Eglise*, 4th ed. (*Ceffonds* [Haute Marne], 1908), English edition, *The Gospel and the Church*, tr. Christopher Home, new edition with prefatory memoir by George Tyrrell (London: 1908); *Mémoires pour Servir à l'Histoire Religieuse de Notre Temps*, 3 vols. (Paris: 1930–31); *The Origins of the New Testament* (*Les Origines du Nouveau Testament*), tr. L. P. Jacks (London: 1950); *Quelques Lettres sur des Questions Actuelles et sur les Evénements Récents* (Ceffonds [Haute Marne], 1908); *Religion et*

353

Humanité (Paris: 1926); *The Religion of Israel* (*La Religion d'Israël*), tr. A. Galton (London: 1910); *Simples Réflexions sur le Décret du Saint-Office "Lamentabili Sane Exitu" et sur l'Encyclique "Pascendi Dominici Gregis"* (Ceffonds [Haute Marne], 1908); *The War and Religion* (*La Guerre et la Religion*), tr. A. Galton (Oxford: 1915); *Un Mythe Apologétique* (Paris: 1939); *Y A-t-il Deux Sources de la Religion et de la Morale?* (Paris: 1933).

The major study of Loisy's thought in the context of the crisis is Emile Poulat's comprehensive volume, the first of two, entitled *Histoire, Dogme et Critique dans la Crise Moderniste* (Paris: 1962). The source for his early development, complementary to the *Mémoires*, is the Houtin and Sartiaux volume. Sympathetic presentations of his ideas are those of Henri Bremond, writing pseudonymously as "Sylvain Leblanc," *Un Clerc Qui N'a Pas Trahi* (Paris: 1931); Maud Petre, *Alfred Loisy, His Religious Significance* (Cambridge, England: 1944); Friedrich Heiler, *Alfred Loisy, Der Vater des Katholischen Modernismus* (Munich: 1947), which discusses the postwar flurry of interest in the possibility of Loisy's reconstruction and the Vatican's rejection of the idea; Adolfo Omodeo, *Alfredo Loisy, Storica della Religioni* (Bari: 1936); Alec Vidler, *The Modernist Movement in the Roman Catholic Church* (Cambridge, England: 1934), pp. 69–139, with a comparison of Loisy and Tyrrell, pp. 179–184. Loisy's contributions to religious studies were assessed by his contemporaries in the proceedings edited by P. L. Couchoud, *Jubilé Alfred Loisy: Congrès d'Histoire du Christianisme*, 3 vols. (Paris–Amsterdam: 1928). Criticism came from orthodoxy and from the radical left. In addition to a considerable body of periodical writing (see Poulat, *Histoire*, passim, and Lucio da Veiga Coutinho, *Tradition et Histoire dans la Controverse Moderniste, 1898–1910* [Rome: 1954], pp. xv–xvi), more elaborate analyses are Jean Rivière, *Le Modernisme dans l'Eglise, Etude d'Histoire Religieuse Contemporaine* (Paris: 1929), pp. 154–179; Marie-Joseph Lagrange, *M. Loisy et le Modernisme* (Paris: 1933); Coutinho, *Tradition et Histoire*, pp. 15–42, 112–113; G. Martini, *Cattolicesimo e Storicismo: Momenti di una Crisi del Pensiero Religioso Moderno* (Naples: 1951), pp. 195–256. The radical left's response to Loisy is discussed in detail in Poulat, *Histoire*, pp. 316–363.

The major manuscript sources for George Tyrrell's life and thought are the British Museum bound volumes Ad. Mss. 44927-31, 45744, and 45754 (the latter comprising the von Hügel correspondence) and the unbound Petre Papers, Ad. Mss. 52367-82, of which the first two listings are the complete Tyrrell-Petre correspondence. Other useful materials are typescripts and manuscripts of a limited number of articles and books, material relating to the circumstances of Tyrrell's death and burial, and Miss Petre's diaries. The most important of the letters, with a few exceptions, are published in the volumes noted below. An unsystematic running bibliography of Tyrrell's books and major articles is contained in the text and notes of Volume II of the *Autobiography and Life*. I have drawn primarily on the following: George Tyrrell, *The Autobiography and Life of George Tyrrell,* ed. M. D. Petre, 2 vols. (London: 1912); *Christianity at the Crossroads* (London: 1910; reprinted New York: 1966); *The Church and the Future* (L'Eglise et l'Avenir), "by Hilaire Bourdon," printed "for private circulation only," n.d. (appearing 1903); *Essays on Faith and Immortality,* ed. M. D. Petre (London: 1914); *The Faith of the Millions: A Selection of Past Essays,* 3rd ed., 2 vols. (London: 1904); *Hard Sayings: A Selection of Meditations and Studies* (London: 1904); *Letters,* selected and edited by M. D. Petre (London: 1920); *Lex Orandi, or Prayer and Creed* (London: 1903); *Medievalism: A Reply to Cardinal Mercier* (London: 1909); *A Much Abused Letter* (subtitled "A Confidential Letter to a Friend Who Is a Professor of Anthropology") (London: 1908); *Nova et Vetera: Informal Meditations,* 4th ed. (London: 1905); *Lex Credendi: A Sequel to Lex Orandi* (London: 1906; *Oil and Wine,* "New Impression" (actually a second edition with new preface and appendixes) (London: 1907); *Through Scylla and Charybdis, or The Old Theology and the New* (London: 1907); M. D. Petre, ed., *Von Hügel and Tyrrell: The Story of a Friendship* (London: 1937).

Johannes Jacobus Stam's *George Tyrrell: 1861–1909* (Utrecht: 1938) is a careful and chronological discussion of the development of Tyrrell's thought from a critical Catholic point of view. A biographical treatment, at once critical and sympathetic, is J. Lewis May's *Father Tyrrell and the Modernist Movement* (London: 1932). Loisy assessed the friendship and theological differences of Tyrrell and Bremond in a short book entitled *George Tyrrell et Henri Bremond* (Paris: 1936). Rivière's critical treatment (*Modernisme,* pp. 192–223) contrasts with the sympathetic discussion by Vidler (*Modernist Movement,* pp. 143–184). Tyrrell's early writings were analyzed by Ernest Dimnet, *La Pensée Catholique dans l'Angleterre Contemporaine* (Paris: 1906). Tyrrell's ideas (and those of Loisy) were discussed in conjunction with the philosophy of William James by René Berthelot, *Un Romantisme Utilitaire, Etude sur le Movement Pragmatiste* (Paris: 1922), Vol. III. There was a good deal of polemical writing assessing Tyrrell's break with the Church, of which Raoul Gout's *L'Affaire Tyrrell* (Paris: 1910) can be regarded as typical. Recent assessments can be found in Coutinho, *Tradition et Histoire,* pp. 43–62; Martini, *Cattolicesimo e Storicismo,* pp. 143–192; W. S. Smith, "George Tyrrell and the Modernists," *Christian Century,* Vol. 80 (April 1963), pp. 490–492.

The William L. Sullivan Papers are still in the process of being cataloged in the Archives of the Harvard Divinity School Library. It would appear that all likely material in the possession of the estate, with the exception of one box of correspondence "of a very personal nature" (from a letter by one of the executors dated 2/19/41), is now available. The principal materials for Sullivan's early history are the personal diaries and notes and the manuscripts from the Kansas City period. There are also three boxes of typescripts of 156 sermons, most of them taken in shorthand and subsequently typed, and in some cases corrected (1912–16, 1917–22, 1931–33); two boxes containing various versions of *Under Orders* and the correspondence relating to its publication; 44 folders containing drafts of sermons, reading notes, correspondence, and materials relating to Sullivan's work with the Unitarian Laymen's League, to the collection of meditations and sermons published in 1961 (*The Flaming Spirit*), and on parish life and work in New York and Germantown. In addition, the Papers include the manuscripts of early books; the tract on *Evolution;* two novels, one unfinished, one unsigned; assorted book reviews and clippings, and copies of magazines containing published articles as well as copies of printed sermons. There is no material before 1895, and no material that can be definitely dated for the period 1900–10.

In addition to the Papers, I have drawn on the following: William Laurence Sullivan, *Letters to His Holiness Pope Pius X, by a Modernist* (Chicago: 1910); *The Priest: A Tale of Modernism in New England,* 3rd ed. (Boston: 1914); *From the Gospels to the Creeds* (Boston:

1919); *Epigrams and Criticisms in Miniature* (Philadelphia, Pa.: 1936); *Under Orders, The Autobiography of William Laurence Sullivan* (New York: 1944; reprinted Boston: 1966); *The Flaming Spirit, Meditations and Prayers of William L. Sullivan,* ed. Max F. Daskam (New York-Nashville: 1961); "The Anti-Religious Front," *Atlantic Monthly,* Vol. 145, pp. 96–104; "Catholicity and Some Elements of our National Life," *New York Review,* Vol. I, pp. 259–268; "Fr. Hogan and the Intellectual Apostolate," *Catholic World,* Vol. 74, pp. 783–792; "The Intellectual Apostolate in Japan," *Catholic World,* Vol. 80, pp. 282–293; "The Latest Word of Theology on Inspiration," *Catholic World,* Vol. 84, pp. 217–227, 326–333; "Mr. Mallock on the Naturalness of Christianty," *Catholic World,* Vol. 82, pp. 527–531; "The Missionary Movement in the Anglican Church," *Catholic World,* Vol. 72, pp. 315–325; "Montalembert and Lamennais," *Catholic World,* Vol. 76, pp. 462–475; "Non-Catholic Missions, The Tenth Anniversary," *Catholic World,* Vol. 78, pp. 223–233; "Our Spiritual Destitution," *Atlantic Monthly,* Vol. 143, pp. 373–382; "Responsibility in Book Reviewers," *Catholic World,* Vol. 73, pp. 338–345; "The 'Three Heavenly Witnesses,'" *New York Review,* Vol. 2, pp. 175–188; "The Winchester Conference of Missionaries to Non-Catholics," *Catholic World,* Vol. 74, pp. 1, 90–96.

II THE MOVEMENT

General bibliographies are contained in several studies of the crisis: Emile Poulat, *Histoire, Dogme et Critique dans la Crise Moderniste* (Paris: 1962), pp. 31–42, 648–676; Jean Rivière, *Le Modernisme dans l'Eglise, Etude d'Histoire Religieuse Contemporaine* (Paris: 1929), pp. xiii–xxix; Lucio da Veiga Coutinho, *Tradition et Histoire dans la Controverse Moderniste, 1898–1910* (Rome: 1954), pp. xiii–xxiii. Albert Houtin, *Histoire du Modernisme Catholique* (Paris: 1913), pp. 427–436, and M. D. Petre, *Modernism, Its Failures and Its Fruits* (London: 1918) give unsystematic lists; the progressive literature of the period is listed and briefly analyzed in E. Hocédez, *Histoire de la Théologie au XIXᵉ Siècle* (Paris: 1947), Vol. III, pp. 103–190. Manuscript sources are discussed by Poulat in *Histoire,* pp. 33–38; his formal bibliography is supplemented by a wide range of references through the text. Also of great value is the "bio-bibliographical index" in Poulat's edition of the memoir of Albert Houtin and Felix Sartiaux, *Alfred Loisy, Sa Vie, Son Oeuvre* (Paris: 1960), pp. 325–409. The article "Reformkatholizismus" in *Die Religion in Geschichte und Gegenwart*, Vol. V, cols. 896–903, contains a good list of recent German studies; a list of works pro and con Modernism completes the article "Modernismo" in the *Enciclopedia Cattolica*, Vol. VIII, cols. 1188–1196. Other recent evaluations are listed in Luigi Paggiaro, *Il Modernismo a Cinquanta Anni dalla sua Condanna* (Padua-Rome-Naples: 1957), pp. 183–210.

The only general history of the movement in English is Alec Vidler's *Modernist Movement in the Roman Catholic Church* (Cambridge, England: 1934), which can be supplemented by his *20th Century Defenders of the Faith* (London: 1965), pp. 32–55, and his *Church in an Age of Revolution* (London: 1961), pp. 179–189.

Of general (and sympathetic) contemporary discussions, the most interesting are the books of Houtin and Petre, and the following: Ernesto Buonaiuti, *Le Modernisme Catholique*, tr. R. Monnot (Paris: 1927); A. Fawkes, *Studies in Modernism* (London: 1913); Charles Guignebert, *Modernisme et Tradition Catholique en France* (Paris: 1908); Paul Sabatier, *Modernism* (New York: 1908); A. L. Lilley, *Modernism, A Record and a Review* (London: 1908); Lilley's article in the *Encyclopedia of Religion and Ethics* (London: 1916), Vol. VIII, pp. 763–768; H. L. Stewart, *Modernism, Past and Present* (London: 1932). Systematic Modernist statements of aims to match the encyclical can be found in *The Program of Modernism: A Reply to the Encyclical of Pius X*, tr. George Tyrrell (New York: 1908); *What We Want: An Open Letter to Pius X*, tr. A. L. Lilley (London: 1927); Joseph Schnitzer, *Der Katholische Modernismum* (a collection of French writings on the subject) (Berlin: 1912); Johannes Kubel, *Geschichte des Katholischen Modernismus* (Tübingen: 1909); R. Murri, *La Filosofia Nuova e l'Enciclica contra il Modernismo* (Rome: 1908). The major critical works are the article "Modernisme," by various authors, in the *Dictionnaire Apologétique de la Foi Catholique* (Paris: 1916), Vol. III, cols. 591–695; the article "Modernisme," by Jean Rivière, in the *Dictionnaire de Théologie Catholique* (Paris: 1929), Vol. X (Part 2), cols. 2010–2047; Rivière's *Modernisme* and his article "Chronique de Théologie Fondamentale: La Crise Moderniste devant l'Opinion d'Aujourd'hui," in *Revue des Sciences Religieuses,* January–April 1940, pp. 140–182; the article "Modernisme," by A. Vermeersch, in *The Catholic Encyclopedia* (New York: 1911), Vol. X, pp. 415–421, and his *De Modernismus Tractatus* (Bruges: 1910). A comprehensive article on "Modernism," by J. J. Heaney, appears in the *New Catholic Encyclopedia* (New York: 1967), Vol. 9, pp. 991–995. Among more recent studies of the crisis, in a larger context, the most important are Coutinho, *Tradition et Histoire;* Paggiaro, *Modernismo;* G. Martini, *Cattolicesimo e Storicismo: Momenti di una crisi del Pensiero Religioso Moderno* (Naples: 1951); Yves Congar, *Vraie et Fausse Réforme dans l'Eglise* (Paris: 1950); François Rodé, *Le Miracle dans la Controverse Moderniste* (Paris: 1965); K. Leese, *Die Religionskrisis des Abendlandes und die Religiose Lage der Gegenwart* (Hamburg: 1948).

To the considerable body of general studies of the period, and of special problems relating to the Modernist controversy, the following may serve as an introduction.

For church history in the nineteenth and early twentieth centuries: Jean Leflon, *La Crise Révolutionnaire, 1789–1846,* in *Histoire de l'Eglise depuis les Origines jusqu'à Nos Jours,* ed. Fliche and Martin, Vol. 20 (Paris: 1951); Roger Aubert, *Le Pontificat de Pie Neuf,* in *Histoire de l'Eglise,* Vol. 21 (Paris: 1951); two very detailed works from the liberal point of view by Eduard Lecanuet, *La Vie de l'Eglise sous Léon XIII* (Paris: 1930) and *Les Signes Avant-coureurs de la Séparation: Les Dernières Années de Léon XIII et l'Avenement de Pie X, 1894–1910* (Paris: 1930); A. Latreille and R. Rémond, *Histoire du Catholicisme en France,* Vol. III. *La Période Contemporaine* (Paris: 1962); Adrien Dansette, *Religious History of Modern France,* 2 vols. (New York: 1961); Georges Weill, *Histoire du Catholicisme Liberal en France, 1828–1908* (Paris: 1909); from the integrist point of view, Emmanuel Barbier, *Histoire du Catholicisme Liberal et du Catholicisme Social en France: 1871–1914,* 5 vols. (Paris: 1939); Georges Goyau, *L'Allemagne Religieuse: Le Catholicisme 1800–1870* (Paris: 1909); Kenneth Scott Latourette, *Christianity in a Revolutionary Age,* Vol. I: *The 19th Century in Europe, The Roman Catholic Phase* (London: 1959).

For biblical criticism: James M. Robinson, *A New Quest of the His-*

torical Jesus (London: 1959), which surveys the modern literature in detail; James Peter, *Finding the Historical Jesus* (London: 1965); Avery Dulles, *Apologetics and the Biblical Christ* (Westminster, Md.: 1963); Jean Steinmann, *Richard Simon et les Origines de l'Exégèse Biblique* (Paris: 1960); two older works of Houtin, *La Question Biblique chez les Catholiques de France au XIXe Siècle* (Paris: 1902) and *La Question Biblique au XIXe Siècle* (Paris: 1906).

For Newman, Modernism, and the liberals: Vidler, *Modernist Movement*, pp. 51–59; E. T. O'Dwyer, *Cardinal Newman and the Encyclical Pascendi Dominici Gregis* (London: 1908); J. H. Toohey, "Newman and Modernism," *Tablet*, N.S. Vol. LXXIX (Vol. CXI) (January 4–25, 1908), pp. 7–9, 47–48, 86–88, 122–125; Jean Guitton, *La Philosophie de Newman: Essai sur l'Idée de Developpement* (Paris: 1933); J. H. Walgrave, *Newman the Theologian* (New York: 1960); Edmond Vermeil, *Jean-Adam Möhler et l'Ecole de Tubingue (1815–1840)* (Paris: 1913). Also of interest is a contemporary essay, W. J. Williams, *Newman, Loisy and the Catholic Church* (London: 1906). For the Wilfrid Wards, see Maisie Ward, *The Wilfrid Wards and the Transition*, Vol. I: *The Nineteenth Century* (London: 1934), Vol. 2: *Insurrection versus Resurrection* (London: 1937); Maisie Ward's autobiography, *Unfinished Business* (New York: 1964); Wilfrid Ward, *Problems and Persons* (London: 1903). Two excellent recent studies are Josef F. Altholz, *The Liberal Catholic Movement in England: The Rambler and Its Contributors* (London: 1962) and Hugh A. MacDougall, *The Acton-Newman Relations: The Dilemma of Christian Liberalism* (New York: 1962). Italian developments are surveyed in M. C. Casella, *Religious Liberalism in Modern Italy* (London: 1965), Vol. I, and in a classic study by Arturo Carlo Jemolo, *Church and State in Modern Italy* (Oxford: 1960). For American developments, see R. D. Cross, *The Emergence of Liberal Catholicism in America* (Cambridge, Mass.: 1958); T. A. McAvoy, *The Great Crisis in American Catholic History, 1895–1900* (Chicago: 1957).

For "philosophical Modernism": René Marlé, ed., *Au Coeur de la Crise Moderniste: Le Dossier Inédit d'une Controverse* (Paris: 1960); Maurice Blondel, *The Letter on Apologetics, and History and Dogma*, tr. Alexander Dru and Illtyd Trethowan (London: 1964), which has an excellent introductory essay on Blondel's thought; J. J. McNeill,

The Blondelian Synthesis (a study of the influence of German philosophical sources on the formation of Blondel's method and thought) (Leiden: 1966); A. Hayden, ed., *Bibliographie Blondelienne 1885–1951* (Louvain: 1953); Henri Dumery, *La Philosophie d'Action: Essai sur l'Intellectualisme Blondelien* (Paris: 1948); Maurice Nédoncelle, *Baron Friedrich von Hügel: A Study of His Life and Thought,* tr. M. Vernon (London: 1937), which includes a full bibliography. A good general survey is found in Roger Aubert, *Le Problème de l'Acte de Foi* (Louvain: 1958), pp. 368–392. Two of the most celebrated philosophical works, in addition to Blondel's essay, are Lucien Laberthonnière's *Le Realisme Chrétien et l'Idéalisme Grec,* 4th ed. (Paris: 1904), and Edouard Le Roy, *Dogme et Critique* (Paris: 1907). There is a wealth of published documentation besides that given by Marlé; see, for example, A. Valensin, *Textes et Documents Inédits* (Paris: 1961) and Blondel-Laberthonnière, *Correspondance Philosophiques* (Paris: 1961).

For the intellectual climate: H. Stuart Hughes, *Consciousness and Society: The Re-orientation of European Social Thought 1890–1930* (New York: 1958); Gerhard Masur, *Prophets of Yesterday: Studies in European Culture, 1890–1914* (New York: 1961); George L. Mosse, *The Culture of Western Europe: The Nineteenth and Twentieth Centuries* (Chicago: 1961); Ralph Barton Perry, *The Present Conflict of Ideals: A Study of the Philosophical Background of the World War* (New York: 1918); George Santayana, *Winds of Doctrine: Studies in Contemporary Opinion* (New York: 1912).

Index